My Journey

AS I REMEMBER

My Journey
AS I REMEMBER

DARRELL D. STARK

Library of Congress Control Number: 2008901594
ISBN: Hardcover   978-1-4363-2402-1
                 Softcover   978-1-4363-2401-4

To order additional copies of this book, contact:
Xlibris Corporation
1-888-795-4274
www.Xlibris.com
Orders@Xlibris.com
47321

Contents

Introduction

I met Darrell Stark by accident—by a few coincidences that I feel blessed have occurred in the way that they have. Mr. Stark called the Veteran's Office at the University of Connecticut, where I am a Masters student and an instructor in the Freshman English program. He left a message with the student that fielded the call, saying that he was looking for a student who would be interested in working with him on his memoir—to correct his grammar and do some editing work. The request got passed along to a friend of mine who worked in the office and who thought of me immediately. I was a student of English and looking for a job for the summer to supplement my waitressing income.

I called Mr. Stark right away. I thought that his memoir sounded interesting, and it would probably be pretty easy to correct a few commas here and there. We set up an interview—no easy task amidst his busy schedule of speaking engagements and veteran's meetings—and I went to his home to meet Darrell, his wife Judy and his daughter Darlene.

As soon as I sat down for the interview, I knew this wasn't just a matter of a few errant commas. I was struck right away by Darrell's drive and his dedication to getting his story out to the public. He conducted the interview in a business-like manner; although he was very friendly, it was clear he was taking this seriously and I would too. The show of family support at the interview was the first glimpse I had of how important family was to the Stark's. Over time I would become closer to Darrell and Judy and meet more and more of his family.

When I was offered the position, I was glad that he had chosen me, but a bit nervous. I wasn't sure how I would ever become comfortable with this man who was generations older than me, and who had been through experiences that were so much outside of the realm of my own. And, in many ways, his story offers insight into a world that is different than the world that I live in. However, I have come to learn that at the core his story is something that anyone can learn from and relate to.

His story became accessible to me, at first, as a story of a man who had grown up and struggled along with our country. In many ways his own coming of age mirrors that of the United States. His family struggled and persevered through the Great Depression alongside our young country, and they did it in the Midwest—the region arguably hit the hardest by the devastation. Later, he turned seventeen and joined the Army just as our country entered World War II. As he suffered through atrocities against his humanity as a Prisoner of War, our entire country dealt with the death of its own soldiers. When he was finally liberated and returned home to begin his life, struggling to come to terms with what had happened to him in the POW camps, our country dealt with the returning soldiers and POWs as well as struggled to understand how the Holocaust could have happened right under our eyes.

Darrell Stark came of age with what he calls "wonderful hardships," but while his childhood and life as a soldier is framed and mirrored by our country's history, at the crux of his story are timeless truths that transcend history—the prevailing love of family and the incredible power of one man's will to live.

Over time, I no longer thought of Mr. Stark's story as simply a memoir or a history, but rather as a testament to an amazing life of a man who inspired me and taught me so much over our relatively short time together. One day, as we sat discussing his life after his experiences as a POW, I asked him how he managed to let go of all the evil that he had experienced in order to live the life that he did. He answered, "I'm not a religious man. What I believe in is one word. Just one word. Love." I realized that those weren't just empty words said to impress me with his wisdom, but his real truth. I know that those are words that I will carry with me as I struggle to make sense of my own life. They are words that one can build a great life on and words that Darrell Stark has lived his inspiring life by.

As I sit here, struggling to put into words what a man that I've only known for three months has come to mean to me, I am struck by how much I have learned from him and all that he has taught me unintentionally, through his quiet courage. However, what is most important about both Darrell and his story is that any insights offered are never forced, never preached from up high or from a position of "one-who-knows-better." Instead, both Darrell and his story are quiet and unassuming, seemingly slight at first, but in actuality an all-encompassing story of an everyman who has overcome struggle and adversity to live the life we all only hope for. He wrote his story for those who he felt it might teach or help, but I think he has never realized what a large audience that could be. His story is one that we can all learn from and become inspired by.

Jamie Daniel
University of Connecticut
August 2007

Letter from Frederick Bird

The year was 1955 or 1956, and I was friends with James McHutchinson of Tolland. At that time, all of Ellington, Tolland and Vernon went to Rockville High School, which was located in the center of the Rockville section of the town of Vernon. The old high school is now the court building.

I asked James (Jim) McHutchinson how we had started going to the old Tolland Jail to visit Darrell Stark, and Jim told me that he had belonged to a youth group that was sponsored by the Tolland Volunteer Fire Department—James had met Darrell Stark through this association. Sheriff Sweeney had started a fire dispatch center at the jail and James also knew the older man who was the evening/night dispatcher. Those were the days when no one asked how or why two teenagers were at the county jail. James and I started going there on many Saturday evenings and would often sit on the fire radios when the dispatcher had to go for relief. Once, Jim and I stopped at the jail not knowing that a jail break attempt had occurred. When we knocked on the door, Darrell let us in and told us to stay in the radio room. We were there during the entire State Police investigation, and because of Darrell, no one even asked us who we were. This gave two teenagers a real awakening about real life that we wouldn't have been able to have otherwise.

I graduated from high school and went on to junior college, but during the summers I paid many visits to Darrell at the county jail. I can remember my father and mother saying that they did not worry about where I was, as they knew I was in jail. After graduation from junior college, I spent three years in the military.

I returned from the military in January of 1963. Darrell told me that the old state prison, in Wethersfield, was looking for corrections officers. This was before the Department of Corrections, and the jails were under the county system while the main prison was under state corrections. I took the test and was immediately hired to work on the midnight shift. While at the state prison, I took the entrance exam for the State Police, and in

October of 1963 I entered the State Police Academy. I graduated in January of 1964. My first assignment was at Troop C in Stafford Springs, Ct. With this assignment, I had the chance to interact with Darrell once again.

Since 1956, the wheel has turned many times. Both of us are retired from state service and are now working together on Darrell's book. It has been an honor to be able to assist Darrell with the photography restoration for the old family photographs and to take photographs of the clothing that he was wearing when he was released from prison camp.

Fred Bird
Owner, Fred Bird Photography
Ellington, Ct.

Note from the Author

First, I would like to note that my book represents my memories of my experiences as they happened to me. Although I have read many historical books on the topics covered in these pages, my memoir does not reflect specific research on my part. It is not a collection of historical documents but instead, as the title suggests, it is simply my own memories as I recall them at this point in my life. At times I include my personal opinions about the things that happened to our country during World War II, and at times I also reflect upon the opinions that I have heard through conversations with other World War II veterans at conventions, etc. Although my opinions are always honest and I try to always be respectful, I am sure that there are some who will disagree with me. I respectfully note that I have always written about things as I vividly remember them, despite the fact that they happened to me many years ago.

My memoir begins with a discussion of my experiences growing up during the Great Depression. Although it is my personal experience, I believe that it represents the experience of many Americans during that period of our nation's development, and it is my hope that this book will give my readers a personal story to put to the experience of growing up in Oklahoma during that time.

My primary motivation for this book was to reflect upon my experiences, specifically as a Japanese Prisoner of War. I use the word "Jap" often throughout my memoir because that is the word that was primarily used during the war, and I do not mean the word with any disrespect.

In conclusion, it is my hope that this book will leave the reader with the sense that you should never give up, no matter what the circumstances. I have learned throughout my lifetime that if you are able to keep fighting you will, in many instances, be able to overcome the difficulties that are facing you.

Preface

A Letter of Gratitude

I am grateful to many people; first and foremost my mother, Gladys Pollard Stark, and my father, Frank Hardy Stark. They raised me to always have a will to keep fighting while maintaining a sense of self-worth. They instilled in me a sense of humanity, which fostered a respect for those who were enduring the same cruelties as I was. Most of all, they gave me the foundation to establish the wonderful life that I have had.

Next, I am grateful to my wife, Julia Ridzon Stark, who has been by my side unconditionally for the last sixty years. She has been a true and faithful partner in spite of some difficult times that I have had as a result of my war experiences. Our life together has produced a family that is a constant source of joy and pride for me, and I am grateful to my family for those gifts.

I would also like to take this opportunity to thank all the wonderful people in my community, some whose names I have never even learned. I would like to tell them now that I appreciate everything that they have done for me to give me a sense of belonging.

Finally, I would like to express my deep sense of pride for my country and for all those who have worked so hard and made so many sacrifices to finally win the war. It is hard to adequately express in words the love and appreciation I feel for all those who gave their lives, as well as for all those who persevered and continued to fight until the final days that the war was won. These feelings are too deep for words, but it is my hope that this book will be a testament to my appreciation.

This book would not have been possible without the encouragement of my family and friends, but I would like to express a special appreciation to my daughter, Darlene Dion, and my granddaughter, Stephanie Palmer, for transcribing my shaky handwriting. Also, I would like to extend an additional special thank you to my brother, Donald Wayne Stark, for transcribing one section and editing the entire story. Thank you all so much.

Part One

My First Seventeen Years

Daddy and Mother and my First Years

I was born October 2, 1923 to Frank Hardy Stark and Gladys Pollard Stark, in Wilson, Oklahoma. I was the first of eight siblings who followed in this order: Darrell D, Barbara Ann Rojean, George William, Lee Ray, Gerald Edward, Patsy Gail, Donald Wayne, and Carol June.

My mother and father both came from large families that had moved up from South Texas to Oklahoma while Oklahoma was still Indian Territory. Their families were there when the territory was opened up to white settlement in 1893, and in the land rush both staked out the maximum number of acres that they were allowed by the government.

Both Mother and Daddy had only fourth grade educations. Daddy was the third of nine children, and his father had a reputation for being very mean to his family. Daddy's brother, Uncle Henry, once told me that Grandpa Stark was meanest to Daddy of all the children. As a result, Daddy left home when he was only twelve years old, and he managed to be self-sufficient from that point on. Under extreme circumstances he was able to take care of himself while learning a trade in the oil fields. I am sure that some good people helped him along the way and supplied him with the knowledge that he needed to grow to the kind of man and father that he was. With that trade he was able to fulfill his own needs and care for his family in the future, despite an inadequate education. I knew very little of Grandpa Stark, but I remember him vaguely from our time in Maud, Oklahoma, where we lived for a time in a tent city for oil field workers. He moved there so Mother and Daddy could take care of him, as Grandma Stark had already died before I was born. They took him in and took care of him, but it was an exceptionally cold winter and he died of pneumonia in the tent city. My most vivid memory of him is from the day that he died: I was about six or seven years old and rode on the back of the wagon when they took him to the cemetery.

We came close to losing more in that tent city at Maud than Grandpa Stark. We had an open natural gas heater that we used to keep us warm, and my sister Jean and I had seen Daddy stand in front of it to warm his hands and then turn around and warm his back. One cold morning Daddy had just come home from work, and Jean and I got out of bed and ran to the heater to get warm. We stood in front and warmed our hands, then turned around and backed up to the heater to warm our backs, just like we had seen Daddy do. Jean got too close without realizing it, and before we knew it the back of her nightgown had caught on fire. She was screaming and I was trying to put out the flame. Impulsively Mother grabbed some water, but Daddy hollered, "No!" and grabbed a blanket to wrap her in. That put out the flame, but when they took the blanket off of her we could see that she had been severely burned. Thinking quickly, Mother applied a thick layer of lard to her whole back. There were no hospitals or even doctors near where we lived, so Mother and Daddy had to care for her and treat her until they could get her to a doctor. Although she had been seriously burned, the quick action and loving care of both parents saved Jean's life.

Living on our own as we did, so separated from the luxuries that we are used to now, Mother and Daddy had to be doctors, housekeepers, caretakers and parents. Life in Maud was perilous at times, and Mother can be credited with saving my life also while we were living there. I came down with a bout of pneumonia, and the doctor was unable to come to see me right away. While we waited, Mother took several different types of ingredients and applied them to my chest in a poultice every day until the doctor could get there to see me. When he arrived to check me over he told Mother to keep doing what she was doing; it had been working just fine to make me healthy again.

I am always amazed when I think back on all the work Mother did just to keep us clean and healthy, and to cook for us and keep house. Daddy helped a lot too, perhaps more than most men of his time; he would change a baby's diaper, wash clothes, mop a floor, make a bed or do just about anything in the house to make things easier on Mother. However, when Daddy was away Mother would care for all the children, keep up the house and make sure that we were all being adequately fed.

Mother came from a family of eleven children, eight boys and three girls, of which she was the eighth. Her mother, who we always called

Mammy, was a small woman whose quiet character and wealth of strength gained the respect of all those who knew her. Mammy died in 1959 at the age of eighty-six. Grandpa Pollard was about ten years older than Mammy and he died when I was about four years old. I can remember sitting on his knee in the morning and sharing his coffee with him, and I can remember the day he died. Daddy was holding me and crying, and I was crying in his arms. Although I didn't know Pappy for long, anyone who had known him always said that he was a kind and gentle person with a lot of strength.

Mother and Daddy were married in Wilson, Oklahoma, and Daddy supported them by working in farming and in the oil fields. When I was about three or four my Uncle Henry, Daddy's youngest brother, lived near us with Grandpa Stark. He told me that once, when Daddy was harnessing his team of mules, I walked behind one of them and it kicked at me. Luckily it missed, but Uncle Henry, who was about twelve at the time, could remember running up and snatching me out of danger.

My young life growing up in Oklahoma is one that I remember as full of hardship, but the hardships were faced and ultimately overcome by my family's love and caring for one another. Despite the difficulties facing the young state of Oklahoma, my parents loved each other and their children, and I remember the joyous occasions alongside the difficult ones. Daddy had no chance for success as a farmer in Oklahoma—it was nearly impossible because of poor soil and the lack of rain—so he finally devoted his time exclusively to the oil fields. Working in the oil fields was often referred to as roughnecking, and Daddy had had lots of experience; he had been a roughneck since the age of twelve. He didn't retire until the age of sixty-two, after a lifetime of hard work and toil in the oil fields. What I remember most from my childhood is constantly having to move as Daddy pursued the work that was heavily sought-after and extremely scarce. As a result of the tumultuous nature of the industry, we moved about thirty-two times that I can remember, but the town we lived in most was Asher, Oklahoma. The town had a population of about 350 at that time, located only about twenty-seven miles south of Shawnee. Like much of the state, farming and roughnecking were the only ways to make a living there, so Daddy did the best he could in the oil fields to provide for his family.

Life on the School Lease

For a few years Daddy tried to combine farming with his oil field work, and during those years all that he was able to raise successfully was sugar cane and watermelons. I was about twelve years old, the oldest of the family, so I worked with Daddy a lot that year. At times I resented having to work with him; I was accustomed to being allowed to go into town on Saturday afternoons and didn't like when my work with Daddy interfered with that privilege. I also had a rebellious streak, and one Saturday after cutting cane Daddy informed me that it had to be taken to the mill to make molasses, and that it *had* to be done that day. At noon, after dinner, instead of being able to go into town Daddy informed me that we had to finish cutting the cane and then bring it to the mill that afternoon.

Impertinently, I said no, I wanted to go to town instead. Daddy had to punish my defiance and he put his belt to my behind. That being done, I went back to work and quietly finished the job. We loaded the wagon and took it to the mill, but when we got there we had to go on a slight grade and, when the cane shifted, I fell off the wagon. Daddy could not stop the team in time, and one of the rear wheels ran over my leg. Luckily the ground was soft so there was little damage; the situation could have been much worse if the ground hadn't been so soft. The next time we went into town just Daddy and me, he bought a bag of candy for me and for the other kids at home.

Just about everyone in Asher had to buy nearly everything on credit, and I still remember the kind man who ran the store and made that credit available to everyone—Mr. John McClure. As far as I am concerned, he was single-handedly responsible for ensuring that many good people in Asher could continue to eat and not go hungry. I have no doubt that in those hard times many people in Oklahoma, Texas, Kansas and other states in the Midwest would have starved to death if not for the people like Mr. McClure. After all, our national government did not have the assistance for struggling families that they have now. If you had no job or if you could not raise food due to bad farming conditions, you had to have help or your family could starve. In that time families and friends helped one another just to survive; if you had neither, your chances of survival were slight. As you might expect, there were also a few who had plenty but were not, to my knowledge, helpful to anyone. As a little boy, I don't recall these families being treated badly by the rest of the community, but just that they did not help the rest of us.

After the bad years of minimal farming, Daddy moved Mother and us kids to a house on land that was leased by my Uncle Doc and Aunt Eunie, my mother's sister. The place was called the school lease, and the house on it was not much more than a one-room shack with a leaky roof. Daddy left us there while he went to go look for a job in the oil fields.

My mother was the strongest woman I ever knew. When Daddy left in the old Model T, on his way to the oil fields to try to find the work that would keep us alive, he did the best he could to leave us with enough dry beans, cornmeal, flour, salt pork and potatoes to support her and the five of us kids for a week. It was just us and Mother, and the nearest neighbor was about a mile away—a much farther distance when you are living without a telephone or even electricity. In order to have fresh water we had to carry it from a spring that was quite a distance away.

My Uncle Doc owned about 640 acres in total, and he grazed cows on some of his land. The entire property was fenced in, so he bought a horse and left it there for me to ride to check the fences about once every week. I also rode the horse to school, but we had no saddle for it so I always rode it bareback. My sister Jean and brother Bill often rode it with me, either to school or while we went out to check the fences. I remember one afternoon Bill and I were riding through some trees at a gallop and we came to a low hanging limb. I saw it in time to duck, but Bill didn't, and the limb caught him in the chest and knocked him to the ground. Luckily, he was okay except for a few bruises.

Another memory I have is of Bill and I riding to our neighbor's house, who had a few sons just about our age. Their family also had hogs, and the older brother and I talked our younger brothers into riding one of them. His brother tried and immediately fell off. Bill, however, was somehow able to hang on and ultimately managed to stay on the hog until it went through a hole in the barn that was only big enough for the hog to fit through. Once again Bill was knocked off, and the barn wall caught him in the chest and raked him into the hog wallow. Although he was filthy, he was alright after that experience as well, which was lucky for me since I had been the one to convince him to do it in the first place.

As far as I can remember, Daddy was gone from the house on the school lease for three or four weeks. There was no mail delivery to the house, so he was not able to contact Mother the entire time he was away. I am sure she was worried, not knowing how long she was going to have to feed us kids and where more food would come from if need be, but she never let us know if she was.

Soon enough, the food did run out, and except for cornmeal we had no more of the rations that Daddy had left. About two or three days after the food was gone, Uncle Doc and Aunt Eunie drove over to see us in Uncle Doc's brand new car. I remember standing by the car with my brothers and sisters; it was so shiny, we could see ourselves in the pristine door. Uncle Doc and Aunt Eunie brought us some food and a black dog we named Snowball, as well as some chickens for eggs. The chickens and the dog both ultimately proved useful; the chickens gave us food and the dog was able to catch rabbits that we also ate to survive.

Mother was very resourceful and, looking back, she is likely the reason that we were all able to survive those difficult times. Despite the conditions we lived in, she knew that our hygiene was important. She kept our clothes patched and made the older kids wash themselves every day. On Saturday night we would all take baths in the #10 washtub. She was also an excellent cook. If we were almost out of food, she could take next to nothing and make a tasty meal out of it. Like all of our neighbors, we had no refrigerator, so we seldom had fresh meat. Instead, meat was cured in salt and canned in jars, along with vegetables and fruits; we ate a lot of dry vegetables and fruits during those years. While we were on the school lease land, in need of food ourselves, a little homeless boy of about fourteen came by and Mother let him stay with us. Although we didn't have much we shared what we did have with him. I still remember his name—Wesley—and at times I wonder what happened to him. He was two years older than I was and left after staying with us only a week. I never saw him again.

I remember waking up one night and finding Mother crying alone in the dark. It scared me, because I didn't know what was wrong with her, and I began to cry too. I asked her what was wrong and she told me that she had a bad headache but didn't have any aspirin to ease the pain. She asked me to go to the neighbors and ask them for some. I said I would, even though I was scared to go all that way in the dark—it was almost a mile all told. I ran all the way and woke them to tell them what was wrong. They gave me some aspirin and I ran all the way home, still afraid, but I remember Mother was so grateful when I returned, and about an hour later she was quiet again.

Somehow it seemed that every time we were out of food someone would show up to help us. Once, when we were almost completely out again, we heard a woman's scream. We all ran outside to see what it was, and who was there but our Aunt Ora, trying to hang on to the wooden box that Uncle Henry had tied on to their Model T Ford as a seat for her. Our driveway had a deep slant on Aunt Ora's side, and there was nothing on the makeshift seat for her to hold on to. She was afraid she was going to fall off, but she had somehow managed to hang on and the two of them pulled into the driveway safely. They were on their way to Sulphur Springs to see my Uncle Sim and Aunt Bobby, and even though they were struggling themselves they had stopped by to help us out along the way. They stayed with us a couple of days, and shortly after they left Daddy came home.

We were all so overjoyed to see him! Although he had not been able to find a job in the oil fields he had managed to get a job picking cotton for a short time and had made a little bit of money, enough to keep us in food for about a week. He showed up at the house on foot; I don't remember what had happened to the old Model T, but he was no longer driving it. After he came home from that job he was able to get work on a drilling rig about three miles from our house, where he was paid five dollars for a twelve hour shift. He went into town and paid Mr. McClure for our grocery bill with his first pay. With the next check he bought a car so he could drive the three miles to work instead of walking.

The new car was a used Plymouth with a stick shift. Daddy had already taught me to drive the Model T, and one day when he and I were going to Asher he decided to teach me to drive the Plymouth. I was doing just fine until we started up a steep hill with deep ditches on each side and Daddy decided to teach me how to shift on a hill. I put it in first and we started up the hill and he said, "Put it in second son." I made a mistake and slapped it into reverse and we started barreling backwards before I knew it, with Daddy frantically trying to stop the car with no luck. We ended up in a ditch, and we were stuck there until a neighbor came by with a team of mules and pulled us out.

I assumed at that point that my driving lesson was over, but after we got out of the ditch and back on the road Daddy said, "Darrell, you get in the driver's side." I replied that I didn't want to drive again, but Daddy said, "Yes. Do it NOW!"

Even though I was shaking all over, I climbed into the driver's seat once again. I put it in first and started up the hill again, and halfway up he had me stop. I was nervous; I thought that I was in big trouble. He calmed me down and told me to put it in first gear again and we started off. Then, he told me to put it in second. I made sure I got it in second this time. Eventually we reached the top of the hill and stopped for the main road, and I thought for sure he would have me get out so that he could drive, but he didn't. He sat where he was and told me how proud he was of me being able to overcome my fear. Then he said, "Put her in gear, Son, and go on to Asher."

We lived at that little wreck of a house on the school lease for about three or four months. Mother and Daddy made friends with a few families and we kids made friends with some of the other kids in our little one room school. All the kids carried their lunches with them to school in the morning, and most of our lunches were the same, consisting of biscuits with butter and jelly, and sometimes a little salt pork and dried fruit.

We had a male teacher whose name was Mr. Fields. He was a very mean teacher; he cut switches on the way to school, and one day he decided that he had reason to use it on me. I went home that afternoon with large welts on my skin. Mother saw them and asked Jean and I what had happened. Jean told her that Mr. Fields had given me a whipping at school, but I kept quiet; I was afraid that when Daddy came home from work he would get after me for being unruly. When Daddy did get home, Mother told him about what had happened. He had me take my clothes off so he could look me over. I still wasn't sure what he was going to say, but he just told me to get dressed again and didn't say anything else. The next day Mr. Fields came to school with two black eyes and no switches.

We had no radios or any other types of entertainment like we have now, but we had different ways of entertaining ourselves back then. For example, it was customary to have square dances that rotated to a different family's house each month. After Daddy started making some money and we could afford it, it came around our turn to have a square dance at our house. There was always someone who could play the fiddle or some other stringed instrument, and the adults would sing and dance and have a good time. The children always found ways to entertain themselves and have a great time as well. On the night of the dance at our house, two young men got drunk on moonshine and started a fight. Things got nasty and the dance ended in a big brawl, and Daddy had to tell everyone to go home. That was the last time we ever had a dance at our house.

It was pretty cold at that time of year, and the shack we lived in had no finished walls inside, making it very hard to heat. There was no chimney, so Daddy put a stove pipe through the roof for the cook stove and a tin heater. It was not an entirely safe situation, and eventually a spark or an overheated stove pipe caught the roof on fire. Daddy was able to put the fire out, but the situation scared Mother and Daddy. Soon after that we moved from the house back into town.

Asher

We had lived in town before, at several different houses, and this time we moved into a small, narrow house that was called a shot-gun house. It had only three rooms and no electricity, but it had running water which was a great help, especially to Mother. Daddy was working steady at the time, so he bought her a Maytag washing machine that was powered by a little gasoline engine. It was a bit of a luxury, especially compared to the school lease house where we had to carry water almost a mile to do the washing. Washing day in Asher was on Wednesday, and when Mother and the other women in town cranked up their gas washing machines and started washing their clothes, Wednesdays in Asher could be very loud!

Daddy had me spade up a piece of ground in back of the Asher house for a garden. We planted all kinds of vegetables and ate many of them fresh, and the rest Mother canned in mason fruit jars. Daddy also bought a Jersey milk cow, and it was my job to stake her where she could graze every day and to milk her twice a day. One day I was almost through milking her when she suddenly jumped up and kicked me. The milk bucket was full and I fell off the stool and spilled all the milk I had gotten. I looked up to see two boys, both about a year older than me, laughing at me. I asked them what they were laughing at and the biggest one said he had thrown a stone at the cow to see what she would do. When I heard him say that, I got mad and went for him without even thinking about any possible repercussions. We ended up in one tough fistfight. After it was over I never had a problem with milking again, and as time passed I found him to be a good kid and he and I even became close friends.

The Asher school was about a block and a half from our house, and it was built to accommodate both the Elementary and High School. To keep the two separate from each other the gym was located between them. I wasn't a very good student; in fact, you might say that I was a terrible student. My friend Harry and I, along with two or three others, were always talking and planning for what we were going to do when we got out of school instead of concentrating on our classes. All that talking in class kept us in trouble and kept our teacher, Miss. Archer, mad at us. She sent us to the principal's office a couple of times, but after realizing that she wasn't seeing any change she kept me, Harry and our friend Perry in the room while the other kids were out for recess. She had the three of us bend over the front desk and she whacked our backsides with three solid whacks each. Boy, did they sting! Then she asked each of us if it hurt. Perry and I answered yes, but Harry said no. Hearing that, she gave him three more, and this time he let her know that they did hurt. After school she gave us a note to take home to our parents, and when Mother read it she gave me three more good whacks for not listening in school.

Despite the trouble I got into in school, or perhaps even because of it, we kids had all kinds of fun. All of it had to be created by us, because we had no manufactured toys of any kind, but our parents added to our fun and did things with us that made us happy. For example, quite often at night they would sing to us, and we also enjoyed listening to them talk about things that had happened at work or during their life. Mother had a beautiful voice and we all just loved to hear her sing. Daddy used to joke that the only way he could carry a tune was if someone put it in a bag, but he still added to the fun and the merriment that I remember so fondly from our nights spent together as a family.

We had a knack for getting into trouble, but many of the memories of those times still make me look back and laugh. One such time involved a scheme that one of the neighborhood kids cooked up. There was a small garage in town, and one of our friends noticed some old wheel bearings there. We came up with the idea of making a scooter with them. We got some old boards, and by making a few cuts with the handsaw and attaching the wheel bearing to the bottom of them we were able to put together a makeshift scooter. We took it to the only paved road in town, the north-south highway that ran through Asher. It was considered heavily traveled with about three cars an hour, speeding by at thirty miles per hour. After some practice runs and subsequent changes, we were able to keep up with the fastest cars on the road by picking up speed going down the hill. We especially loved to ride our scooters at night so that we could watch the sparks fly as our wheels met the pavement.

One evening we rode them about three miles north of town to go fishing. We were catching fish and having a wonderful time, but we hadn't told our parents where we were going. When we started back late that night, watching the sparks fly the whole way, we began to see headlights heading towards us. When the car got to us we could see that it was Daddy and the father of one of the other boys. They had been looking for us for a long time and were very worried. Daddy hollered for me to come to him, and by the tone of his voice I could tell that I was in big trouble. I started pushing my scooter along as fast as I could, with the other boys running along with me trying to keep up. The car turned around and caught up with us, and there stood Daddy on the running board with his belt in his hands. When the car got a little way ahead, Daddy jumped off and grabbed me as I went by, and when he caught me he gave me a strapping for not telling someone where we were going. Then he sent me on my way to get home on my own, and when I got to our house Mother was there crying. She was glad to see me, but also very angry, and she punished me as well. After we all calmed down she gave me the supper she had saved for me and I washed up and went to bed. By the time I got up the next morning everything was okay, and I ate breakfast, milked the cow and went to school as normal. When I got there my friends and I compared punishments and talked about the wonderful time we had!

Throughout most of this time Daddy was working, and when we had enough money we would visit Mammy and Mother's brothers and sisters in Ardmore, about seventy miles south of Asher. Uncle Tom, Uncle Pete, Uncle Cletus, Aunt Eunice and Aunt Myrt all lived there. On our way we would stop in Sulphur Springs and visit with Daddy's brother, Uncle Sim. The stop at Uncle Sim's allowed me to spend some time with my cousin, Tom. After leaving Uncle Sim's we began the second leg of the trip, which took us through the Arbuckle Mountains.

The crooked stretch of mountain road that led through the Arbuckle Mountains was exciting for us. We could look down and see the road we had traveled, and I can still remember the route quite vividly. About halfway up to the top there was a gas station and a place to let the old car cool off. We replaced the water that had steamed out of the radiator and started off again. After a bit the road flattened out and we could see the water tower at Ardmore. This was the landmark that got us all excited; we knew we were almost there and we so loved to visit with Mammy and the others. I don't remember a time that we went without taking food or buying a lot of it when we were there. This was a practice we always followed, no matter where we visited, because times were so hard and Daddy and Mother wanted to be sure to give instead of take. When others came to see us, they always repaid the favor and did the same.

Just a few weeks after one of these trips, Mother and Daddy started going to the church just in back of our house, a Church of Christ. They decided to become members and were baptized, and from then on they remained members. On Sundays we went to church in the morning and the evening, and we kids went to Sunday School before the services and attended Bible Study on Wednesday nights. I learned early not to sit next to Mother in church though. Just like in school, I had a problem with talking and fooling around, and Mother found a quick solution to that problem. She would gather some of my flesh between two fingers, squeeze hard, and twist. If I made any noise she would just increase the pain. At first I made it a point to try and keep one of my brothers or sisters between us, but she came up with a solution for that also. She would reach around in back of whoever was between us, quietly grab and pull up at a tuft of my hair, and then shoot me a look. I was quiet during the service after that.

We had some good times in church as well as after the services. One of the most fun times I can remember took place after Bible Study. One of the members of the church was a farmer whose farm was about two miles west of Asher. He had put in a peach orchard and the trees had grown to about four feet high before the drought had set in and he started having serious problems. Since the drought had killed off so much of the vegetation that was usually food for the wild life, the wild rabbits were eating the bark off his trees and killing them. The rabbits always came after dark, so one Wednesday he asked me to go hunting with him after Bible Study, when the dark had set in. I was pretty good with a .410 gauge shot gun, so he would have me stand in the bed of his small truck and look over the top of the cab as he drove through rows of trees. When the truck lights would shine in a rabbit's eyes it would freeze, and I would cut loose on him with the .410. The best part was that the rabbit would be dinner for the next day, and sometimes we could get up to three or four per night.

Aunt Myrt came to our house in Asher when she was due to have her first child. Her husband was in the Army, and she needed someone to be with when the baby arrived. While she was there, her husband came to visit. He was in uniform, and I loved the way that he looked in it, so powerful and strong. From that time on, I knew I wanted to be in the Army. After he left, my Aunt Myrt had my cousin Kenny, and I never saw Aunt Myrt's husband again.

Konawa, Ada and Moore, the Road to the City

After living in Asher for awhile, things became very bad for us again. Daddy couldn't find work and we were getting deeper in debt with Mr. McClure. When things got really bad Daddy had to leave us again to go and look for work. He was gone about a week, and when he came back he informed us that we were moving to Konawa, which was several miles east of Asher; in fact, it was one of the towns that Asher played football against. Just like any other school, I quickly learned that Konawa had its own bully, and the first day I had to have my fight with him, just as I had at Asher. I got along just fine after that, until the day that Konawa played Asher. I was rooting for Asher to win, and the same kid that had bullied me the first day didn't like that I was showing my allegiance for my old school. He took a piece of chalk and started making marks on a brand new sheep-lined coat that Mother had bought me, and we got into it for the second time. When he grabbed me by the coat I bent over and slipped out of it, and we went at it for awhile. After the game and the fight my sister Jean and I were walking home when some kids started throwing rocks at us. Off I went after them, and I had my second fight that day. I escaped with only a few bruises, and Jean and I got home safely and went to school as usual the next day.

We were in Konawa for about a month before moving to Ada, and I was glad to go. In Ada Daddy worked on a drilling rig with his two brothers, Uncle Sim and Uncle Henry. While we lived there I spent a great deal of time trying to find a job to get some of my own money, but there just were not enough jobs to go around. Once in awhile, though, I could make some money baby-sitting for Uncle Henry and Aunt Ora. One night, when I was babysitting my cousins Billy and Betty, I invited over a few of the girls from town that I had become friendly with. We were having a real good time, and the kids were also enjoying themselves, when Uncle Henry and Aunt Ora came home. I thought I would be in trouble; after all, it was quite late and the kids should have been in bed. To my surprise neither Uncle Henry nor Aunt Ora reprimanded me at all, but instead they started up a conversation with the girls. I was embarrassed, and also hesitant to think what might happen when the girls went home and I really got an earful, but when they left all that happened was that Uncle Henry teased me something terrible. They still asked me to baby-sit the whole time we lived there, but that would only be for a few weeks before the oil well was drilled, Daddy was laid off, and we had to move again.

We packed only the essentials: the cotton mattress, the wood burning cook stove, the bed clothing, our personal clothes, and Mother's sewing machine. Mother was a very good seamstress; she made all her own patterns, cut and sewed shirts for Daddy and us boys, and made dresses for her and Jean. At the time I was growing up the poverty was so rampant that few people had any money to spend. Mother was so creative that she was able to make clothes out of the large flour sacks that we bought to make our bread. Some of the sacks were made of colorful printed cloth, which she used to make dresses for herself and my sister, and some were made of solid colors which she used to make shirts for Daddy and us boys. I can't remember if we had a car with a trailer at the time of our move or if Daddy had traded the car for an old truck by that time, but we were most certainly packed in tight between all of us kids and our belongings.

Daddy had heard that there was work at an oil field near Oklahoma City, so we took off headed in that direction. In a few days we arrived in Moore, Oklahoma, and Daddy immediately started looking for a house for Mother and us kids to live in while he went out and looked for a job. There were many vacant buildings in Moore, and he found a vacant store to put us in. It was a large building with just a single large room that had big glass windows in front. There was no place for the stove pipe to go, so Daddy cut a hole in the roof and put in a pipe so he could start the fire. The kids pitched in by starting to unload the car and putting our mattresses down, and Mother set to work putting together a good meal for us all to eat. The next morning Daddy left us to go find a job.

We enjoyed the spacious living quarters, and I was able to find a job quite quickly with a local dairy farmer. I worked for fifty cents a day, and when Daddy came back and said he had found a job we immediately started looking for a house in the area to move to permanently. He found a four room house about two miles west of where we had been, and it was close to the one-room school. It was a nice little house, but it had no electricity or running water. My siblings and I that were of school age were enrolled in school, and Jean and I were put in the same grade because she had skipped a year in Asher while I had been held back a year. Bill and Ray were behind us. It was a nice school with about ten or twelve kids besides us and with the exception of Miss. Archer from Asher, the teacher was the best I ever had. She was able to teach, keep order and get us to enjoy ourselves, all at the same time.

Mother would keep after me all the time about keeping my knees and elbows clean. I washed every day and scrubbed my hands before every meal, but when it came to my knees and elbows I just didn't work hard enough. One day at school I fell and hurt my knee pretty bad. The teacher wanted to look at it, but I remembered that morning that Mother had told me that my knees were especially dirty and that I needed to wash them. I refused to let the teacher see how bad my injury was, and instead pretended that it didn't hurt all that much, but my sister Jean told her that the reason I would not let her see my knees were because of how dirty they were. After that, my knees and my elbows were always kept clean.

We were still at that school at Christmas time, and the teacher put together a show where each of the kids would do something that was entertaining. Mother could play several stringed instruments and had taught me how to play chords on a mandolin, so I played the mandolin and sang along with it. I enjoyed myself, but that was the last time I ever played an instrument of any kind.

We didn't have Christmas decorations in the way that we are accustomed to now, but Mother and Daddy always told us about Christmas and always had something for us every Christmas morning. There were never toys, but there was candy or fresh fruit, which in itself was very hard to find. Usually we would get just an apple or an orange, but we were always happy for that. We had heard that mistletoe was a Christmas decoration, and it was very plentiful where we lived, so we started hanging it all over inside of our house. We didn't know that if a girl walked under it she was supposed to be kissed. If a girl walked in our house at Christmas time and got kissed under that mistletoe, I doubt that she would have willingly walked under the mistletoe again!

Oklahoma City

We stayed in Moore until the end of school before moving on to Oklahoma City where Daddy got another job. They were drilling oil wells in the city at that time, so Daddy rented a house there and we all moved in. I quickly got a job for a man who delivered ice. It was hard work for a kid like me, because the blocks of ice were so heavy, but I did it for quite awhile until finally Mother made me quit because she felt the work was too heavy for me. We had a movie house not too far from where we lived, and we all just loved going to the movies. Most of the films we saw were silent, but they were still fun. At that time wrapped bread was just beginning to be marketed and sold in the stores, and Wonder Bread had a promotion deal with the movie house where you could get into the movies for free with a certain number of Wonder Bread wrappers. Every kid in town begged their parents to buy Wonder Bread, just for the wrappers, even though most of us loved our mothers' homemade bread and biscuits much more.

We would also try to sneak into the movies from time to time, but most often we were promptly caught and thrown out. We would always keep trying, and sometimes they would look the other way and let us get away with it. If we did manage to sneak in, we would spend the whole movie sliding down in our seat like a snake whenever the usher walked by, nervous that he would catch us and kick us out. Once the usher passed by we could sit up again, but it didn't even matter if we missed part of the movie that way—we had probably already seen it many times before. I always enjoyed going to the movies and other types of entertainment, and because I loved it so and seldom had enough money to get in, we saw a lot of movies in between dodging the ushers as they walked the aisles.

I remember living in Asher when a carnival came to town. Jean and I wanted to go to the tent show, but we had no money to get in. We walked around to the back of the tent to crawl under, but here we ran into a little problem. The carnival workers had tied a monkey to the back of their tent, right in our path. We had never seen a monkey before, so to us this was almost as exciting as getting to see the show. The monkey was sitting on some crates, and at first he just looked at us, but then he started making a lot of noise, jumping up and down and causing quite a commotion. However, since he was so small we weren't afraid of him. We weren't afraid, that is, until we started under the bottom of the tent and the little monkey got me by the leg and bit me. Turns out he was a bit of a guard monkey, because that was the end of trying to see the show without paying!

While we were in Oklahoma City my cousin Hoyt, who was about my age, came and stayed with us for a couple of weeks. He was the son of Uncle Lonnie, my mother's brother. Hoyt was very light skinned, and the sun was always shining hot at that time of year in Oklahoma City. One day, he and I decided to go to a pond about a mile from where we lived. We walked around the pond for awhile looking for frogs or spotting a snake now and then, but we were getting hotter and hotter by the minute. We looked and saw that there was no one around, so we decided to take off our clothes and jump in the pond; I remember the water felt so wonderful on that hot day. We were having a great time when we heard someone laughing, and when we looked up we saw three girls standing by our clothes. They just stood there, laughing, while we pleaded with them to let us go. We were both getting burned by the sun at that point; Hoyt especially was just cooking because of his fair skin. Finally we told them that we were coming out whether they left or not, so they left—and took our clothes with them! We both jumped out of the water and started after them. They ran a short distance but then dropped our clothes, so we put them back on and headed home. We both had blisters on our backs, but Hoyt was so bad that he was sick for a couple of days; Mother had to treat us both with some type of salve. I don't know where those girls came from, and I don't remember ever seeing them again. By the age of thirteen I was starting to think about impressing girls, but after that day I was turned off for awhile.

Daddy had always taught me to respect girls and women, but for a short while after the embarrassment of that experience it was hard for me to do. Not long after this, I was to have one of the toughest fights of my young life because of a remark made to my sister Jean. I felt like I had to defend her name because she was my sister and she had been insulted, and it was my duty as her older brother to stick up for her.

A lot of times, we had to find ways to entertain ourselves, and so naturally a lot of our ideas of games to play came from the movies; we were especially interested in all things to do with cowboys and Indians, which was a popular movie genre at that time. In one of the movies we had seen the Indians building a tunnel, and so we decided to dig one in the back of our house. The backyard had no lawn, so Mother and Daddy just let us go at it. You have never seen a bunch of kids work so hard—every kid around was involved in the construction of that tunnel, even the one I had the fight with. The engineering that went into it would make the building of the Panama Canal pale in comparison! We searched everywhere for material to cover it with, and we dug it and played in it for several weeks, at least until a big rainstorm came along and put an end to that adventure.

Daddy and I were always close during those years, even if he did have to strap my behind to discipline me from time to time. I especially enjoyed the occasions when he would bring me to work with him. I thought it was so exciting to see the big steam boilers and the tall derrick up close. The thing I remember best was when I would go on the night shift. It was cold, and he would lay some clothing on the bench by the boilers to make me a bed. I would lie down and he would cover me and tell me to say my prayers, then he would kiss me goodnight. The heat from one of the boilers would put me into a sound sleep, and I would wake up with the sun. One of the rigs that I went on with Daddy was on the lawn of the Oklahoma State Capital—the rig still stands in that location today, as a monument to the state's oil fields and the workers. I also remember when Daddy took us to the Oklahoma City Museum in Oklahoma City.

Back to Asher

When work became scarce for Daddy in Oklahoma City it was time to move back to Asher. We had to pack up only the essential belongings, leaving the rest behind. It was nice to see all my old friends in Asher again; we would go fishing in the South Canadian River, about a mile south of town. In the name of fun we would look for quicksand or try to find ourselves some other semi-dangerous adventures. By this time I had become a pretty good driver, in the Model T as well as with a stick shift. No one was required to have a driver's license at that time, so Daddy would let me take the Model T Ford by myself every once in awhile even though I was only twelve or thirteen. I would pick up some of my friends and we would go for a ride. One morning I asked Daddy if I could go driving, but he said no. It was one of those days when, after three months of no rain, we had received just enough to make the red clay streets as slick as ice. Daddy had just come home from work, taken a bath in the #10 washtub, ate the breakfast Mother had left him, and he was now in bed fast asleep. I guess I was starting to feel just a little too confident and independent, because when I thought he was sound asleep I quietly went and cranked up the old Model T. It started up after a couple of cranks, and soon enough I was in it and driving it as fast as that Model T would go, which on this particular morning wasn't very fast due to the slick streets. I had to go around the block because the Model T couldn't climb the slick hill by the house. When I came back to the street where the incline was, Daddy was waiting for me. He jumped on the running board and grabbed the steering wheel, and we went back to the house where received a talking to as well as some leather to my behind.

During this time I started to gain an interest in girls and one of them that I noticed in particular was a daughter of a very wealthy family, at least in my eyes. They lived next to us and, like us, had no running water or electricity in their house. Her father was the school janitor, however, and that gave them more money then my family had. Another girl who I was interested in was a girl in my class at school. I didn't know how to act around either of them, but I got my first kiss from the beautiful daughter of the janitor.

Around this time in Asher I met a boy at church, Max, who I became very good friends with. His father sold some sort of patent medicine which was supposed to cure everything, although to this day I do not know what it was exactly. His father got his supplies in Lawton, where my cousin Hoyt lived. Max and his family were going to make a trip to Lawton for supplies, and since school was out I asked Mother and Daddy if I could go with them and visit my cousin. They said yes, and I was able to visit Hoyt for about a week. While I was there I was able to see mass production in action for the first time. My uncle was a deliveryman and salesman for

Wonder Bread, and my cousin Willadine worked in the bakery. She took me on a tour of the bakery, and when I saw all those bread wrappers all I could think was that I wanted to go to the movies. I sure had a great time while I was there, and I would certainly have liked to stay longer.

I rode back home with Max's parents, and on the way home we just barely avoided a very serious accident. We were driving at night on a dirt road in open range country, which means that live stock were free to roam wherever they wished. The headlights on cars at that time were so dim you had to strike a match to see if they were on, and we were doing about twenty-five or thirty miles per hour. Suddenly, and seemingly out of nowhere, we came across a huge horse in the road, and it was only through a combination of good driving and some luck that the horse moved at the right moment that we were able to avoid a serious accident and arrive home safely.

I arrived back home to find Daddy out of work again. We had to start cutting and selling stove wood, thrashing pecans, or doing whatever we could to make a little money to buy food with. Soon, things were so bad that we were forced to move again.

Union Valley

Daddy heard that drilling had started up again near Ada, so we loaded everything we could fit while still allowing room for us to sit, and off we went again. Counting Mother and Daddy there were eight of us at that time. We ended up in a little town near Ada called Union Valley. It was so small that it did not have much more than one store and a one-room school, and we moved into a house right across the street from the school. Daddy found a job shortly after we arrived there, and all of us kids started school.

I was in seventh grade at that time, and because I didn't like school I did as little work as possible. Once, while I was walking to school, Miss. Archer drove by and picked me up, and I rode into school with her. She asked me why I didn't work a little harder, and told me that I had the ability to be an excellent student. We talked as we drove along, and she complimented me by saying that she enjoyed talking to me and that I was very articulate. Our conversation was very uplifting for awhile, but I knew that the main thing that soured me on school was that every time I started a new one I would have to fight a bully, even though I just hated fighting. Daddy would always say to me: "Darrell, don't you ever start a fight, and always be polite. But don't ever be pushed around by anyone, because if you allow it to happen you will be pushed around all of your life."

People who worked in the oil fields, like Daddy, were very good people for the most part, but they worked in a hard and dirty job and often became hardened toward life. At times they carried that hardness home with them, and as a result many of their children became bullies. Although I was apprehensive at first, I finally found a very good situation at the Union Valley school. The teacher was a man, and Mr. Fields, the switch cutter, immediately came to mind. However, this teacher was the opposite of Mr. Fields. He took an interest in every one of us kids, and he was always searching for ways to make things a little bit better. Through his kindness and friendship he made a lasting impression on me and others as well. He would even come over to his students' houses sometimes, just to talk, and we all liked him very much.

One of the big changes that he made was in deciding to put a bell on the schoolhouse. He went to work and built a belfry, which was no small task, and then he needed to complete the harder job: to get the bell up to the roof. The bell he had chosen was about three hundred pounds, and he came over and asked Daddy to help him hang it.

He couldn't have asked a more qualified person, because Daddy worked with heavy objects all the time in the field, and most of the time he was the derrick man, which meant that he worked about eighty feet up in the derrick. As was necessary for his job, Daddy was a very strong man. He was 5'10" and weighed about 175 pounds, and he was as solid as a rock. He was also a very good athlete; when we were young he bought boxing gloves and taught all of us to box. We would have boxing matches with each other and with our friends. Daddy was also an outstanding wrestler, and he would teach us all various wrestling holds, some of which he learned from experience and some from college athletes who were working in the oil fields. Although he taught us how to fight, he always taught us not to be mean or bully.

Daddy agreed to help hang the bell. He said, "Come on Darrell, let's go and help get that bell up so we can hear it ring." We worked hard all day to get it up. It took quite a lot of planning and execution, but we got it up and the kids at that school always had a bell after that. I always enjoyed hearing that bell ring, especially knowing that I had helped to get it up there.

While we were in Union Valley our family got a dog. It had short legs and a long body, but it could catch a rabbit in no time flat. We still had my

.410-gauge shotgun which I used to shoot rabbits and quail, and Mother could cook them for a delicious dinner.

During this time I went to work for a farmer up the road from us who raised cattle, pigs, chicken and ducks. The way that I started working for this farmer is a story in itself. I had never seen a duck before, and I was hunting near this farmer's land when I saw my first one. Although I wasn't sure exactly what it was, it looked like it would be good to eat, so I put my .410 to my shoulder and shot my first duck. The farmer heard the shot and came to see what it was. I had just picked up the duck and had it in hand when the farmer came over to me and asked why I had shot his duck. He was a little angry, but when I explained that I hadn't realized it was his he eventually cooled down, and we became friends. He asked me if I'd like to do some work for him and I said yes. He gave me the duck to take home, so I brought it home for Mother to cook for dinner. It turns out that cleaning a duck is a much harder job than cleaning a chicken, but she managed to make a meal out of it.

The first job the farmer had me do was cultivate a large corn field across the road from where we lived. He took me to the barn where he had a team of mules, and after showing me where the harnesses were he left me to harness the team and get to work. I did, but soon realized that the cultivator was a two-row cultivator, which I had never used before. I had only used a one-row with a horse or mule, so the farmer had to show me how to operate this one, but I caught on quickly. I worked about six hour days for a dollar a day. Although it was hard work I always felt good doing it, and that was the first time I realized that I could do man's work.

While we were living in Union Valley I met a very pretty girl at school. She lived about a mile up the hill from where we lived, and we became good friends. She would visit us or I would visit her at her house, and things were going great with us until we found out we would have to move again for Daddy to find work—we were going back to Asher. Before we left, however, I got my second kiss from a girl.

As usual, moving meant taking only what was most important and leaving the rest behind. This time we took a battery powered radio with us. We would only play it for about an hour a day because we didn't want to run the batteries down. We always listened to "Amos and Andy," and another show that we enjoyed featured a couple of Texas string bands that we could sing along with.

When we got back to Asher there was no work of any kind. Once again we were buying food from Mr. McClure on credit, just to get by.

Eventually it came time to move again, in the hopes of finding work for Daddy somewhere else.

Holiday, Texas

Daddy heard that there was drilling starting in Holiday, Texas, which was about two hundred miles from Asher. By this time we had an old Model T truck that we loaded down with all that we could fit. We filled the gas tank at Albert Browder's gas station, where I had been working pumping gas for fifty cents a day, usually for no more than three or four cars a day. Putting gas in a car was a lot more work then than it is now. First you had to pump it by hand up into a gallons-metered overhead glass container. Once you had pumped it in, you would use a spicket and let gravity do its work while it flowed into the customer's tank until he had the amount that he wanted. At that time the price of gas was ten cents a gallon, but most people couldn't afford it.

We were lucky if our old Model T averaged ten miles per hour. When night came Daddy would pull off to the side of the road and he and Mother would fix us something to eat and make up a bed for the kids. When we woke up breakfast would be ready, and we would wash our face and hands, eat, and get back on the road again. The fact is, we never thought about it being a hardship; we enjoyed the adventure, and I started to get the wanderlust myself. When we went over the Red River into Texas we were very excited and started to sing. When we arrived in Holiday Daddy rented a little shotgun house like the one we had lived in at Asher.

After we had settled into the new house, Daddy went looking for a job and all of us kids started school. Jean and I were in the eighth grade, Bill in sixth, Ray in fourth, Ed in second and Pat was too young to go to school yet. We only lived about four or five blocks from school, and at this school I never had to fight the school bully to prove myself as I had so many times before. I became good friends with a boy named Wayne the very first day, and he and I were to have many good times together.

Daddy wasn't able to find work right away, so he started looking for people to sell stove wood to. Luckily, he was able to find quite a few customers fairly quickly. He found a place where he could cut wood, and he started cutting about three ricks a day (a rick is one-third of a cord). He would receive a dollar and fifty cents per rick, which was enough for us to get by. Sometimes after school Jean, Bill and I would take the old truck, load it up, and deliver the wood to Daddy's customers. I had trouble driving the Model T up big hills, so I started backing it up because reverse worked much better. Daddy worked very hard during that time, cutting wood, and even though his hands were tough he would get big blisters on them. He tied rags around them and just kept cutting, and we continued helping with the hauling, and it continued that way until Daddy was able to get a job in the oil fields.

Our house sat behind the barbershop on Main Street, and I became friends with the barber. He had a shoeshine chair in his shop, and he asked me if I wanted to shine shoes for him to make some extra money. I agreed, and he set me up with everything I needed in exchange for agreeing to sweep the floor and the front porch of the barbershop, and soon I was in business. I made ten cents for every shine, and sometimes I would get a five cent tip. On average I would get about four to five shines a week, which was very good since most people couldn't even afford shoes! There were a few wealthy people in Holiday and the surrounding area that made up my customer base.

There was a railroad that ran through Holiday which facilitated some shipping that ran in and out of town, most of which was related to farming or ranching. In Holiday they raised cattle and some grain; the oil fields were just starting and some of the drilling supplies came by train. One day a coal car came in, loaded with crushed stone. I was down near the tracks and a man came over and asked me, "Boy, do you want to make some money?" I said yes so he took me to where the carload of crushed stone was and said, "Do you think you can unload this car for me?" I asked him how much he would pay me, and he replied that I would make fifteen cents an hour and that he would put the shoot up for me to shovel into. Well, it turned out to be a job that I wished I had never taken because it was the most backbreaking and seemingly unending job I had ever tackled. I had my sister Jean and my brother Bill help me, and I remember that I gave them something for their help, although I'm sure it wasn't much.

Daddy finally found a job in the oil field, and since he was working pretty steady he was able to give up the job cutting wood. He earned enough money to buy a better car, but he kept the old Model T truck and let me drive it pretty much whenever I wanted to. My friend Wayne and I would occasionally drive it outside of town, and one day when we were driving we noticed a prairie dog town. I noticed all the prairie dogs were standing on their back legs barking at us, and I drove over to check it out, but as soon as we did all the little prairie dogs disappeared. I had never seen a prairie dog before and decided that I wanted one for a pet. Wayne and I came up with the brilliant idea that we would catch one for me to take home as a pet by pouring water into one of their holes to force them out. We thought for sure that we would be able to just grab one that came out; surely it would be just as simple as that. We headed back to town, about a mile away, to get a fifty-five gallon barrel to fill with water and drive back out there. We did just that, but when we filled the hole with water, no prairie dogs came out. We drove back and forth to town several times to get more water, but we were never able to get a single prairie dog to come out of its hole.

On one of our trips to get more water for the prairie dog project I was driving down a hill when all of a sudden I saw a wheel from right off our Model T go by us. At about the same time the back part of the truck on the driver's side dropped, and our project was stalled for awhile. We fixed the wheel and went back to our project, but after a lot of hard work and seeing only a few Diamondback rattlesnakes come out of wet prairie dog holes, we admitted defeat and went home without a new pet. Later on, however, we were able to get two of them when they were just pups. We fed them from a bottle filled with condensed milk, and they grew up to be great pets and watch dogs.

A few milestone events happened while we lived in Holiday. First, Jean and I both graduated from eighth grade. Also, Daddy started a business, opening up a vegetable stand on Main Street. He bought various types of vegetables for sale and put them on display, covering them with a canvas to keep the sun off. He put Jean in charge of the stand, but it was a short-lived enterprise. Holiday was a small town, and the few people who did come by had no extra money to spend on fresh vegetables. Also, it was hot and dry and the stand had no refrigeration to keep the vegetables fresh. It seems the little vegetable stand was doomed from the start, but Daddy was working steady at that point so he just took the loss and went on.

By that time my mother was pregnant with my brother Bud, number seven. When it was close to the time of his birth Daddy started leaving the car at home and riding into work with someone else. He also allowed me to go to work with him once and spend the day so that I would know how to get on the rig. He told me that if Mother should tell me to go I was to leave at once, and I was to stay close to home until it was time.

I was asleep when the time came. Mother woke me and said, "Darrell, you and Jean go and get Daddy." We were out of there as fast as we could, but we were having one of the rainstorms that came only once every three months or so. All the roads were nothing more than dirt tracks with deep ruts, and they were all filled with water. There was no windshield wiper on the Model T or the car, and between bad vision and the bad road conditions I was having a very hard time getting to Daddy. When we arrived at the rig Daddy was out of his work clothes and in his clean clothes waiting for us. I'm sure he had been able to see us for quite awhile before we arrived, even despite the bad weather, because he had been working about eighty feet up while the crew was pulling the pipe out of the holes to change bits.

As soon as we got there Daddy jumped in the driver's seat and started for home as fast as he could. When we got home Mother and Daddy sent all of us kids to a neighbor's house. It felt very unsettling for us as there were so many things happening very fast, but the next morning we were able to go back home and greet Mother, Daddy, and our new little brother. Mother and Daddy asked me if I wanted to give him a name and I said yes. I named him after my good friend and fellow prairie dog hunter, Donald Wayne. That was March 26, 1938.

A few days after Donald was born we heard a noise from the sky, and I looked up and saw something I had heard but never seen before—an airplane. It had a wing below the body and one above, and it was flying very low over the town. It circled the town five or six times before landing just outside of Holiday. Everyone in town was excited and a lot of people immediately rushed to where the plane had landed, including Jean, Billy and I. By the time we got there a lot of other people had already gathered around the airplane, and the pilot was offering a ride around the town for a dollar. The first person gave him a dollar, and I watched as he got in the seat behind the pilot and got strapped in. The pilot twirled the propeller and started the engine, climbed in and revved the motor, and soon enough the plane was in the sky. It was so exciting just to watch, and I knew I had to give it a try. I had a dollar in my pocket, and when the pilot landed I made sure that I was the next one to go up. I was nervous and excited all at once. This time the pilot kept the engine running while I was strapped into my seat, and in just a few minutes after giving him my dollar, we were in the air! It was one of the most exciting things I had ever done. We told Mother about it when we got home and she didn't like it, but Daddy thought it was great.

Beside the railroad track that ran through town there was a grain elevator that was used to move the grain that would be shipped out by train. We had seen a grain elevator before, but we had never been in one, and since this one was not far from where we lived curiosity finally got the best of us. One day Jean, Bill and I decided to go take a look at it up close. It was round, built of corrugated steel, and about sixty to eighty feet high. We went inside to look around, and we saw a platform with a railing all around it. It was obviously not a stationary platform, as there were lifting cables attached to the top of it. The cables extended up to the top of the elevator, over some pulleys, and were eventually attached to another platform with railings around it, identical to the one on the floor. They were joined by the cables in such a way that when one was lowered the other would rise. There was a ladder to the top, so we climbed the ladder to check things out from above. When we got up there we found that the elevator was sectioned into different enclosures with grain stored in every one, except the one that we were in. We went back down to investigate further, and soon found out that there was a brake that controlled the platform as it rose to the top of the elevator and lowered the other to the floor. We set the brake so that the platform wouldn't move, and then we climbed to the top again. When we got up there we found what they used to fill the elevator shafts with grain, and when we went over the side into a shaft filled with grain, we started to sink. We didn't go down very far, but we could have easily been buried in about fifty feet of grain. Instead, we were able to fill the top car with grain to get out alive.

When we had gotten out, we climbed back down the ladder and after all three of us had gotten on the platform below we released the brake. The weight above was enough to just get us off the floor, so I set the brake and got out. I told Jean to release the brake and be sure to stop the platform when they go to the top. She did release the brake, and when she did you would have thought they were propelled by rockets, with the speed that one went up and the other down! The one going up went so fast that Jean had no time to put the brake on, and the one going down was heading right toward me, just as fast. I had to move fast just to get out the way, and when it hit the floor we could see that we had done some serious damage to the machine. The one that Jean and Bill were on continued up for another three or four feet and then dropped back down with a jerk. I ran up the ladder as fast as I could; Jean and Bill were both crying, but they were okay besides a few cuts and bruises. We climbed back down that ladder as fast as we could and ran out of there. The grain elevator was far enough from town that no one had heard the crash as the elevator hit the floor, and you can bet that we never told anyone about the damage we had caused. Later, Jean and Bill would joke and tell me that I had tried to kill them that day, and we would all have a big laugh about our day in the grain elevator.

Back to Oklahoma

Things started going badly again, so Daddy traded the car for a truck and we loaded all the things we really needed and started back to Asher. When we crossed the Red River this time we were glad to be back in Oklahoma. We were some distance from Asher when we lost a wheel on the truck, and Daddy couldn't find anything to repair it with. After talking with some local people he was able to find a man with a truck who would haul us to Asher in exchange for our broken truck. We unloaded everything from one truck to the other, and Mother and our baby brother rode in the cab while Daddy rode in the back of the truck with the rest of the kids. When we got to Asher Daddy had to find a place for us to live, and quick, since the man who had driven us there had to return home. Daddy found a couple of rooms in back of the hardware store on Main Street, and we all moved in.

The next day Daddy went looking for a job, and he found one on a Wild Cat drilling rig, which was set up to try to identify a new oil field from which to drill. While we were living in Asher our cousin Estelle, Aunt Lottie's daughter, came to visit us for awhile. She was Jean's age and a lot of fun to be around. Once she and Jean were playing in back of our house and discovered a nest of bumblebees in the ground. We lived in a time where you created your own entertainment, and Jean and Estelle created their own that day by disturbing those bees and then seeing which one of them could get away and not get stung. This game developed into quite a contest, and after watching them for awhile I came up with the bright idea to put on some heavy clothes, cutting two eye holes in a paper bag, and just walking in to show the bumblebees who was boss. Everything went just fine until one bee got into one of the eye holes and stung me on my forehead, just above my nose. I ran for cover, tearing the bag off my head as I went. Within a short time both of my eyes were so swollen that they were nearly shut, and I could hardly see. That was the end of that game for me.

When school started again I enrolled with Jean in the ninth grade and went out for Freshman Football. I was enjoying it, but I could not keep my mind on the book work. I would sit at my desk, just staring out the window and daydreaming about being somewhere else. To add to my desires to be somewhere else, during a visit from Uncle Henry and Aunt Ora I overheard them talking about going out to California because things had gotten so bad in Oklahoma. I also learned that I had two uncles that had moved to California when I was small, Daddy's brother, Uncle Hawley and Mother's brother, Uncle Odd. I had heard of California—lots of people from Oklahoma were starting to move out there—and I started to fantasize about going out there too, to find this better life that everyone kept talking about. I got the addresses of Uncle Hawley and Uncle Odd, and I continued in school, doing whatever work I could to make money to save in order to go to California. After football season had ended I heard that I could get a ride to California for ten dollars, and I went out to Shawnee to check it out. I found out that I could get a ride in a car that was being transported from a car dealership out to the West Coast for resale. They let me know when the next trip would be made and that I could get a ride for only ten dollars—it was as simple as that. I told them to hold the ride for me and I went home and told Mother and Daddy about the arrangements I had made. I told them I wanted to go out to California to visit Uncle Hawley and Uncle Odd. Although they didn't particularly like the idea, they agreed to let me go. I had some money, but not quite enough, so Daddy gave me a few dollars too. The day before I was to leave I said goodbye to my friends at school, and the next day I put the few clothes I had into a bag and headed out. I hitchhiked my way to Shawnee and paid my ten dollars. The driver and the other passenger got into the front seat, and I climbed into the back of the nicest car I had ever been in, and with that, I was on my way out to California.

On my way to California

I had no knowledge of California; I didn't know what it would be like, how far away it was, or even what my uncles were like. They didn't even know I was coming! It was late and it was cold when we left for California, and there was no heat in that beautiful car. That didn't bother me though, because I was just excited to be going on the greatest adventure of my life. I had always had an adventurous streak as a boy, and although I was apprehensive I was also excited about my upcoming adventure in California. We traveled north from Shawnee until we reached Route 66, then we headed west. As we drove I got acquainted with the two men I was traveling with, and they were both very friendly. We drove all night and I eventually fell asleep, and when I woke up we were pulling into a gas station that had a café. They were going in to eat but I declined; I was hungry, but I only had five dollars and I wanted to make it last all the way to California.

After awhile the country started to look a lot different than the country we had left behind in Asher. It was much flatter in most places, and the hills that we did see were much more visible than they had been in Asher because there were no trees on them. We drove until the middle of the afternoon when we stopped for gas and for something to eat. I was very hungry by that time, so I went in with them and ordered a hamburger with fried potatoes and soda pop for fifteen cents. When we got on the road again, I had a full belly. I remember going through Amarillo, Texas, and the feeling of excitement I had when we crossed the border from Texas into New Mexico.

We started our second night on the road, and I was sleeping when all of a sudden the sound of someone hollering jerked me awake. We had been driving in rain when I fell asleep, and while I slept it had gotten cold enough for the rain to freeze on the road. The driver had lost control of the car, causing it to spin off the road into a gradual decline that tipped the car on its side. The passenger in front hollered, "Turn off the key!" Then he hollered even louder, "Turn off the damn key and get out!" We started climbing out of the windows and doors, and when we eventually got out we had to stand in the freezing rain for an hour or longer before someone came along, because there was hardly any traffic on Route 66 at that time of night.

Finally someone came by and saw us, and other cars started stopping to help too. When there were enough people to turn the car back on its wheels we all pushed it back to the highway. Once we got it up and back onto the highway everyone was trying to figure out if and how we could restart the engine. They opened the hood and checked the oil, satisfied that it would be okay, so the driver got in, hit the starter, and started us running. He let it run for awhile, and shook hands with all of the people who had helped us get back on the road. We got in the car and were on our way again.

I was wet and cold for a long time, but after putting on the few extra clothes I had I was able to get warm enough to go to sleep. The next thing I knew, I was feeling very hot. I opened my eyes and the sun was shining very bright; we were stopped and the other two men were asleep. I sat for awhile before deciding to get out and look around, and when I got out I was amazed at what I saw. It was so beautiful; the view was unlike anything I had ever seen before. There was a cliff about a thousand feet high, and the area around it contained the most beautiful colors I had ever seen in nature. The entire area was completely covered in trees. I was standing there, spellbound, when one of the other men came over and said, "Ain't that the prettiest thing you ever saw?" I agreed; it was. By this time the other man was up too, and we all enjoyed the view for a bit until the driver said, "Well, let's hit the road," and we were on our way again.

As we drove the scenery continued to change, and I was enjoying every bit of it. After a few hours of driving it seemed that there was less and less color and more small trees; they were a type of tree that was different from any I had ever seen. I was fascinated with the scenery and continued the stare out the window; one of the men told me that we were in Arizona now. I started looking for something different, expecting the scenery to change, but it stayed the same for the rest of the day. It was almost dark when we stopped at a trading post where they had gas and a café. Everyone was tired and hungry, so after the car was filled with gas we went into the café for something to eat. I was starving by that time, so I had fried potatoes and onions, a bowl of pinto beans, a large hunk of cornbread and a large glass of butter milk, which cost me about thirty-five cents. After we ate the driver said, "We'll stay here for the night." There was a small building that the driver and the other passenger slept in, and I stayed in the car. I slept in the back seat as soundly as a baby. They woke me the next morning and asked me if I wanted to eat, but I said no. While they were eating I went to an outside toilet to relieve myself and also found a place where I could wash my face and hands.

When they came out of the café we loaded up the car and drove for quite awhile, and the scenery started changing again. The trees starting getting bigger and bigger the further we drove and one of the men informed me that we were getting close to Flagstaff, Arizona. Not long after that we came to a town where we stopped to eat before we were on our way again. As we drove I could see that a lot of the trees were at least a hundred feet high, and I was amazed at how different they were from anything I had seen around Asher. I was fascinated by everything we passed and all the new things I was seeing. I saw the houses that the Indians lived in and liked the way they looked. We drove for the rest of the day, and toward evening we started down a long hill that was windy and crooked. Just before dark one of the men said, "We should be in Needles pretty soon." I asked where Needles was and he informed me that it was just over the bridge that crossed the Colorado River. That was the first I had ever heard of the Colorado River, and I was even more exciting when the man told me, "When we cross the bridge we will be in the state of California." I kept quiet about how excited I was, but I couldn't believe I was almost in California at last.

It kept getting hotter the further we went, but I kept awake and alert, watching for the bridge. Finally we came to it and we crossed the Colorado River into California, driving into Needles. We stopped at a gas station and restaurant, a new name for café, and after gassing up and eating we found a place to sleep. I stayed in the car again, and was sound asleep when they woke me in the morning. It was still dark when we started driving; they told me that we started driving so early because they wanted to cover as many miles as they could before the desert got too hot. We drove for a long time before the sun came up, and when it did I started to see what the desert sun looked and felt like. As the sun got higher I understood the difference between this heat and the heat in Oklahoma; it got hot in Oklahoma at times, but it was nothing like this.

We drove until once again we had to get gas and something to eat. After we started driving again I started to see more and more towns. I had given the driver my Uncle Hawley's address in Inglewood. It was starting to get dark when he told me that he would drop me at my uncle's house before he dropped off the other passenger.

Uncle Hawley and Aunt Evelyn's house in Englewood

We got to Uncle Hawley's just after dark and the streetlights had just come on. I took my few belongings out of the car, and both men got out and shook my hand and wished me good luck. As they were leaving I looked at the house and noticed that there were no lights on. It was drizzling rain, and I was very tired. There was a house next door with lights on, so I left my small bag of things and went to the front door of the house next door. I knocked and asked the man who answered if a Hawley Stark lived next door. He said no and my heart missed a beat. Then he said, "There's a Harry Stark that lives there." I went back to the house and sat on the front step for awhile, not wanting to disturb them if they were asleep since they didn't even know to expect me. I was getting more wet and feeling very miserable, and finally I decided that I would try to get in the house and wait where it was dry. I tried the front door, but it was locked, so I walked around to the back of the house. It had a screen door, but when I tried to open it I realized that it was locked from the inside as well. I took out my pocket knife and made a cut in the screen that I could put my hand through to unlatch the screen door. After I opened the screen door, I tried the solid door only to find that it was locked. I stood there for awhile, not sure what to do, but I realized I could be miserable or I could try to find an open window to get in. I finally found one that I could open so I pushed it up and climbed in, but I still had to climb over a bed. By the time I got in my night vision was getting good, and there was also quite a bit of light from the street. I worked my way to the front door, opened it, brought my bag in and shut the door again.

I made my way to the living room, which had a large couch in it. I was wet, but I was even more exhausted, so I sat on the couch for awhile, then eventually took off my shoes to lie down on the couch. The next thing I knew someone kicked me, and I awoke with a start. The room was bright with light and I saw a man standing above me with a hammer in his hand. He yelled, "Hey you SOB! What are you doing in my house!"

I asked him, "Are you Uncle Hawley?"

He lowered the hammer and said, "Yes. And who the hell are you?"

I told him it was me, Darrell, and he asked, "Darrell?" Then he put the hammer down on the floor and started asking me all kinds of questions about how I got there. Finally he said, "Darrell, you are as dirty as hell. Come with me."

He took me to the bathroom and turned on the light. They had electricity in their house, and there was a big tub. He walked over and turned on handles and more handles, and water started running from them. He said, "Come here boy," and he had me put my hand under the flow of water and showed me how to adjust it to my comfort. He told me to turn it off when the tub got half full, then he got me a wash cloth and towel and some clothes of his to put on when I was done. When I had gotten undressed I got in the tub and stretched out, and it was one of the most wonderful feelings that I had ever experienced. It was surely a lot better than a #10 wash tub. I laid there and enjoyed it for a long time, but after I finished and got dressed it was time to meet my Aunt Evelyn and my cousin Jimmy, who was their only child. He was only nine or ten years old and was a little confused about everything that was happening in his house that night, but Aunt Evelyn was as loving as could be. She made me feel comfortable and at home, and told me to come on in the kitchen. All four of us went in and she turned on the light, and I saw a kitchen unlike any that I had ever seen in all my life. She had an electric refrigerator instead of an ice box, a kitchen sink instead of a dishpan, and, most impressive of all, the house had electric lights instead of coal oil lamps, as well as hot and cold running water.

Uncle Hawley, Jimmy and I went over and sat down at the dining table, and they started asking me about everyone at home. Soon, Jimmy became very interested in hearing about his cousins that he had never met. In just a little while Aunt Evelyn had plates on the table, and she set out a good meal for us to eat. After we ate they took me to where I was to sleep, and showed me where everything was. They turned down the covers on the bed and said, "We'll see you in the morning. Sleep as long as you want." I turned off the light and got in bed, and I was out like a light. When I woke up Aunt Evelyn was the only one at home, because Uncle Hawley had gone to work and Jimmy had gone to school. Aunt Evelyn said, "When you get out of the bathroom I will have your breakfast ready." When I came out, which was not too long, she had a plate full of food on the table for me. After I ate I asked her where my clothes were and she said, "You'll have to wear Uncle Hawley's for awhile. I am washing yours, and when they are done in a few minutes I will hang them out to dry."

I noticed that the sun was shining and I was glad that it wasn't raining anymore. After eating and talking for awhile she said, "I think your clothes are done." She picked up the empty plate and put it in the sink and said, "Darrell, come on." We went to a back room that was used as a laundry room, and she went to the washing machine and started putting my clothes through a ringer, and I took them as they came out. That was the first time I had ever seen an electric washing machine. We went outside to hang them to dry when I noticed a tree with orange fruit on it. I asked Aunt Evelyn what kind of tree it was and she said, "Darrell, that's an orange tree." I walked to it and found it loaded with oranges. I asked her if I could pick one and she said that I could pick as many as I wanted to eat. I had seen oranges before, but I had only been able to eat one at Christmas as a special treat. I pulled one off the tree, and I can still remember seeing the juice pop up to the surface, and the smell of it as I was eating it. I can almost taste it now. Seeing it on the tree and picking it for myself to eat has made it a vivid memory that always stays with me.

When Aunt Evelyn finished hanging my clothes we went into the house. I opened the screen door that I had cut a hole in the night before, but I didn't say anything about it. When we got in she said, "Sit down and relax while your clothes are drying. I am going to do some house cleaning." I asked her if I could help, but she told me just to sit down and take it easy. I did, but we continued talking and getting to know each other while she was working, and it was the beginning of a loving relationship that would last our entire lifetime.

When she finished cleaning she said, "I think the clothes are dry," and she went out the door before I could say that I would go get them. I wanted to go because I was afraid that she would see the hole in the screen, but she was gone just a few minutes before she came back in and said only, "Darrell, here are your clothes. Go get dressed and we will go into town." When I came out, dressed again in my own clothes, we headed into town.

All the streets were paved and lined with a kind of tree that I had never seen before; they were tall with white trunks, and Aunt Evelyn informed me that they were eucalyptus trees. There were also palm trees, as well as other types of vegetation that I had never seen. When we got into town she took me to a clothing store and started me with about three changes of clothes with underwear. Then she bought me a new pair of shoes and some socks. We had a sandwich and an ice cream cone, and after we were done shopping we walked around town and talked. She asked me about school and I told her that I didn't like it much. On our way home we picked up Jimmy at school, and shortly after we got home Uncle Hawley came in through the back door. He had a little smile on his face, and he asked me, "Darrell, did you try the back door last night?" My heart stopped, and I took a few deep breaths before I answered him that yes, I had. He could tell I was scared, and he looked at me and said, "Ah, hell, boy, that's alright. I'll fix it." I told him I was sorry, and that was the last I ever heard of it.

While we were waiting for supper Jim asked me to come outside with him, and he and I went to the back of the house where there was another building. He opened the door and brought out his bicycle to show to me. I had seen a bicycle before, but I had never ridden one. He asked me if I wanted to ride it and I said no. He asked me why not, and I told him that I didn't know how. He looked surprised, but he only said, "Then I will teach you." Before we were even called for supper I could ride that thing like a pro, and Jim was as happy as could be because he had taught me. He was ten and I was sixteen.

We had a wonderful meal and I really enjoyed talking and catching up with them. During the conversation Uncle Hawley asked Aunt Evelyn, "Did you get the boy some clothes?" She said that yes, she had, and Uncle Hawley said, "That's good." After I took my bath and got ready for bed Uncle Hawley said, "Darrell, I'll pick you up tomorrow at noon and you can take a ride with me." As I went to bed I realized that only twenty-four hours after cutting the screen and climbing through the window, I loved these people who, I was sure, loved me as well.

The next morning I woke up in time for us to all have breakfast together, and Uncle Hawley went off to work. Aunt Evelyn asked me if I wanted to go with her to take Jim to school, but I said I would like to stay and, if Jim didn't mind, ride his bicycle. Jim got a big smile on his face and said yes, and Aunt Evelyn said it was okay, but she reminded me to be back at noon to go with Uncle Hawley. As soon as they were gone I was on that bike and riding all over town. I had a wonderful time, and although I arrived back at the house a bit tired I was anxious to go with Uncle Hawley.

He came in the backyard at noon, driving a truck that had a large tank on it. He said, "Boy, get in," and I climbed up into the truck. We started talking about everyone in Oklahoma; he was very interested in what they were all doing and what was new with his family. During the conversation I also found out that he had his own business related to the oil field industries; the tank truck was a part of it.

I stayed with Uncle Hawley, Aunt Evelyn and Jim for about two weeks, and during that time I did a lot of things I would never have had the opportunity to do otherwise. I saw the Pacific Ocean and went to the Los Angeles City Museum where I saw all kinds of wonderful things, including Lindbergh's *Spirit of St. Louis* airplane. I also went to watch a bicycle competition that Jim was in, which was really great as well.

I hadn't said anything about Uncle Odd and Aunt Ivey, but I wanted to see them too. One evening at supper I mentioned to Uncle Hawley that I would also like to visit them while I was here. Uncle Hawley asked me where they lived, and after giving him the address he told me that he would see if they were in the telephone book. That was quite a surprise to me, because although I knew that they had a telephone, the idea of looking someone up in a book puzzled me. As it was, this was the first house I had seen with a telephone, and I was having a hard enough time getting used to that idea. He took out a small book and looked for awhile, and soon enough I heard him on the phone talking. He came back and said that he had talked to them and that they wanted to see me as well, and Uncle Hawley promised that he would drive me to them the next day. The next morning we all got in the car and the whole family drove me to my next big adventure.

My next big adventure: Uncle Odd and Aunt Ivey's house

When we got to Uncle Odd's they were all waiting, and everyone was friendly with each other—Pollards and Starks have always enjoyed each others company. Uncle Hawley, Aunt Evelyn and Jim stayed for about three hours before leaving to go home. I hated to see them go, but they assured me that they would see me again soon. When they left Aunt Ivey said, "Darrell, get your things and follow me." She took me to a nice bedroom and showed me where the bathroom was. It also had a bath tub, just like at Uncle Hawley and Aunt Evelyn's. She told me that she was glad that I came and that they wanted me to feel at home, which made me feel much more relaxed. They had three children, two boys and a girl. The boys were quite a bit older than me, but the girl was about my age. They were all very nice and did everything they could to make me feel comfortable; the first week I was there someone took me somewhere every day. I had so many great experiences, like fishing on the pier, going to an amusement park or just riding around and seeing oranges, lemons and the other vegetation that grew in abundance near their house. Even with all the love being given to me though, I was beginning to miss Mother, Daddy and my brothers and sisters. I wanted to go home, but I was flat broke, so first I had to find a job of some kind in order to make some money.

By this time I had grown close to my cousin Aubrey. He was working every day and I asked him if he knew where I might get a job. He answered, "Maybe I can get you a job where I work. I'll ask tomorrow when I go, and if I can, you can ride to work with me."

I could hardly sleep all night and was restless all day, waiting for him to come home with the verdict. When I saw his car drive up I became even more nervous, that was how badly I wanted and needed that job. He got out of the car with a big smile on his face and told me, "Darrell, you start work tomorrow. You'll be paid two dollars a day." I couldn't believe my luck; the most I had ever made in Oklahoma was one dollar a day. The next morning, after not sleeping much, I was up. Aunt Ivey gave me a good breakfast and after I ate and Aubrey said it was time to go, she handed me my lunch as I was walking out the door. She did that for me every day that I was there.

When we got to work I couldn't believe the size of the building and all the cars that were parked outside. I went inside with Aubrey and once again I was amazed. There were people everywhere and it seemed that everyone was doing something different. I was taken to the office where I was formally hired, which in itself was a new experience for me. After I was hired they took me to my work station where I was introduced to my boss. He told me I would be loading and unloading trucks and delivery supplies for the workers in the factory. The Joy Shoe Company was a production line factory that made women's shoes, and that was who I worked for while I was in California. The work I did was hard, but I enjoyed it, and I worked there for two or three weeks, until I felt I had enough money to make it home. I asked Uncle Odd if he could call Uncle Hawley and ask him to pick me up, because I wanted to see them before I went back home to Oklahoma.

Uncle Hawley agreed to come and pick me up in a few days, so I went to work where I thanked them and told them I appreciated what they had done for me, and I said my goodbyes. Two or three days later Uncle Hawley came and got me, and I said goodbye to the aunts, uncles and cousins that I had come to love and who had been so wonderful to me during my visit. On our way to Uncle Hawley's I talked about going home and hoped I could get a ride back to Oklahoma in the same way I had gotten there. Uncle Hawley and Aunt Evelyn asked me to stay for awhile and go to school out there, and Jim said, "Please stay." It made me feel wonderful to have them ask me to stay, but I was homesick for those I had been with all my life that I loved so much. I told my aunt and uncle that I was so glad I had come to stay but that it was time for me to go home.

Uncle Hawley understood, and he told me, "Okay, we'll see what we can do tomorrow about getting you a ride home." We sat and talked awhile, and when I went to bed I lay there thinking about all the wonderful things I had done and seen, but I was also feeling in a hurry to get back home to my family.

The next day, after Uncle Hawley and Jim were gone, Aunt Evelyn started looking for someone for me to ride back to Oklahoma with. Before the day was over she had found me a ride back. It was a ten dollar ride and they were going to pick me up at the house two days later, in the afternoon. The next day Aunt Evelyn washed all my dirty clothes and packed my bag, which was larger than the one I had come with. That evening we all went to a restaurant and had a nice meal, and that night we came home and talked and laughed about how well we had all gotten acquainted.

The next morning I had breakfast with everyone. I said my goodbyes to Uncle Hawley before he left for work and then to Jim when we took him to school, and then Aunt Evelyn and I had time to have a good talk before my ride came to pick me up. Two young men arrived about two o'clock. Aunt Evelyn walked me to the car; I'm sure she did it because she wanted to satisfy herself that they would be alright for me to ride home with. She talked to them for awhile before giving me a big hug and telling me, "Be good, and go back to school."

Back Home in Oklahoma

I was sad to be leaving people that I had learned to love and become comfortable with, but mingled with that sadness was excitement to be going home. I was looking forward to seeing Mother and Daddy and my siblings. The two men that I was traveling with turned out to be very friendly, and we had a good trip back. We went back to Oklahoma by way of Las Vegas because they wanted to go over the Hoover Dam, which had not been open very long. It didn't mean anything to me because I didn't know anything about it, and when we crossed it late at night I was tired and not very impressed. We proceeded on past the dam and picked up Route 66 east, and about three days later we were back in Shawnee, Oklahoma.

The two men dropped me off, and I walked to the highway that had about three cars an hour and stuck out my thumb. The first car passing stopped and drove me the twenty-seven miles to Asher, where I was dropped off at Mr. McClure's store. I went in and Mr. McClure said, "You are back!" He told me that Mother and Daddy had moved, and I felt my heart skip a beat until he told me that they still lived in Asher.

I walked home, and when I walked up to the house Mother spotted me first. She was so happy to see me, and rushed out to greet me, crying, holding my little brother Bud in her arms. Ed and Pat were there, and they greeted me as enthusiastically as Mother had. Soon after, Bill, Jean and Ray came home from school, and we were all overjoyed to see each other.

They were all asking me questions about my trip, wanting to know about California and about our uncles, aunts and cousins. My sister, Jean started teasing me when she saw the new clothes, calling me "fancy pants" now that I had gotten back from California. A few hours later Daddy came home, and it is beyond any words I can think of to describe how great it felt to have all nine of us together again.

Mother and Jean went to work in the kitchen to cook me a good Oklahoma meal. After we ate, Jean got the dishpan and heated some water on the stove to wash all the supper dishes. By this time it was starting to get dark so we lit the coal oil lamps on the kitchen table and talked and laughed all together. Daddy had put a large tea kettle full of water on the stove to heat, and the old #10 washtub was brought in and set on the kitchen floor and filled so it was half full. When the tea kettle of water was hot it was taken off the stove and poured into the tub to make the water warm. When this was done, Mother and Jean started bathing all the little ones. When they were bathed and taken to bed the older boys washed up and went to bed too. Daddy emptied the tub and put clean water in it, saying, "Darrell, we are all going to bed. You look dirty, so you had better take a bath before you go to bed."

After they all left I took off my clothes and set my feet in the water. I felt like the happiest sixteen year-old boy in the world, because I was with the eight people that I loved most. Once I had bathed and put on clean clothes, I blew out the coal oil lamp and worked my way to the cotton mattress on the floor, covered with a sheet. I lay down beside my brothers Bill and Ray, and I fell asleep listening to their breathing, feeling complete joy to have them lying so close beside me.

When I got up the next morning Daddy had already gone to work. I saw the kids off to school, and Mother and I sat and talked about the people in California and those in Oklahoma. She told me that Uncle Henry and Aunt Ora, Uncle Sim and Aunt Bobby, and Uncle Carl and Aunt Mert had all moved to Illinois, as they had heard that there was work in the oil fields there. Once we had something to eat I told Mother that I was going to see some of my old friends. I was able to find most of them; Max and Perry were still in school, but Harry and most of the others had already dropped out and were just hanging around. They wanted to work, but there just wasn't any to be had, so there was nothing to do but hang around all day.

After only a week at home I was starting to become restless. One day Daddy came home from work and said they had finished drilling the well they were on and he was now out of work. He said to Mother, "Let's go see Mammy for awhile." She agreed, and we decided to leave in a few days.

The next day was Sunday and we all got up and went to church. It was so nice to see everyone, and they were all happy to see me back. There were about thirty people in our church and I knew every one of them. Except for a handful of them, everyone there was as poverty stricken as our family, and they had all been that way for so long that they had conditioned themselves to survive the hard times and to continually fight to make things better. Because we were all living through the same hardships we all felt a sense of camaraderie, and no one felt inferior to anyone else. Even the six who were better off often gave what they had and deprived themselves to help those of us who were worse off, and they were loved by everyone for it. Our church became a community and even a family for all of us.

Furthermore, before Mother and Daddy became members of the church, Daddy used to swear as bad as all his brothers. Mother was always after him not to swear in front of the kids, but nothing stopped him. Nothing, that is, until the day he was baptized; after that I never heard him curse again.

That Sunday we went home after church and had a good Okie fried chicken dinner that we topped off with a vanilla wafer pudding. That afternoon I asked Daddy if he still had the boxing gloves. He said yes and asked me if I wanted to box a little. I said sure, and he went and got the gloves. We put them on and started punching each other lightly while weaving and blocking. Soon, I started feeling confident, and I was picking up the pace and punching pretty hard. Daddy picked up the pace too, and the next thing I remember Daddy was squatting by me asking, "Are you okay son?" He had hit me harder than he meant to and had knocked me cold. I was fine though, and everything turned out okay; we had a great time the rest of the day.

The next morning we got up early, had breakfast, and loaded the car with the things we would need for our visit to Ardmore. We had a 1938 Ford Sedan at the time, with considerably more power than the Model T, so we went over the Arbuckle Mountains with ease, despite the fact that there were more of us this time. We got to Mammy's house, and shortly after we were there Daddy went to the store. In a short while he and Uncle Tom were back with a lot of groceries. We stayed at Mammy's for about three days and then went the thirty miles to visit Uncle Lonnie and Aunt May and our cousins. When we got there everyone came out to the car to see us, and we all went into the house, bringing in some of the groceries with us, including a bunch of steaks that Daddy had bought. We didn't realize the windows were open, with no screens, and we were talking with everything laid out on the table when Uncle Lonnie's coon hound jumped in the window and grabbed the steaks. He jumped back out and kept on going so that none of us could catch him, and the next time we saw him he had a big belly and a very lazy look on his face.

Uncle Lonnie and Aunt May's oldest son, Earl, was about my age, and he and I were very happy to see each other again. They lived on a farm not far from the Washita River, and I always looked forward to going fishing when we visited them. The morning after we had arrived, he and I were up early and on our way, two bamboo poles in hand. We were distracted on our way, however, when we went past some pools of water that hadn't been there before and heard a big splash in one of them. We went over to check it out and found, to our amazement, that the pool was full of large fish. The Washita River had previously overflowed its banks, and now that it had receded it had left all the fish landlocked in small pools. We rushed back to the house to tell Uncle Lonnie and Daddy about the fish, but they said that they were carp, too bony to eat. In fact, they told us, they weren't good for much more than fertilizer.

That was all we needed to hear. Earl asked, "Can I take the team and wagon?" When Uncle Lonnie asked him why he replied, "To haul fish in." Uncle Lonnie looked at Earl as if he was out of his mind, but he just shrugged his shoulders and said, "Sure."

We promptly harnessed the team of horses, hooked them to the wagon, and headed for the pool with all of our cousins following us. When we got there we started pushing the fish into a narrow part of the pool, but things didn't go as smoothly as we had anticipated. Some of the carp weighed up to six pounds, and there were also snakes in the water to contend with, although they mostly tried to get away from us. Earl moved the wagon down close to the pool and as we caught the fish we would put them in the wagon. We were having a great time, and you couldn't have paid us enough money for as hard as we worked. We loaded the wagon and got back in, heading back to the house. When we arrived everyone came out to look at what we had done, and Uncle Lonnie could do no more than ask, "Now what are you going to do with a wagonload of rotten carp?"

While I was visiting with Earl he told me that he planned to join the CCC. I asked him what it was, and he told me that it was something like the Army. I was interested in joining the CCC as well, and Earl's idea also planted the seed in my mind to join the Army in the years to come.

Colorado and the CCC

After our enjoyable visit we were on our way home again, and on the way I talked to Mother and Daddy about joining the CCC. They told me to go ahead, but Mother said, "Just six months." A couple of days after we got home I went to Shawnee and filled out all the papers, bringing some home for Mother to sign. The CCC stood for Civilian Conservation Corps, and it was a government program set up to help families going through hard times. A young man could enlist for just six months, and he was sent to work in the national parks and other government facilities. I was paid thirty dollars a month for my work; I kept seven and twenty-three went to my parents. That was enough money for Mother and Daddy to feed all eight of them very well.

The next day I packed the few belongings I had and hitched a ride to Shawnee, where I enlisted in the CCC. I took a bus to Oklahoma City, where they put me up in a hotel overnight. The next morning I met some of the other enlisted boys and they took us all to a café. We had breakfast and walked to the train station. There were enough of us to fill a whole car.

I was very excited; this was the first time I had ever been on a train. Shortly after we pulled out, the boy sitting by me started talking to me, and he and I were to become good friends. I also met a friend of his who had enlisted along with him. We were told that we were going to Colorado, which was exciting to me as this was another place I had never been and marked the beginning of another adventure in my life.

We were on the train for about three or four hours and we were having a great time talking and watching the scenery go by. As we moved along with the window open, we went around a long curve and I could see the big old steam engine belching smoke and steam. At about noon the man in charge of all of us walked down the aisle and told us to watch toward the front of the car; when he raised his hands we were to get up and follow him. About twenty minutes later we saw him talking to the conductor, then he turned and raised his hands and we all got up and on were our way.

We didn't know where we were going, but after walking through several cars we came to one that had tables set with white tablecloths. We sat down and people started bringing us food; we were all served the same good meal. It was the first time I had eaten in a dining car, and the excitement of another first experience brought us almost to Kansas. The country out there was flat, barren, and dry, but it was an amazing experience to sit by the window and watch the flat country go by at a speed unlike anything I had ever experienced. By the time we had finished supper we were well into Kansas and at about nine o'clock that night we were in for another surprise. Four or five men came in the cars and asked the boys to stand in the aisle, and before we knew it they had made our seats into a bed with white sheets and pillows and a drape between each person. You were close to the next person, but you had just enough room to undress before bed. I didn't undress, though, because I was afraid that someone might see me, and the next morning when talking to everyone else I realized that no one else had undressed either. Also, they were all as surprised as I was to find that the seats could become a bed.

There was no place to bathe, so we could only wash up in the lavatory. We had breakfast at 9:00 a.m., and as we rode I noticed the tremendous changes in the countryside. Then we went into an area with high walls on both sides where a large river ran beside the railroad tracks. We rode through this canyon for quite awhile before the train stopped and we were told that we could get off the train and look around. When the train whistle blew again it would be the signal for us to re-board.

I got off the train and got one of the biggest surprises of my life. I looked up and saw that the wall was at least two thousand feet, straight up, and at the top there was a bridge that ran from one canyon wall to the other. The man in charge walked by and one of the boys asked him what it was that we were looking at. He replied, "It's Royal Gorge, Colorado." The train whistle blew then, and we were back aboard and on our way. We continued quite a way before we came out of the gorge, and it was a sight that I will never forget.

The distance from Oklahoma City to Grand Junction, Colorado was about one thousand miles. In that time we were able to see everything from Kansas, with its flat and monotonous landscape, to mountainous Colorado. After we passed through Royal Gorge there were tall, snow-topped mountains and beautiful rivers, along with something else I had never seen before—large beaver dams with small lakes built up in back of them. The water was always clear, not red like I was used to in Oklahoma.

When we arrived in Grand Junction we got off the train and traveled by road to Montrose, some sixty miles away. The scenery was nice, but again very flat, with mountains all around us on each side. The CCC camps were always outside of town. Ours was a pretty good sized camp, housing about three hundred of us. When we arrived we were welcomed by the camp commander and then divided into groups of ten, with a barracks leader for each group. Our barracks leader took us to our barracks and assigned each of us to our bunks. On the top bunk we found all the bedding we needed: two sheets, two blankets, a pillow, three towels, three washcloths, a bar of soap, a toothbrush and a comb. At the foot of our bed was a locker for our clothes and personal items. I was very impressed with how clean and organized everything was, including the beds all made up the same way. After we were shown our barracks, the leader took us to the latrine to show us where the toilets and showers were. That was the first time in my life I would hear the word latrine, but not the last.

After the latrine he took us to the supply room where we were all fitted with clothes: three changes of shirts, pants and underwear, and five pairs of socks. We were given a hat and a new pair of shoes as well. Boy was I glad to get them too, because the clothes that Aunt Evelyn and Uncle Hawley had given me were looking threadbare.

Finally he took us to the mess hall and I saw something else for the first, but not the last, time: a mess tray with various compartments for your food. We were shown the mess line, and when I went through I was confused by all the choices of food. While we were eating our leader came by and gave us each a list of the rules that we were to follow while we were there. After we finished eating he took us to the aid station and had us looked at, then we went back to the barracks and he taught us how to make our beds. They kept us busy all day, and before we knew it the day was over. The other boys came in from work detail and I made friends with the boys whose beds were next to mine. They had been in the CCC for some time, and they knew how everything worked; they were very good to me and taught me the ropes.

When the lights were out on my first night I lay in my bed in that room of sixty boys that I barely knew, and felt apprehensive about things to come. I fell asleep eventually, and when the whistle blew in the morning it felt like I had only been asleep a very short time; it was time for my first full day in the CCC.

The day started with a trip to the latrine, for health and sanitary reasons, then back to the barracks to make the bed as we had been taught to do the day before. Once we had made our beds we stood by them for inspection and headcount, then it was off to breakfast, which was as ample as our meal had been the night before. I wasn't used to getting fed so much food at one meal. After breakfast we were sent back to our barracks to await further instructions.

Later that day we were all interviewed and asked if we had anything in particular that we wanted to learn while we were there. I didn't know what to say, since I had never been exposed to any type of trade before, so they assigned me to work detail and told me to watch for something I would like to learn. If I let them know they would try to teach it to me. The next day I went to work cleaning out a pond with a huge drag line, and I was assigned to work with the operator. I helped prepare the machine for the days work, and basically followed the orders of the operator for the day. I stayed on that job for a couple of weeks, and it wasn't too bad. The operator was a nice, older man, and he took an interest in me, showing me everything he could about the machines. I could tell he was training me to eventually operate the drag line on my own.

One day he said, "Do you think you could run the machine on your own?" I said I thought so, so he got up and let me sit in his seat, and he showed me how to pull up the bucket and how to stop it. He warned me not to put the brake on too fast when I was lowering it, as a sudden stop could cause the whole machine to turn over. He also started to teach me how to throw the shovel out, and I was doing well and was happy with my progress until eventually, when making a long throw, I applied the brake with too much power and almost turned that whole big machine over. The operator was so nervous that he was shaking, but when he calmed down he said only, "Now that was close." He wasn't angry, and I was more embarrassed than scared.

When we got back to camp that day I asked if I could be assigned to another detail, and they assigned me to the Black Canyon road detail. It turned out to be a good move for me; I was with about twenty other boys that I got along with real well, and our supervisor was a very nice man too. We worked in the mountains, and although it was quite a long ride in the truck we had a lot of fun going up and coming back. On one of the trips we were servicing a gravel road when we came to a covered wagon pulled by a team of mules, and there were about five hundred sheep around the covered wagon. We had to stop until the shepherd could get his wagon to the side of the one lane road to let us by. When he finally got to one side we still had to wait for him to get off the wagon and work with his sheep dog to get all those sheep off the road for us to go by.

The road we serviced ran from the main road in Montrose, up the mountain, and back down to the bottom of the canyon where it ran by the Gunnison River. At the end of the road by the river there was a nice little house and a building that housed all kinds of equipment. There was a chain link fence that covered a hole large enough to drive a truck through. I got acquainted with the site as well as the nice man and his wife that took care of it, and one day our crew leader asked if two of us wanted to go to the bottom of the canyon and deliver the mail to the caretaker. Several of us wanted to go, but I got chosen to go with another boy. The road down was about two and a half miles from where we were, and it was a pretty steep grade with switchbacks; at times we could look up and see the boys working on the road above us. Going down the hill wasn't too bad, but coming back was a real hard walk. It was so hard, in fact, that the boy that I went with said he didn't want to ever go again. I did it once a week though, for as long as I was there, because I liked that man and his wife.

They were always glad to see me come, and the woman always had two good meals for us to eat, with a new dessert each time. The man took care of the gates for the water tunnel that was dug through the mountain to supply the Montrose Valley with water from the Gunnison River. The large tunnel we saw was a service tunnel for the main tunnel, and the gate was a safety measure. The large building was the machine shop, well-equipped with all different machine tools, and the caretaker knew how to operate all of them. During my time there he showed me some of the tools he had made.

On one of my visits I asked them how often they went to town and they said about three times a year, but they received supplies about once a month. The last time I took the mail down I found that the machine shop was in bad shape; a boulder the size of a car had rolled off the mountain and landed right on the machine shop. However, they didn't seem too upset by it; it had happened to them before. His wife had a good meal for us and, after we ate, I started climbing the road back. That was the last time I saw those two nice people.

I had been in the CCC for about two months and I had made a lot of friends already, among them the two that bunked next to me. I was sorry when their six month enlistments were up, and I missed them when they were gone. After they left I asked the leader if I could move to the end bunk next to the wall and he agreed.

It turned out to be a good move. After three or four days they brought in some more boys to replace the ones who had just been discharged, and when I came back to camp that evening after work I met the two boys who replaced my discharged friends. I quickly became aware that it was bully time again. When I spoke to them they were always nasty, along with two of the others across the aisle. I tried to make friends with them, but they made it their mission to give me as much trouble as they could. They were giving some other boys the same kind of treatment. The one sleeping next to me was the leader of the other three, and he especially was just plain mean. I was in a situation that I had never been in before, and I wasn't sure how to handle them.

At the camp we were assigned to K.P., or Kitchen Police, on a rotating basis, and about ten days after the bullies arrived I was assigned to kitchen duty. To alert the others to meal time we had to ring a large bell, and that evening I was told to go and ring it. I was about to ring the bell when the four bullies walked by, and the one that slept next to me picked up a stone and threw it right at me. It was coming toward my head, and when I dodged to miss it I yanked the bell rope real hard at the same time and the support at the top came loose, bringing down one side of the support, bell and all. I put my hand up to try to stop it from falling, and a nail from the board hit the fleshy part of my hand by my thumb, and went straight through. The bully who threw the stone only laughed as he went by, but a couple of boys behind them came as fast as they could to help me. When they saw that the nail had gone right through my hand they didn't know what to do, but I told them just to hold the board. Eventually I was able to pull my hand down and free myself of the nail. They accompanied me to the aid station where I was treated and released.

I gave a report as to how it had happened and was sent back to my bunk. When the four bullies came in they were still laughing; I was so angry that I couldn't even say anything. I was sure that if I were to get in a fight with one of them I would have to take them all on, so after the lights went out that night I laid awake and devised a plan. When the whistle blew the next morning to wake us up I got out of my bed at once, stepped over to the bed of the bully who had thrown the stone, and tapped him on the shoulder. He looked up with surprise and at that moment I reached down and flipped his bed as hard as I could. When he got up I made a fist with the nail-hole hand and hit him as hard as I could, knocking him out cold. In about one minute the fight was over. I looked at the other bullies, but they gave no indication that they wanted to fight, so I gathered the things I needed to wear and headed to the latrine. As I walked down the aisle no one said a word, and when I came back the bully who had thrown the rock and his friend that slept next to him were gone, but the two across the aisle were still there. They came over to me and apologized for the way they had acted, and several boys congratulated me, saying that someone should have whipped their asses when they had first arrived. I was questioned about it, but to my knowledge no one was ever punished.

Before my six month stay was quite over, two of the boys from Shawnee asked me if I would like to take a trip home with them. We were given permission to be gone for seven days, but if we weren't back by the eighth day we would be considered AWOL. I said I would go, because I wanted to see everyone at home. However, I would end up wishing that I hadn't because it turned out to be the most awful trip I had ever taken.

It was a thousand mile trip, and with the time spent visiting we had to rush to not be AWOL on our return. We set off in a Model A Ford Coupe at the hottest time of the year. My seat was the rumble seat, which was a seat for two that sat in back of the main seat. The main seat itself was enclosed, but in the rumble seat I was completely at the mercy of Mother Nature, which was boiling hot sun all day and cold air all night. On the way home we stopped at the Royal Gorge Bridge and looked into the gorge, and I could see the river and the railroad tracks that had brought me there. When we got to Shawnee they dropped me off at the road to Asher, and I was able to get a ride with the first car that went by. It was good to see everyone well and happy and to find that Daddy was working, but in only three days I had to meet the boys in Shawnee for the hot trip back to complete my enlistment, as I still had almost eight weeks left. Luckily, when my enlistment was up, the CCC sent me back home by bus.

Olney, Illinois

When I arrived home after my discharge I found that Daddy was out of work and had gone to Illinois after my uncles. He had left the '38 Ford Touring Car and a trailer to haul all our essentials, and I was to bring the family to Illinois when I came home from the CCC. We stayed in Asher for a few days after I came home, waiting for a letter from Daddy to let us know where we were to go. During that time I had a good visit with friends. Things had not changed much in my absence; they were in the same state of unemployed poverty that we had been in all our lives.

When we received the letter from Daddy, I was happy to hear from him and anxious to be on our way. It was the only trip when I would ever drive the whole family, and I felt quite a bit of responsibility for it. I was only sixteen years old, but there was never any doubt that I could do it. We all loaded the trailer and once again put what we could in the car, and the seven of us got in and started the 650 mile trip to Olney, Illinois. The weather was beautiful when we left and, even though we were quite packed in the car, we were having a good time. We drove north to pick up Route 66 east, to St. Louis.

Mother had made food so we could eat as we drove, and we made good time. We made it to the Oklahoma-Kansas border just after dark, and there was very little traffic on the road by that point. Shortly after dark we began to see lightning flashing behind us, and although it was still quite a distance away I was worried that it would catch us and that all the things in the trailer would get wet. Mother was worried, but for another reason—she was petrified of lightning. The storm gained on us for awhile and then stayed behind us at a consistent speed for hours, but it never caught us.

By morning we had made it well into Missouri, and by about three o'clock we were in St. Louis. It was a new experience for me to have to drive in a city. One of the things that especially impressed me was that, as we were climbing a hill, a bicyclist caught up with the slow-moving truck ahead of us and grabbed onto the truck bed. The truck pulled him to the top of the hill and once they reached the top the bicyclist left the truck and passed it, and I never saw him again. When we arrived at the bridge over the Mississippi we were all very excited. We were amazed by the size of the river and the boats we saw on it, and we all began to feel very anxious to see Daddy and the new place where we were going to live.

We arrived at the Olney house about an hour before dark and found Daddy there waiting for us. We were all overjoyed to be reunited once again. Daddy took us in, and the very first thing he did was to turn on the electric light. It was the first house we ever lived in that had electricity, and we were all so happy to be in the best house we had ever been in. It was a two-story house with four rooms on the first floor and two upstairs, a full bath and closets. Downstairs we had a full kitchen, living room, dining room and one bedroom.

After we had all looked the house over we began to unload the cotton mattresses for our beds, and we took them upstairs and put them on the floor. When the sheets and quilts were brought up, Jean made up our beds on the floor. Even after we put our clothes in the closets they still seemed almost empty. Shortly after all of our things were unloaded, Mother and the rest of us were so happy to be putting the dishes and cookware away in a kitchen equipped with a sink, a countertop, running water and kitchen cabinets and, most of all, electric lights. The dining room had a large table with eight chairs, and it was the nicest table I had ever seen. Our living room had a big potbelly stove, also the first I had ever seen.

We got our kitchen stove set up and Daddy started a fire in it, and Mother and Jean went to work. Not long after that we had our first meal in our new house. After we ate we all took baths and went to bed. I had a wonderful night's sleep in our new house, especially because I was worn out from driving all that distance without any sleep the days before.

When I woke the next morning I was anxious to get out and see what the town looked like and to see if I could find some way to make some money. When I came downstairs the only one there was Mother; Daddy had already gone to work. Mother made me a good breakfast and while I was eating she told me that Daddy had been picked up by a fellow worker so I could use the car if I wanted to. I was happy to hear that, and as soon as I finished eating I was out the door and on my way into town.

I found Olney to be very clean and neat, and all the streets were paved. As I drove along I saw a solid white squirrel cross the road in front of me, and soon enough I had seen several others. When I stopped to put gas in the car, which was ten gallons for one dollar, I asked about the white squirrels. The gas station attendant told me that Olney was the home of the white squirrel; they were protected by the government. While we were talking I asked him if he knew where I might get a job, and he told me that the only work in the area was out of town on a large farm. He gave me directions and I promptly drove out to the farm where I talked to the farmer. He gave me a job stacking wheat, a dollar for a ten-hour day, and he told me that I could start the following day. When I got home I was happy to tell everyone that I had found a new job already.

When Daddy got home I asked if I could use the car to drive to work and he said yes, he would be able to ride to work with the same man he had driven in with that day. I worked for about two weeks before the farmer ran out of work for us to do. The farmer and his wife were kind and caring people, and every day that I worked for him they would bring good home-cooked food and ice cold drinks out to the field for us. After that job was over I looked everywhere for some work, but there was none to be found.

I told Daddy and Mother I was going to go to Fairfield, where all my aunts and uncles lived, to try to look for work there. They agreed, so I put together the few things I had, walked to the highway, and hitchhiked the sixty miles to Uncle Henry and Aunt Ora's house. They were glad to see me, and I had a good visit with them and the rest of my family that lived in the area. I tried hard to find a job while I was there but there was none to be had. While I was there I came across many men with families that couldn't find any work, and it was just impossible for a sixteen year-old to find any.

After about two weeks I went back home and continued to try to find a job there, but to no avail. Sometimes, out of boredom, I would go out to work with Daddy, and those trips were always full of enjoyment and amazement. On one of the night trips they performed what they referred to as a round trip, which consisted of pulling all the pipe out of the well, replacing the bit and running the pipe back in again. When this was done the man in the derrick, which was some eighty feet up, had to disconnect the pipe and then stand it in the derrick. Once all the pipe was pulled out they replaced the worn bit with a new one, and by about 2:30 or 3:00 a.m. they were reversing the process and running the pipe back in. I woke up and ate some of the food that Mother had made for me and Daddy and after while I decided to go up on the derrick floor and watch the men work.

In 1940 there were no safety rules that restricted anyone from entering an oil field work area. I climbed up to the derrick floor and watched the precision and teamwork between the driller and the two floor men as they worked with the thousands of pounds of steel pipe on a slippery, muddy floor. If one of them was slow in his part of this very precise procedure it could easily become a serious problem.

After I stood there for awhile and watched the pipe lowered into the hole, the driller heard Daddy whistle from eighty feet up. He stopped all movement, and when the noise had subsided Daddy hollered that he wanted me to climb up to where he was. The driller called me over and asked if I wanted to go, and I said sure. He asked, "Have you ever been in a derrick before?" I answered that I hadn't, and he warned me, "When you start to climb, don't look down." I said okay and began my first eighty foot climb. I had just started when I heard Daddy holler, "Darrell, DON'T look down!"

In no time I was standing on a platform of an oil drilling rig, eighty feet in the air, enjoying a feeling of apprehension and excitement while standing next to my dad. Daddy showed me where to stand and told me not to be afraid of the way the rig would shake and move, that feeling was normal and even good because it showed that the derrick was adjusting to the weight. He had a safety belt on, with a rope attached that gave him enough length to stretch out over the edge of the platform with only his feet planted firmly on it. Soon he hollered, "Let's go," to the driller. I was glad he had warned me about the movement, otherwise I might have thought the derrick was coming down, but I eventually became relaxed after being up there for awhile.

My dad was talking to me in spurts, showing me and telling me what the different things were. After watching him do his dangerous job with speed and complete confidence, as well as absolute pride and joy for his work, I realized that if the pace for the work was set by the way Daddy did his job, the other men must certainly have gone home tired. Daddy was great at what he did, and it showed in his work. While I was up there with him that morning the sun was just coming up, and he pointed it out to me saying, "Darrell, look at that." He pointed to the sun just as it was coming over the horizon, and that beautiful scene and moment shared with my father has remained freshly imprinted on my memory for my entire life. Shortly after the last pipe went in the hole we climbed down, and that was the first and the last time I was ever in an oil derrick.

A Short Trip to Oklahoma, then on to Texas

I was still trying to find work of any kind in Olney, and one day when I had the car I went to see the farmer that I had worked for before and talked with him about a job. He told me he could use me for about a week, so for the next few days Daddy let me use the car and I was able to earn seven dollars helping the farmer. While I worked that week I decided that I wanted to take a trip back to Oklahoma to see Hoyt and some of my other cousins. When I got my pay I told Mother and Daddy that I wanted to go back to Oklahoma for a couple of weeks. Mother had reservations but they both said okay, and the next morning I was walking back toward the road to St. Louis. I was there for just a little while when a man stopped to give me a ride to St. Louis. That was the first leg of the longest trip I was ever to make as a hitchhiker.

The round trip was about 1440 miles. When I got to St. Louis it became difficult to get a long ride, and as a result it took me quite awhile to get out of the city. Finally, I got lucky. A man came by who was able to give me a ride all the way through Missouri to Miami, Oklahoma. He drove steady all day before letting me off near a café. I went to get something to eat but was turned away because they were closing, so I had to leave the café as hungry as I had ever been. I hadn't had anything to eat since breakfast.

There was almost no traffic on Route 66 at that time of night so I started looking for a place to lie down and sleep for the night. The weather was warm and dry and I spotted a large billboard sign off the highway about two hundred feet, so I walked to it and found a smooth spot where I laid down, using my few clothes for a pillow. The next thing I knew the sun was shining in my eyes, so I got up, dusted myself off, and walked to the café. I went inside and, after washing up, was able to have a good breakfast. When I got back to the highway I caught a ride to Oklahoma City, and from there I went out to Lawton. I was there for about two weeks and I had a great time, and after the two weeks were through I hitchhiked back to Olney.

Just two weeks after I returned home from Oklahoma Daddy was out of work again, which meant it was time to move. This next move was to be the farthest one yet; we loaded the trailer and the nine of us piled into the '38 Ford, headed for the southern part of Texas. We were looking for oil field work or a job picking long staple cotton, which paid about a third more per hundred pounds than picking regular cotton.

We were all excited about moving somewhere new, but we had no idea when we set out just how far we had to go. The trip was about eight hundred miles and Daddy did all the driving. We slept beside the road at night, usually by a stream so we could find some fresh water for cooking and washing. Whenever we crossed from one state to another we would start to sing and have a good time. It took about a week to get to Houston, and then it would be a day or so before Daddy would find a way to start making some money.

Eventually he found a black sharecropper who had about twenty acres of long staple cotton to pick. We had picked cotton before, but never the long staple kind, so this was a new experience for us. The sharecropper gave us a one-room shack to live in, and while we were there Mother, Daddy, the girls and Bud slept in the shack while Bill, Ray, Ed and I slept in a small barn near the house. We slept just as well as the ones in house, because our bed was a load of the cotton we had just picked, in a trailer to be delivered to the cotton gin. The farmer's cotton field was just outside of Sugar Land, Texas, and his house was not too far from the shack we lived in. He and his wife were very nice; they would bring a gallon of milk over every day and occasionally butter and vegetables. One day, when he was going to bring a load of cotton to the gin, he asked me if I'd like to accompany him. I said sure, but I didn't know what to expect.

I had never associated with a black person before; in fact, I had only seen a few before meeting the nice sharecropper and his wife. After he and I delivered the cotton to the gin he told me, "I'll take you to eat with me."

We drove to a café and got out of the truck, and I started for the front door. He told me, "No. I can't go in there. You come with me," and we headed for the backdoor. That was my first experience with segregation and at first I didn't understand why we were using the backdoor. When we went in I found that it was all black people, and they all looked at me with questioning faces. After a short while, however, I felt at ease. After we finished eating a good meal he asked me if I had ever tried peach brandy. I answered that I hadn't, so he ordered one for each of us and told me just to sip it. I did and found that it was very good.

When we returned home I discovered that while I was gone a man had come and repossessed the '38 Ford, and now we were without transportation. We had almost finished picking the field of cotton, and with no oil field work around we would be forced to move again. Daddy started looking around for a vehicle to get us to where he could find work, and he finally found an old Nash Touring Car that he could buy with part of the money he had made picking cotton. The day after he bought it we loaded everything we could on the top and inside, left just enough room for us, and left everything else behind. Again, all nine of us were on our way to Oklahoma, about four hundred miles away.

I turn seventeen and join the Army

While we were in Sugar Land I turned seventeen years-old. Reflecting back upon my youth I realize that my sixteenth year was the year that I developed much of my confidence and self-reliance. I had traveled seven thousand miles, and during the course of that traveling I had learned to overcome difficulty on my own. In the beginning of my seventeenth year, however, my family found ourselves in circumstances that reminded me of being back on the school lease in Asher, when things were just about the worst they had been for our family. Daddy just continued driving the old Nash Touring Car, and Mother and us kids tried sleeping and were sometimes hungry or cranky. This went on for three or four days, until we finally crossed the Red River into Oklahoma.

Not long after we crossed the river we came to a small town called Teral that was as far as we could go; I can't remember if it was because we were out of money or the old car wouldn't make it, but it was the end of the road for us. Daddy had to find a place for us to live, and soon he was able to find a one-room shack about a mile southeast of town. We were there about two or three months with Daddy doing whatever job he could find to get just enough money to feed us all. Finally, he had to tell Mother that he was going to have to leave her and the children and find a job.

Daddy had done some work for a farmer close by before he left us to find something better, and after Daddy left I picked up doing some work for the farmer. I trapped animals for fur and I helped him with his trap lines. The farmer caught animals, skinned them, and sold their pelts, and I helped with this process. I also milked his cows, and although the pay was small the gallon of milk I got every day was priceless. One morning, while we were checking the traps along the creek, we were surprised to see that we had caught a mink. It was the first one I had ever seen, but the farmer knew just what it was and became very excited when he saw what we had trapped.

I continued to work for the farmer until the middle of February. By this time we were in very bad straits when Mother received a letter from Daddy. He told us that he was in Oklahoma City, where he had found work. The very same day the farmer I worked for drove into our yard with a big smile on his face, saying, "Darrell, I have something for you." He gave me fourteen dollars, which was my part of the money he had gotten for the mink pelt.

After he left I asked Mother, once again, if she would sign for me to go into the Army. She had refused when I was sixteen, and she did once again. I was very determined though; even though I knew very little about the Army I felt certain that it would be something better than where I was. When she said no again this time, I did what I felt I had to do, and I told her that I was going to go to Oklahoma City to find Daddy and have him sign my Army papers.

The next morning when I awoke I put on my clothes, gave Mother ten of my fourteen dollars and, with great sadness, left seven of the eight people that I loved with all my heart. As I walked away I hoped that the ten dollars would be enough to get them through.

I walked two miles to the highway and hitched a ride all the way to Oklahoma City. When I got there I immediately started looking for oilrigs, and because Daddy was so well known and well-respected by the men in the oil fields, I was able to find him without much trouble. Someone told me where he was rooming so I went to the rooming house where the man at the desk told me which room he was in. I went to his room and knocked, and Daddy came to the door. He was surprised to see me, and he came out asking, "Darrell, what are you doing here? Is there anything wrong?" I said no, and he put his arms around me and gave me a kiss before making me something to eat.

He asked me lots of questions about everyone, but soon he wanted to know why I was there. I told him I wanted him to sign the papers for me to go into the Army, and he asked me why I wanted to go. I told him that it was something I wanted to do, something I thought I would like and that would make my life better. He was quiet for awhile, but he put the food on the table for me to eat and continued talking to me while I ate it. Finally he told me, "Son, you go get those papers tomorrow, and when I get home from work I will sign them for you, because there is nothing here for you to do."

The next morning I went in search of an Army Recruiting Office, and when I found one I went in and talked for awhile with the recruiter. He took down all of my information and gave me the necessary papers. I took the papers back to Daddy's room and sat and waited for him to come home. When he came in he looked them over and signed where he was supposed to. I returned the papers to the recruiter first thing the next morning, and he told me to report the following morning to be sworn in. Just like that, I had succeeded in joining the Army.

I spent the whole of that day just walking around, feeling excited and apprehensive, and anxious to tell Daddy what I had done. I was back in the room by the time he came in from work, and I quickly told him all that had happened; I was to report the next morning for a physical, and if I passed I would take my oath to become an Army man. He expressed that he was happy for me, and whatever other emotions he may have had he didn't say. His expression contained both happiness and sadness. He made us something to eat and we talked the entire evening. When I laid on the pallet that he had put down for me to sleep on, he knelt down beside me, kissed me, and told me, "I am proud of you and I love you. I want you to be a good soldier and to be sure and say your prayers every day." The next morning, when he got up to go to work, I got up with him so that we could have our coffee and breakfast together.

I reported to the Army Recruiter who took me to a large building where I was given my physical along with other men. Everything was fine, and when I had finished with the examination I was sent to another area of the building where I waited with a group of others for about three hours. The wait ended when I received the first order of my time in the army. In a loud, authoritative voice the recruiter ordered: "ATTENTION. You will assemble here in front of me, and form a column of four." He could see that I knew what he wanted, a result of my time in the CCC camp, but there were others who were confused.

In a short time, however, our group of fifty was in order. We were ordered to raise our right hand and repeat our oath as the administrator relayed it to us. Upon completion of the oath, on March 5, 1941, myself and forty-nine others were congratulated and welcomed as members of the United States Army.

Before we were dismissed they asked if any of us would like to go to the Philippines. The Philippines sounded good to me, even though I didn't know where they were, so I held up my hand along with another young man. We were called forward while all the others were moved out. They took us to a room where they gave each of us a food pass and a train ticket to San Francisco, along with directions and arrangements for our transportation after the train ride. When we were finished we were told that we had the option to take the train the following day or that we could have three days before going if we wished, but we had to give him an answer while we were there. I told him that I would be leaving the next day, and he shook my hand and wished me well.

When I finished at the Army office I went back to Daddy's room. When he came home from work he was surprised to see me there already, and he wanted to hear all about what had happened. I told him that everything had gone well, that I had been sworn into the Army and that I was going to the Philippines the following day. I am sure that he didn't know where the Philippines were any more than I did, but he and I were glad to have one more night together. We had another good talk, and he told me how anxious he was to get Mother and all the kids with him again. We talked about me and my plans for the future as he made up my pallet for me to sleep on.

My sleep that night was very restless, as I'm sure Daddy's was as well; I could hear him moving around all night. The next morning we woke up and had breakfast together, and when he gave me a hug and a kiss before walking out the door, I could see the tears in his eyes. We looked at each other, but I was unaware these were the last looks we would exchange for five long years.

As I am writing and remembering that time, a time that was so important and influential in my life, I am left with much more than my decision to enter the Army. I think about Mother and Daddy and all my brothers and sisters and the things that our family shared in together. I think of what Mother and Daddy taught us: to love one another, to always practice a strong work ethic, to respect others and to honor the notion that all men were created equal, a concept that also meant that we were not inferior to anyone, despite our financial situation.

The unstable and difficult conditions that I grew up in were caused by the Great Depression. Although the Great Depression affected the entire country, Oklahoma and other Midwestern states were hit the hardest because the situation was compounded by the horrible drought. The conditions were not conducive to growing food, making it difficult for anyone to even eke out a living, never mind make a profit, and because of this harsh reality many families had to constantly move just to survive. With the exception of very few people, everyone we knew and all of those around us were very poor and in the same situation as we were. I know that it was because of Daddy's hard work, determination, and skill at what he did that we were able to survive, and we were better off than many of the others. We moved a lot, but it was what he had to do for us so that we would survive. I also credit my Mother for being able to take charge of us and keep us healthy and safe whenever Daddy was away. The way that I grew up may have been hard, but I have found that those hardships, as well as the freedom I was given to grow and prosper in spite of them, would become the largest contribution to my survival in the future. I realize now that the first seventeen years of my life *were* hard, but they were wonderful hardships, crucial hardships, that became essential to my later survival.

The Old House

I'm just an old house upon a knoll. Standing alone in the cold. Thinking
back of times gone by, of love, of laughter, or a baby's cry.

Children playing on my floor, down they slide on the cellar door.
A stick, a hoop, a wagon ride; a rubber ball bouncing on my side.

But now I'm cold as I stand alone, all rooms empty, as all have gone.
If I could cry, tears would fall, no more
pictures hanging from my wail.
Oh, how I miss chairs galloping cross my floor. An oven filled with
Biscuits and very little more. That warmth is gone now passed with the
Wind and rain, with the falling of the
snow through a broken windowpane.

Memories still linger of times I hold dear,
of a sharecropper's family of eight little
ones of a wife and three daughters and five healthy sons.
They toiled the soil around me with sweat from their brow.
From daylight to dark with two mules and plow,
the land reaped their living for a good many years and there was
serenity and happiness with occasions of tears

It was sometime in the thirties that things fell apart.
The wind and the sand plucked the strings to their heart.
No crop to harvest and not even a dime.
Left them helpless and hopeless with a long hill to climb.
They pulled the old T model up next to my door
loaded their belongings and left an empty floor.
How sad it was as they pulled away with tears in
their eyes and no place to lay.
This is just part of the history that has passed my way
as I stand here alone day after day.

-Author George Stark-

This picture was taken around 1930. It is of an old oil rig in Oklahoma. Daddy is in the center.

This is a picture of Mother and Daddy.

This is a picture of me with my sister Carol and my brother Bill.

My brothers and sisters.
Front row (from left):
My sister, Pat, myself,
and my brother, Bill.
Back row (from left): My
brothers Ray, Bud and Ed.

This is Grampa and Gramma
Pollard, taken in Oklahoma.
We lovingly called them
by the names of Mammy
and Pappy. This picture
was taken between the late
1800s to the early 1900s.

This is the picture of a
school class in Asher,
Oklahoma in the late 1930s.
My brother, Bill, is in the
back row.

This is my Great-Grandfather Stark, born in 1836 in Louisiana.

3rd from left is my Uncle Sim and catfish caught in Oklahoma.

This is my Grandfather Stark, born in 1860, with three of his sisters.

Part Two

War

My First Military Order

On March 6, 1941 I set out to fulfill my first military order—to report to Angel Island, California. I showed them my train ticket at the station in Oklahoma City and was sent to board. When I boarded the train that day I was a seventeen year-old boy: almost six feet tall and weighing only 165 pounds. I had on the same clothes that I had on when I left Mother and my siblings; they were clean, but very worn out. I thought about Mother and Daddy and my family as I sat there in the car, and I was filled with emotion. I felt fear, but also wonder at what was immediately ahead of me in my life; I was also more excited than I had ever been.

It was only after I had boarded the train that I found out that there wouldn't be a bed made for me on this trip; I would be sitting for the entire length of the trip, except when I got up to use the bathroom or to visit the dining car. There were very few people in my car, and I sat alone for the entire first day. At about 6:00 p.m. I went for something to eat and then returned to my seat to try to make myself comfortable with the two seats, blanket, and pillow I had available. I fell asleep shortly after dark and slept until almost daylight. When I got up to use the bathroom I found that in my deep sleep I had split my worn pants in the back, right down the middle—a big problem since I had no undershorts and nothing to change into. I was embarrassed, but I had to use the bathroom so badly that I stood up, gathered the two sides of my pants in my right hand, and held them tightly together as I walked down the aisle and through the car.

Luckily everyone in the car was asleep, so I was able to use the bathroom, wash up, and walk back to my seat in the same fashion, holding my pants together and hoping that no one would wake up and notice. For the next three days and nights every move I made was potentially embarrassing, but I was careful to try to avoid any situation where someone might see the problem I was having. I was able to avoid embarrassment and even enjoy my time on the train, taking in the beautiful sights along the railroad.

When we finally arrived in San Francisco I followed the next part of my order, holding my pants all the while, and as twilight was coming to the late afternoon sky I found my ride at a small pier by the bay. I could see the paved streets snaking up steep hills and homes more beautiful and ornate than any I had seen before. By the time we pulled up to a dock and the driver informed me that we had arrived at our destination, it was dark. I got out and, with his directions, I walked a short distance down the dock until I came to a boat of about sixty or seventy feet. It had a roof over it and long benches on both sides and its name, *The Cox,* was written on the side. When I walked on board holding my seat I realized I was the only passenger. A man checked my pass and another released the boat from the dock, and with that I was off on my first trip on the Pacific Ocean.

I didn't know where Angel Island was, so I didn't know how long of a ride to expect. We were not gone long when we pulled into a dock and one of the men said, "This is Alcatraz," but that didn't mean anything to me since I had never heard of Alcatraz before. While stopped at the dock the men loaded a large pile of clean sheets, pillow cases and towels on board, and once those had been loaded we pulled away en route to our next stop, Angel Island. I stepped off the boat thinking that, despite the torn pants, I had successfully completed my first Army order.

No sooner had I stepped off the boat than someone approached me and asked me to follow him. He took me to a supply room where I was issued three sets of blue denims and a fatigue hat, underclothes, socks, a new pair of shoes and a barrack bag to carry it all in, as well as bedding and towels. Next I was escorted to the barracks where I was issued a bunk, and then they showed me the latrine and the mess hall. My escort said, "When you have showered and made your bed, you can go and eat."

As soon as he left I grabbed a set of my new clothes and immediately changed out of my split pants. I threw all of my old clothes away and stepped into a wonderful full shower. Clean and dressed in my new clothes I headed for the mess hall where, besides the mess hall crew, I was the only one in the building. They made me a good meal, and I ate and thanked them and headed to my bunk, where I was to meet some of my fellow soldiers, other men who were also waiting to go to the Philippines. They were all very friendly, but their talk and mannerisms were very different than what I was used to in the Midwest. One, a young man from New York, was the first person I had ever met from the East Coast. He was just as green as I was about the Army, but he had been there for a few days and he helped me to get adjusted to the routine. We were to have no basic training until we got to the Philippines, so we were able to get adjusted to Army life without the rigors of training right away.

On the morning of my first full day I was awakened by a bugle at reveille, and it sounded so good that I did not mind the early wake-up call. After latrine call and breakfast I was escorted to a medical exam room and given another physical as well as all my immunization shots. There were quite a few men who had been in the Army for a long time, but most were young men of about my age. I noticed a few men who looked real sharp, especially because of the stripes on the shoulders of their uniforms. I was impressed, but just kept walking when I passed them. Soon I came face to face with one young man with the stripes on his shoulders, and I heard him holder, "SOLDIER!" I continued on my way and he repeated himself. There was no one nearby and I realized that he was speaking to me. When I turned back toward him he said, "Come here!" By now I realized from the tone in his voice that I had better do what he said, and when I walked back toward him he asked me, "Don't you know that you are supposed to salute an officer?"

I said that no, I didn't know that, and he replied, "You are to say 'No sir'." Pointing to his lieutenant bars he added, "When you see these you always salute." I didn't even know how to salute, so he showed me and I repeated what I was shown. He returned my salute and dismissed me, and so passed another first for me. However, until I could tell one foot from the other I was busy saluting the ones with stripes on their sleeves and boards on their shoulders, as many of the others were doing as well.

Most of the time we were free to do as we pleased, but after a few days it started to get boring despite the fact that they tried to keep us busy with movies or a sing-along in the evening. They also had a library where you could go and read or take out books, which was an altogether new experience to me, and that was my favorite part of Angel Island, as I had always enjoyed reading. However, I was soon ready to move on to the next phase of training and to head for the Philippines to start my real Army experience.

Crossing the Pacific

On March 30th we were all assembled and told to get our bags packed and ready to move out the next day; we would be leaving as soon as the morning mess was over. I barely slept that night and instead just lay awake, anxious about what was to come.

When reveille sounded I was out of the bunk and in the latrine, fast, and it was a good thing because everyone in that place was on the move. Shortly after we ate they began ferrying us to a large pier where I saw one of the largest ships I had ever seen. It was the United States troop carrier, *The Republic*. We boarded with our barrack bags and were shown where our bunks were and how to find them when we left them and returned again, which was important because the ship had several decks. The sleeping conditions were bunks piled four high; there was just barely enough room to get in, and you could only sit up if you leaned over.

After I was settled and had put my barracks bag at the foot of my bunk I went back up to the main deck to look around. What I saw amazed me: from the deck I was standing on you could look up and see four decks above you, each with rails around the deck and officers milling around and watching all of us in our blue denims. We were crowded on the deck, and as I walked around I witnessed some men gambling. It was the first time I had witnessed that, and in no time there were blankets spread out all over the deck for shooting craps as well as many other types of card games. I had never gambled before, but I was interested when I saw money changing hands. I stopped and watched a card game and asked someone what the game was. He told me it was called blackjack. It looked pretty easy to me, and soon one of the players got up and the dealer asked me if I wanted to play. I told him I didn't know how, but he said, "Sit down and I'll show you."

I agreed and he quickly went over the rules and told me I could play for a dime, but not more than a dollar. I put down a dime, and when he dealt the cards he took my dime. The next time I put down forty cents, but the dealer took that too. I got up and left the game and that dealer never even did what Mother and Daddy had always taught me—say thank you when someone gives you something. That was the end of my gambling in the Army.

At about four or five o'clock there was a lot of commotion, and I was told that we were about to pull away from the pier. Sure enough, soon after I felt the ship moving as we left the dock. I was excited and interested to watch as we pulled away from land, but I was also getting very hungry. They announced that we could go and eat by deck and section number, and when my number came up I went down to eat as quickly as I could. I was one of the first ones so I grabbed a tray and went to the food line. They had many items to choose from, including one of my favorite meals—hot dogs and beans. I loaded my tray and sat down at a stainless steel table with benches attached to each side. The table was just wide enough for two trays with about four inches to spare around them, and it had a raised edge all around it to keep the trays from sliding off during bad seas.

I sat down in front of the tray filled with my favorite foods. The boat was moving up and down slowly, but I was eating and enjoying my food as the room filled up with more men that had arrived to eat. Suddenly, one of the men sitting opposite me stopped eating and got a funny look on his face. Before I could move he threw up in his tray and into my hot dogs and beans. That ended my first meal on *The Republic*.

I got up off the bench to leave and empty my tray of the dirty food, and it was then that I realized almost everyone in here was getting sick. I got out of there as fast as I could, and when I stepped over the doorway I found myself standing in about two inches of slippery puke. Eventually I reached topside and found a place to wash off my shoes. After I had done that I was able to stand by the rail and enjoy the big, slow waves as they softly lifted then lowered the ship.

As I stood there, just before sunset, I witnessed one of the most beautiful scenes of my life. The ship had come to a stop and I could see a sailboat coming towards us in the distance. It was coming very fast and it looked as though it would ram into us. Then it turned all at once, sailed right up alongside our ship and slowed down, almost to a stop. It pulled up to a platform attached to our ship, and I realized there was a man standing on it. When the sail boat had maneuvered into the appropriate position, the man was able to jump onto it, and they were on their way again.

The man who jumped onto the sailboat was the pilot who had guided us out to sea. The sailboat headed for San Francisco and we continued past the Golden Gate Bridge, on to the Pacific Ocean and to our destination— Hawaii. The trip over was very nice; we had calm seas and beautiful sunrises and sunsets, and I was able to see different kinds of sea life in the crystal clear waters. One day I was sitting in the library enjoying a good book, when I started to feel seasick from the movement of the ship. I was able to stop myself from getting sick by getting out into the fresh air, and that was the only time in my life I have experienced seasickness.

After about a week, we arrived in Hawaii. We pulled up parallel to a large pier and docked the boat. We were excited to be there, as we had been able to see Hawaii for quite awhile before we finally landed. We had not seen land for so long and we were anxious to see what Hawaii was like. We were only there for a few days, and we were not allowed to go ashore, only onto the pier for a short time. While we were there we were entertained by a stage show on the ship where native entertainers performed Hawaiian music while hula girls danced. It was a good show and another first for me.

I also enjoyed watching the native divers who we could see swimming and diving around the side of the ship, waiting for a coin to be thrown into the water so that they could dive for it. They could reach unbelievable depths with no equipment, just holding their breath. I realized that they must have been experiencing extreme poverty, because they would dive just as far for only a dime, nickel or even a penny. When they came up for air they would take a deep breath, put the coin in their mouth, and wait for another coin. They would dive for quite awhile before they were eventually relieved by a partner.

In the evening of the second day the ship started making preparations to go out to sea again. I was glad to start moving again, but at sea there was very little to do. Most of the time I was able to talk with someone who already knew the ropes and in that was I was able to learn a lot about Army life. One of the soldiers I liked to talk to was from Texas. He was on his second enlistment and had completed a tour in the Panama Canal. He had requested the Philippines for his second tour. He was an artilleryman and knew what his assignment would be when we arrived in the Philippines. He told me that was true of all of those who had the sheaves on their sleeves.

During the first night out from Hawaii I went to my bunk, got a blanket and a pillow, and went topside to find a place where I could lay down and be comfortable. The seas were calm and there were a lot of soldiers sleeping on the deck where they could because it was much better than sleeping in the tight quarters below. At about ten o'clock in the evening I was lying on the deck, trying to get to sleep. Almost everyone around me was already sleeping, a big moon was shining and a soft bugle sounded, and I started to feel a strong wave of homesickness for the first time since I had left. I wondered how Mother and Daddy and my brothers and sisters were, but I had no way to get in touch with them. Communication was unbelievably slow between civilians, not to mention that I did not even have a permanent address for them. I thought about them for awhile, but eventually I was able to fall asleep and rest very soundly through the night. When I woke up I enjoyed the beautiful ride from Hawaii to the Philippines. On a Friday,

April 12th, we heard a message on the PA system that we would cross the international dateline at midnight and the chaplains would be holding Sunday Services.

On April 14, 1941, a Sunday, we were on our way to Manila, Philippines. On that leg of the trip we saw flying fish over the sides of the ship, giving us something to watch and enjoy as we rode. We learned that on April 21st we were to report to a certain area of the ship in groups as we were ordered. I reported with my group and was issued a complete World War One uniform: dark green wraps for leggings that were made of heavy wool, and hats. It was a cold climate uniform despite the fact that we were in the tropics. We were told that we had to be dressed in full dress uniform, and these were what we had received so our only choice. The next morning, April 22, 1941, I arrived at Manila, Philippine Islands.

Manila, Pearl of the Pacific

The last day on the ship we were restricted to our bunk areas and ordered to get into our dress uniforms. I had no problem getting into my pants and shirt, but the tie tripped me up—I had never worn one before. Luckily, some of the others had, and one of the soldiers who had worn one was kind enough to show those of us who hadn't how to tie it. In some cases he even made the knot for us. The leggings were a different story altogether. Although he showed us how, *watching* and *doing* were two completely different things. We were all waiting for our leggings to get wrapped when our section was called to disembark. We found that we had better watch the feet of the soldier in front of us, because it would be very easy to step on the part of his leggings that were not wrapped and were dragging out behind him. I can only guess that we were the worst looking bunch of fully dressed soldiers that had ever stepped onto that pier.

After we were offloaded at Manila, we were marched to a truck and loaded on, ready to head out for our basic training. As we were moving along, I was focused on taking in everything that we passed by. I saw some of the most beautiful buildings I had ever seen, and many were built with materials that I had never seen before. As we drove through the city we were met with wonderful aromas that were mingled with the smell of raw sewage. It was hot and humid, and I sat on that truck in total misery in the heavy wool clothing. I kept my mind off it though, with the excitement of everything that I was seeing as we drove. We were in the truck for quite awhile before we finally arrived at our destination—a large area of open space with small tents in neat rows. There were also two or three very large tents, one of which was our mess tent.

We came to a stop and were ordered to dismount the truck and form a line. When we were properly in line, an officer informed us that we were the worst looking bunch of men he had ever seen. As he spoke, I became aware that I was looking at the greatest man I had ever seen. He was dressed in a tailor made khaki uniform and a campaign hat, and his belt and shoes were shined as bright as can be. He told us that, despite our disheveled appearance, when he was through with us we would look and perform as soldiers should. He dismissed us and we were shown the latrine and told we would have one half hour to use it. We were reassembled after that and marched—leggings dragging—to the mess tent. We enjoyed a good meal and were told to remain seated after we had eaten in order to receive further instructions. We were assigned our tents and ordered to report to them; there we were met by a drill instructor and shown how to make our beds. He instructed us on all the procedures of the camp. We made our beds and were ordered to change to our blue denims and to turn in the wool pants, hat and leggings. That was good news to me; I don't know how we would have gotten by in those hot uniforms with the Manila heat and humidity.

Company M, 31st Infantry, Machine Gun Company

We were at Basic Camp for about six weeks, during which time we became well trained in performing as an Army unit, and we came to take a lot of pride in ourselves. We were given extensive physical training, we learned to march, we learned the proper procedures of good soldiering, and we were instructed in self-defense and first aid. Our training was scheduled to have lasted longer, but the rains started and the camp quickly became a field of ankle-deep mud that was impossible to maneuver in. Close order drill in those conditions was nearly impossible, so we were ordered to pack our belongings in our barrack bags for a move to our respective units.

Prior to our move, they asked anyone who was interested in joining a machine gun company to step forward. It sounded exciting to me, so I stepped forward along with several others, and they loaded us up and took us back to Manila. After a long drive we stopped and were ordered to offload with all of our belongings, and I became a member of Company M, 31st Infantry, at the Estado Mayor.

They promptly led us to our barracks, which were very impressive. They were as clean and uniformly neat as anything I have ever seen in my life. As you entered the building, to the right was the company commander's office and non-commissioned officers' quarters, and to the left was a double-wide door to the mess hall. Past the mess hall were the quarters for the rest of the company.

I received another surprise upon being directed to our bunks. My bunk was already made and had a footlocker that was highly polished. We were told to place our barrack bags on our footlocker and our barrack boy would put our things in it, in compliance with the rules. Shortly after I was there the bunk boy that was assigned to my group of ten appeared before us with a big smile on his pock-marked face. He introduced himself as Bilon. He was about five feet tall with a slight build, and looked to be about thirty years old. He had been with M Company for several years and knew the rules as well as or better than anyone else in the building. After I was there for awhile, I came to know the pride that Bilon took in what he did, and I also learned of his amazing strength. He could pack the bed clothes and towels for all ten bunks into a bundle, tie the bundle, put it on his head, and walk with his arms at his side, whistling all the while. He was one of several Filipinos who worked in our building, and they did all the work of keeping the soldier's spit-and-polish, which included preparations for full barracks inspection. They shined our shoes, laid out our uniforms, and prepared our clothes for laundry. We also had Filipino barbers and kitchen workers who did all the KP. The total cost to us was two pesos and seventy-five centavos per month, which amounted to $1.37 per month of our thirty dollar pay, a fee that was absolutely worth it in exchange for the work being done for us.

Those of us who had just come in were assigned to different squads, and after we had placed our barrack bags at our bunks we were shown the latrine, which was outside the main building in an east-yard. We relieved ourselves, washed up, and reported to the mess hall for our first meal in our new home.

When we had finished eating we went back to our bunks, where it was time to get acquainted with more new people. I met some of the men in my squad for the first time that night. Over time I learned that all of the men in my squad, with the exception of one, were all very good soldiers, and I will have more later in reference to the one who wasn't. I was just beginning to feel more at ease when, at about six or seven that evening, I was surprised by the sight of Bilon putting our mosquito nets down for the night, because I expected to do it myself. We were ordered to remain by our bunks at bed time and to be by them the next morning after having breakfast with our squad.

It turns out that we were told that we had to eat with our squad, in part, as an introduction to the proper manners for the dining table. We learned that our squad leaders all sat at one of the table, and there was no conversation except to ask someone to please pass whatever you needed. When passing it, you had better not use it before it reached the person who had asked for it. Most of the meals were served family style, but for breakfast we went through a line, cafeteria style, where they would prepare our eggs however we wanted them.

After the new arrivals had finished eating we were told to report back to our bunks for further orders. About an hour after breakfast we were marched to the 3rd Battalion supply room and issued our full dress khaki uniforms, which included a tie and new Florsheim dress shoes, a campaign hat, pistol belt, first aid kit, a shelter half and a .45 caliber pistol with a holster. That was the first time I had held a weapon in the Army; in basic training we had received no firearms training. After signing for our pistols we were marched back to our barracks.

The building that we stayed in was formerly a Spanish stable before the United States had taken the Philippines from Spain. As a stable, it was built with about twenty feet of overhang on both sides so that riders could take their horses out of the stable and groom them in all kinds of weather, protected from the elements. The walls on both sides were only about four feet high, and the remaining six feet between the walls and the roof were open and screened in. This all made for a very comfortable building; perhaps the most comfortable in the 31st Infantry. The floors were concrete and finished to a bright polished shine, and inside of them were four rows of bunks with ample space between them. At the back end of the building was the day room for our recreation. It was quite large, and part of it extended on piers over the Pasig River, which was about half a mile wide and emptied into Manila Bay, not far from our barracks. The day room had pool tables, a library, ping-pong and a barber shop.

Under the large overhang our platoon was taught the workings of the .45 caliber sidearm and the .30 caliber water-cooled machine gun. There were two other platoons in the building with us, one of eighty-one millimeter mortars and another of .60 caliber air-cooled machine guns.

When I arrived back at the barracks and went to my bunk with my new equipment, Bilon was there with a big smile on his face. He started putting my issue in order, and I found that my uniform would be tailored to fit me perfectly. For the rest of the day we were free to use the recreation room and walk around outside to look the area over. In front of our barracks was a big horseshoe driveway with shrubs and a few trees. The lawns were beautifully manicured and a flag was flying overhead. I noticed that one of the trees had some kind of fruit on it that I had never seen before. I was looking at it, puzzled, when one of the sergeants came by and asked me if I knew what kind of fruit it was. I said, "No sir," and he said, "Come with me."

We went to the tree and he picked a tree-ripe mango off of the first mango tree I had ever seen, and he told me to take a bite. I did, and I can still remember how delicious it was. The sergeant left with a big smile on his face.

Duties, Recreation, and a New World

The next day we began our duties as members of Company M, 31st Infantry. I was assigned to the second squad of the second platoon. My platoon leader was Corporal Neff, a Yangtze veteran and a long-time member of the Army. When we were in front of the barracks the platoon leaders started to bark their orders and the whole company was in perfect formation within five minutes. We went through the whole procedure of counting off and doing calisthenics, then began a mile run in column order. When we returned we were told to police the area, which means that you must pick up every piece of trash on the lawn or in front of the barracks, no matter how small. Then we were ordered to formation before we were dismissed for breakfast.

After breakfast we were ordered to our bunks to stand by for morning inspection, which was conducted by the First Sergeant and one of the officers. We were responsible for our inspection even though the bunk boy prepared everything for us. After inspection we were assigned by platoon to learn all about the cleaning, care, maintenance and operation of our machine gun: to detail strip it, to field strip it blindfolded, and to set it up for firing. Eventually we were taught how to fire support for rifle companies, how to pack our World War One backpacks, and how to don our gas masks. Throughout, we received extensive training in close order drill and learned the most important rule: that we must keep our weapons clean and well oiled at all times.

We were busy every morning from 5:00 a.m. until noon. From 1:00 p.m. on, if you had no restrictions, you could receive a pass and be free to go where you wished as long as you were present for reveille. After my first day I witnessed something that made a big impression on me. The soldier in the bunk next to me was still in his bunk when I came back from latrine, and soon one of the sergeants came to his bunk and shook him. He responded, and the sergeant talked to him and he talked back, but he still didn't get up. In a flash the sergeant dumped him on the floor, and that was all I saw before I had to leave the barracks to go to formation. When I came back in later, the soldier was gone. I found out that he was trying for a mental discharge, and I guess he got it because I never saw him again. Following that, we new recruits were restricted to the barracks for about a week before we were allowed another pass.

At the end of our first week we received our first pay. It was in pesos, and after accounting for deductions for the Philippine help, we had about fifty-seven pesos left. As soon as I had that first paycheck, I took off to my first visit to the PX. I bought a carton of Piedmont cigarettes, one peso per carton, and various kinds of candy and other snacks. On my first pass I went to the movies in the regimental theatre. One of the men in my squad who had been there for some time went with me and showed me around. Just across the street from our battalion was the Manila Post Office, and across from that was the Manila Metropolitan Theater where stage shows were performed. Both were large, beautiful buildings, and past them was a beautiful park with an open market.

As we walked, I could see a stone wall of about twenty feet high, with a large, well maintained lawn bordering it. When we got closer I saw an opening in the wall to allow for the street we were on. As we walked through the opening I found the wall to be about twenty feet wide at the bottom and tapered to about twelve feet wide at the top. Inside the wall I found what seemed like a new world for me, with narrow streets lined with buildings on each side. Some of the larger buildings had beautiful Spanish architecture unlike anything I had ever seen. The entire enclosure was called the old walled city, and had been constructed by the Spanish as a fortress.

Inside the walled city, little ponies pulled small carriages called carretas, which were pony-drawn taxis. After the movie we took one of these over the Pasig River to downtown Manila, and I immediately began my cultural education about the Philippines and the vast differences from US culture. The poverty in the Philippines was much more visible than the poverty I was used to in the states. I witnessed things I had never seen in America: blind people begging for money, little boys trying to sell their sisters, and women with one foot on the curb and one on the street, urinating with their skirts down. At the same time, well dressed Filipinos would walk by and not put one centavo into the container the beggars were using. I also saw soldiers passing by and not putting anything in. I soon found out why after dropping a fifty centavo coin into a blind beggar's cup. My friend Ray Pierce immediately yelled, "No!" but it was too late. In thirty seconds we were surrounded by poor beggars, all looking for a handout.

We were down in town for about three hours that day, and during that time I visited my first barroom. We went in and Ray asked me what I wanted to drink. I told him that I would have whatever he was having, which happened to be vodka. Well, I drank enough vodka to get very drunk. I don't remember how we made it back to our barracks, but I do know that I had just gotten into bed when the bugle started to blow and it was already time to get up. Oh, I wanted to stay in that bed! I was sick to my stomach and my head was pounding, but I knew I had to get up. I certainly didn't want the sergeant flipping my bunk with me in it. In spite of feeling lousy I was able to do everything that was required of me that day, with the exception of eating breakfast, and that was the last time I was ever drunk.

There were many new and different things to get used to in the Philippines. I remember seeing that, when some people smiled, their teeth were *black*. Not just brown, but actually black, from chewing beetle nut. On one trip into town we walked along the boulevard by Manila Bay where there were no beggars. Only the very wealthy lived there, and you could walk along and enjoy the sights by the bay and see the hulls of a few of the ships that were sunk during the Spanish-American War. The bay was especially nice during sunset or sunrise, or during a full moon.

There was a swimming pool nearby, at a large Olympic-size stadium near the barracks, and we used it often. I just loved it. The only water I had to swim in back in Oklahoma was a shallow pool or a red colored pond, and for a diving board we used the dead limb of a tree. This new pool amazed me, because it was Olympic-sized and had a large diving board. On my first visit there one of my friends climbed to the top diving board, which was about twenty feet high, and did a beautiful swan dive. After watching him I thought to myself, "Wow, I'd like to do that." After he came up from his dive and swam back to where I was, I told him that I'd like to do the dive like he'd just done. He asked me if I had ever dived from that height and I told him, "No, but I'm sure I can." He and I climbed to the top, but when I got there and saw just how high it was I started to have some reservations.

Despite my fear, I had made a commitment and had said I would do it, so I wasn't going to back out like a coward. I let him dive first, and when he had come up and swam out of the way, I made my first and last dive from twenty feet. I was in my Army shorts and it was a perfect belly flop that almost killed me. I hit so hard that the button on my shorts was imprinted on my belly, and stayed there for quite some time. After that I never made any efforts to improve my diving skills.

Despite the fact that we were in training, our time in Manila was often a time of innocent fun. Our work was not overly strenuous and I remained safe and healthy during my time there. Looking back, I realize now that it was the end of an innocent time and a state of mind that I would never return to after the war had taken its toll on me.

An Increased Pace and Guard Duty

About two months after arriving in Manila, the pace of training was dramatically increased. We were beginning to take long marches with our wool shirts on and often with our gas masks on for extended periods of time, all with the sun beating down, the temperature at one hundred degrees and the humidity high. No matter how tired I was after a fifteen mile walk, when we were met and escorted in by the 31st Infantry band, their marching music made me swell with pride. When we approached and heard that music, it was as though it was showcasing our sense of accomplishment. My shoulders squared up, and we all marched as if on parade.

My first guard duty was at the Finance Building, which was by the piers at Manila Bay. It was a large, one-story building and my post was inside. I was to take regular patrols through the building and I was given a .45 automatic for appearance—it had no ammunition. I was stationed at 11:00 p.m. and relieved at 6:00 a.m. It was always very quiet and I had very few lights to walk by; there was just barely enough for me to make my rounds without running into something. The first night I was posted there I was extremely tired; I had never had such a hard time staying awake. At about four o'clock I heard a very loud banging on the door, which certainly woke me up.

I went to the door and hollered, "Who goes there?"

I heard my answer from the Sergeant of the Guard, who yelled, "Open up!"

"Yes sir," I answered, and promptly opened the door.

"What took you so long?" he asked.

"I came as fast as I could," I said.

He asked, "Were you sleeping?"

"No sir," I answered.

He told me, "Resume your duties soldier, but be more prompt next time."

He left, and I locked the door and remained awake but miserable, tired and feeling scolded until my shift was relieved at 6:00 a.m.

We had a competition program to create the sharpest and neatest looking soldiers possible. If you were graded as the best in your platoon for a week you were stationed at guard duty Post #1, at the Headquarters main gate at the Cuartel De España in the old walled city. You stood at attention for two hours, and the only time you moved was to salute an officer who went by. I was on duty four hours off, two hours on, and four hours off. The reward was a carton of cigarettes and a weekend pass, although I soon found that the reward wasn't worth the pressure. After one tour of guard duty at Post #1, I made it a point never to get it again.

Another guard duty I received at Cuartel was at the guard house, where I guarded a prisoner who had been court-martialled and sentenced to hard labor. He was being held at the guard house before he would be sent back to the States to do his time. To comply with the hard labor order he had to dig a hole the size of a grave, and it was my duty to make sure he did not escape while doing so. If he did, I was told that I would have to do his time. For that duty I was issued a 03 bolt action rifle, a weapon I was not familiar with and that, once again, did not have any ammunition. It was common procedure not to issue any ammunition to those on guard duty. When the prisoner finished digging the grave I called the Sergeant of the guard who promptly came over, smoked a cigarette, threw it in the grave-sized hole and told the prisoner to bury it. That was all the prisoner did all day long.

On August 13, 1941, the 31st Infantry celebrated the twenty-fifth anniversary of its organization. The entire week before the anniversary we were subject to a constant program of inspections and close order drills. I thought we were good before that week, but the day of the big parade, when the entire regiment paraded, we were better than we had ever been. I felt a sense of camaraderie and shared experience among the other soldiers as we all paraded with our heads held high.

Some time after August 13th, Captain Gonzales left M Company, and 1st Lieutenant Thomas Bell was promoted to Captain.

Training at Fort McKinley and in the Field

In September we were trucked to Fort McKinley for a week long weapons training, particularly for our .30 caliber machine gun and the .45 automatic pistol. We fired .22 caliber machine guns mounted on .30 caliber frames until we were completely adapted to every phase of the gun's operation. We also had extensive training on the .45 automatic and some with the use of the 03 Springfield rifle. The last couple of days that we were there we all fired the weapons for record, and I did very well with the .30 caliber machine gun especially.

When we fired for record we were able to use the .30 caliber barrel in the gun, and what a difference it made! You could feel the power as you held it. One of the soldiers in my platoon, who was used to firing the machine with a .22 caliber barrel, was sitting and waiting for the order to begin firing. He didn't realize that it had been changed, and when he pulled the trigger and that .30 caliber blast started, he stopped firing, jumped up and started running. He was later moved out of the company and sent back to the U.S. for discharge.

When Lt. Bell was promoted to Captain and became the company commander, the pace of training became even more pressing. We worked longer days and drilled more and more in the use of our weapons. On one occasion we were trucked out to a training area that was a two day march from Manila. We trained under field conditions for a week, meaning that we had to sleep in tents made from our shelter halves; two men put their shelter halves together and slept under one tent.

We covered about fifteen miles per day in our march back, equipped with full field packs and wearing our wool shirts in one hundred degree heat. We had some men fall out, but the majority of us were able to do just fine because of our previous training. Our pith helmets also helped us to manage the heat. Pith helmets were light-weight hats with a wide brim all around. There was a two inch band that set down on our heads and suspended the rest of the hat out to allow air to flow through. Our heads were shielded from the sun and stayed cool the entire time we were marching.

After our first day on march we bivouacked at a small barrio. We had set up our tents and had gone to the mess trucks for an evening meal when we saw a group of men standing by a palm tree about sixty feet tall, talking and looking up to the top of the tree. I heard the sergeant say to one of the Filipinos, "Hey Joe, can you climb that tree?"

"Yes sir," he said.

"I'll give you a peso if you climb up and cut off five of those coconuts for me."

The surprised man answered, "Yes sir!" and immediately got his bolo, hung it across his back, and started up the tree just as easily as if he were walking on flat ground. He took the bolo off his shoulders and we watched the coconuts fall. Within ten minutes he was back on the ground, cutting off the ends of the coconut and pouring the milk into canteen cups.

There was a large lagoon nearby, and everyone in the company wanted to take a swim. We were walking to the water when we came to a group of women, all with no clothes on, who were doing laundry on the edge of the lagoon. They washed their clothes by laying them on a flat object and hitting them with a paddle. When we got to the water about twenty feet from where they were we took off our clothes and started wading into the water. I could hear the women laughing and they were all pointing at us and making gestures to one another, but we didn't understand why. I was too busy enjoying the water, still wading in about waist-deep and 150 feet from shore, when suddenly one of the men near me let out a cry of pain and started running for shore. About the same time, more and more men started yelling and running to shore.

I didn't know what was happening at first, until suddenly I felt a pain that felt as if someone had placed a hot iron on the cheek of my butt. I started to run with the rest, and when I got to shore I saw that I had a red spot about the size of a saucer that would not stop burning. I put my clothes on and rushed to the first aid station, where I had to wait to be seen. The corpsman told me that we had been stung by some kind of jelly fish that lived in the water. Although he gave me something for the pain it still kept me up most of the night.

When the bugle was blown at about four o'clock the next morning I was still suffering in pain from the bite, but feeling a bit better. Nonetheless, we still had the fifteen mile march to Manila, and I started to prepare myself. By six o'clock the company was assembled and we were on our way. When we got within a mile of our barracks in Manila, the 31st Infantry band met us and led us the rest of the way, playing spirited marching music all the while. When that music started you could always sense the unity of step in the entire company, and I felt a lot of pride and satisfaction when we had finished the march. When we arrived at the front of the barracks in formation, Captain Bell told us that he was proud of us and that we would be on light duty the next day.

Back to Manila

When I got inside the barracks I realized that my bunk sure looked good. I could hardly wait to take a good shower and, that done, to have a good meal in the mess hall. I was in my bunk by eight o'clock that night, and I still remember how good that mattress felt after a hard week of work and sleeping on the ground. When reveille sounded early the next morning, I felt like I had just fallen asleep. Despite our fatigue, we all reported for formation, and before dismissal we were told that we could receive a pass at one o'clock. After breakfast I went back to my bunk and lay down, and I fell asleep for a few hours. When I woke up I felt great, and my jelly fish wound had stopped bothering me. I laid out my full dress uniform and took everything I needed for my shower so that I could leave after dinner.

After dinner I got a pass and was getting ready to go to the post theater to see the movie, *Sergeant York*. Ray asked me what I was going to do with my break, and I told him that I was going to go see a movie. He said, "Wait for me, and I'll go with you."

I said okay, and one of the other men in my squad said he wanted to go too. When everyone was ready we took off for the post theater. Ray suggested, "Let's stop and get a bottle of vodka to sip on." I wasn't in favor of it, but I didn't say anything.

After we bought the bottle and opened it they both took a drink before passing it to me. I put it to my lips and pretended to drink, but I didn't really take a sip because I didn't want to get drunk again. The entire time we were in the movie they were sipping at the bottle, hiding it so we didn't get caught with alcohol in the theater. I enjoyed the movie and we got through it without getting caught. On our way back to the barracks I had my hands full with my two good friends, both drunk as skunks. I managed to keep them on the sidewalk and out of the street where they might get hit by a taxi or spook a carreta pony.

My luck failed, though, when we reached the Metropolitan Theater. There were a bunch of taxis waiting for customers to come out when the play was over, and the Filipino drivers were leaning against their taxis, waiting for business. We walked by and all the drivers laughed at the two drunk soldiers. In his drunkenness, Ray angrily confronted one of the drivers and punched him as hard as he could in the face. In a second every taxi driver outside the theater was after us. They backed us up the sidewalk and up into the theater entrance, where there was a trimmed hedge about eighteen inches high on either side. My two drunk friends both tripped over the hedge and fell on their backs outside of the entrance. As all this was happening, I continued yelling for the Sergeant of the Guard at the main gate of the 3rd Battalion, not far away. Suddenly I was confronted by a taxi driver holding an eight-inch switchblade knife. He held it toward by stomach and asked, "Are you Joe?" I said no, and he folded the knife and walked away. We had averted disaster.

Within a few minutes the MP's arrived and were going to arrest all of us, but I talked them into letting me get the drunks back to the barracks. With some difficulty I got them back, and as soon as I could I was in my bunk, sleeping off the chaos of the day. I was awakened by a commotion, and I woke up to find Ray standing there with a bolo he had bought for a souvenir. He said, "I'm going out to get one of those gook sons-a-bitches, and you're going with me." I told him no and went back to sleep. When I woke up the next morning he was still there and sound asleep.

No one was injured as a result of our total stupidity at the movies, and we were never called in or questioned about it. However, about a week later there were several transfers made to and from M Company, and my two friends were transferred to Headquarters Company.

While I was in Manila I also participated in a track meet for the whole regiment. I didn't know anything about track, but I was chosen to run the last leg of the relay. I insisted that I wouldn't know what I was doing, but the sergeant said only, "You'll do just fine. We will show you what to do."

At race time they put me where I was supposed to be and told me that when my teammate came around the bend I could start running, and when he passed the baton to me I was to take off, as fast as I could, to the finish line. When he came around and passed the baton to me he was about twenty feet in front of the pack. At the handoff I extended my arm toward the baton, and after receiving it I was able to extend the lead for our team for a short while until I was hit with a cramp in my right leg. It was so bad that I hit the ground and caused a big loss for my company, not to mention an embarrassing loss for me. All my friends told me to forget about it, but in spite of their support I felt bad about the loss.

On October 2, 1941, I turned eighteen years old in Manila. I had a couple of friends who wanted to go downtown to Manila, have a good meal and see a movie to celebrate my birthday. After the meal and the movie one of them said that he wanted to get a tattoo, so the three of us went to a tattoo parlor where he had a tattoo put on his chest. He had some finishing work added to it while another friend picked out a tattoo for his arm. They asked me if I was going to get one, and I told them no.

"You're just plain chicken," they said.

I insisted that I wasn't and, to prove it, I told them, "Okay. Go ahead and put one on my arm."

"What do you want put on it?" the tattooist asked me.

"The same thing he is having on his arm," I answered, pointing to my friend who was currently getting his tattoo.

"Which arm?"

"The left one," I answered.

The tattooist went to work, and when he had finished I looked down to find that I now had a picture of a beautiful girl with no clothes on, with her long hair strategically positioned in front of her body to shield herself. I had a sore arm for the rest of the week, but I was too ashamed to go to the doctor to have them examine my arm. That bashful girl will be with me for the rest of my life. Although I don't regret having gotten her, I sure was scared to tell my mom about my tattoo!

I am sure that by October of 1941 there was a lot of news about the possibility of the United States and Japan going to war, but as an eighteen year-old I was not keeping up with the news. The pace of our training was increasing every day and we were being kept too busy to worry about current events. We were in the field more than we were in our barracks, we ate field rations, we practiced various procedures for setting up our machine guns and we made our bivouac area safe and sanitary for a company of one hundred and forty men, and although we bitched about all we had to do at times, I felt a sense of pride and satisfaction that I'm sure the others felt as well.

A Feast to Remember

Just before payday on the first of November, Ray Pierce came over from Headquarters for a visit, and he wanted to know if I had any money for us to go out with. I said no, but one of our friends in my squad said, "Hey, I just got some money from home. If you two want to go out this evening, it will be on me."

We asked him, "Are you sure?"

"Hell yes!" he answered.

I got dressed in my full dress uniform and got a pass for the evening and we headed for downtown Manila. Our friend with the money took us to the nicest restaurant in Manila, and it was quite an experience for me. I had never been to such a fancy restaurant before. When we sat down and received our menu, I saw that I didn't even know what some of the meals were, and I was shocked to see the numbers listed for the prices. I asked our host, "Are you sure you can pay for this?"

He said only, "Do you think we would be in a place like this if I couldn't pay?"

Ray said, "You better be damn well sure."

Our friend said, "You can order anything you want. Everything is okay."

We ordered, and even though I didn't know what I had gotten it sure tasted good. When we had finished our host convinced us to order a dessert and an after meal cigar. After all his wonderful hospitality he asked for the bill. They gave it to him, and when they had handed it to him he told the waiter that he didn't have any money. Ray and I couldn't believe it; we wanted to punch him! The surprised waiter told us to remain seated and that he would be back with the manager. Ray and I just sat there, dumbfounded, but there was nothing else we could do. When our waiter returned with the manager he asked us if we could pay the bill, but we all said no.

The manager told us to stay where we were, and the waiter stayed to guard us. When he returned to our table he had a Manila police officer in tow. We had to show him our passes and he took all the information he needed before informing us that our commanding officer would be notified and that we would have to pay our bill. Then he released us with the instructions to report back to our company.

When we got out of the restaurant Ray and I wanted nothing more than to whip our host's ass, but all we did was swear at him and curse him out. It didn't seem to bother him at all. The next morning, the host and I had to report to the first sergeant. We were both chewed out and informed that we would each have one-third of the bill deducted from our pay. I'm sure that Headquarters did the same for Ray, and I was left to pay off the bill from my fancy meal in Manila.

We Move and War Follows

In November the fear of war was so palpable that even eighteen year old, naïve soldiers felt that something was about to happen. We were informed that Manila would begin having air raid drills, so if the air raid alarm was sounded at night we were all to put out any lights and pull our air raid curtains. Anyone who didn't obey would be arrested on the spot. M Company was ordered by Captain Bell not to issue any passes except for the post theater. We started doing more of our field work on the lawn around the old walled city.

After one of our training sessions I was heading to the latrine when I saw Bilon and three other bunk boys sitting on the floor under the overhang. He had that big smile on his face, and I went over to speak to him. I got there and saw that I was interrupting their dinner. I apologized, but Bilon said, "No Joe, that's okay. You eat with us." I said no thank you and went on my way, but I was surprised to see what they were eating. It consisted of about a gallon of white rice in a mound on a large banana leaf. On another leaf there was a pile of fish heads that looked as if they had been deep fried, along with a couple of different vegetables. They didn't use any utensils or plates; they ate with their hands and looked very comfortable doing so.

About a week later, at assembly, we were told that we would be moving to Fort McKinley. We were to put our personal belongings in our foot lockers and from there they would be moved out of the barracks until further notice. Later that day, with full field packs, we were loaded on trucks and put on our way. That was the last time I saw those barracks, my foot locker or Bilon. I had learned so much in my six and a half months there, and although the lessons had come slowly at times, it had been a productive time of growth, both in my personal outlook on life and in my knowledge as a soldier.

When we arrived at Fort McKinley we settled in and began to make preparations for war. I was assigned to a team of soldiers whose job it was to load .30 caliber machine gun belts, which would be attached to the guns when they were firing, and put them into wooden boxes. We had daily inspections of our full field packs, .45 automatic pistols and our machine gun. We were issued World War One steel helmets and received a lot of instructions on the use of gas masks. We were all starting to wonder if and when we would be going to war with Japan. I began to feel that it was only a matter of time. The younger men could see a change in the sergeants who were veterans of World War One, and we were encouraged by the positive attitude they kept up for us.

I went to bed on December 7th with everything as it had been in the months before. When I awoke on December 8th I was in the process of doing my assignments, as usual, when our platoon was ordered to assemble in front of our barracks. We assembled as we were told and our platoon leader asked that we remain quiet. When he started to speak I could see a change in him. He announced that Pearl Harbor had been attacked and that the United States and Japan were now at war.

When he finished his speech, one of the young soldiers said with confidence, "We will whip those Japs in two weeks." We young men had no clue what we were about to embark on, and when the young soldier said that we all gave a loud cheer. I didn't know then that instead of two weeks it would be three years and eight months from beginning to end. In that time, we would change from the innocent young men who cheered for a quick victory, to aged and changed men with a maturity and understanding that few men acquire in their lifetime.

We were dismissed, and as I began to process the information I found myself experiencing all types of misgivings and questions about what was to come with war. I had grown up in a strict religious family and had learned that it was a sin to kill anyone. However, the training that I had received from the Army told me that it was my duty to defend the United States and that I must, in a time of war, kill the enemy if necessary. I was very concerned about all the unknowns that suddenly faced me, but I was sure that I would do what I was ordered to do because of my responsibility for the lives of my comrades and my loyalty to the Army.

Within a few hours we were all loaded on trucks and moved to a bivouac where we stayed for a couple of days before we were moved again. We were starting to see Jap bombers and we could hear explosions in the distance from the bombs they were dropping. On the fourth night we were all loaded on trucks and moved to Nichols Field. We traveled in trucks with no headlights; I don't know how those drivers were able to make it but they did, somehow. Those of us in the back of the truck were unsure of where we were going and if we would even make it there, but we finally arrived at about 3:00 a.m.

As soon as we arrived we were moved by platoon, carrying all of our equipment with us, and stationed around the parameters of the airfield. At our station we set up our machine guns with sand bags. Then, we were ordered to dig in to prepare for the impending attack. I was shown where to dig my fox hole and I started work with my entrenching tool. By daylight we were as ready as we could be, but we had no camouflage for our foxholes or for our machine guns. We were stationed just below the crest of a shallow depression about three hundred feet wide with a gully at the center about three feet deep.

Shortly after daybreak one of the noncoms came by and told me and Lloyd LaDue that the mess truck was located among some trees and to go and have some breakfast. He told us that as soon as we received our food, we were to put our mess kit covers on and bring our food back and release the crew that was on the gun. We could eat while they were gone to get their food.

LaDue and I had just finished eating and had washed our mess kits and scrubbed them clean with sand when all hell broke loose. Machine guns started blasting and, before I had a chance to fire, there was a US P-40 fighter plane over our position, flying as fast as he could about one hundred feet off the ground. Just behind him was a Jap zero fighter with the big red ball on both wings. The Jap pilot had the canopy back on the cockpit, and we could see that he had his flight cap and goggles on and a white scarf around his neck. He flew over and banked in such a way that looking down, he could see us as clear as day as he flew. After they flew over it became as quiet as it had been before it all happened.

We had no latrine trenches dug, and one of the sergeants had gone to the gully and dropped his pants just before it all began. Just as he squatted to do his thing, we were being strafed by a zero fighter. We returned fire the best we could, but we couldn't get enough elevation to do him any damage; our machine gun wasn't mounted on an antiaircraft tripod. There were not any injuries, except perhaps to the pride of the sergeant who was caught in the gully with his pants down. That old World War One veteran came up out of the gully cussing up a storm. He was as mad as could be, calling the Jap plane a goddamned butterfly that wouldn't let him have his shit in peace.

We remained at Nichols Field for a few days and were strafed every day, but we had no bombs dropped on any of our positions. However, there was heavy bombing in the area of the hangars, and we could hear and feel the explosions; we were only about four or five hundred yards from where they were dropped. The entire time we were at Nichols Field we were only served two meals a day, before daylight and after dark.

K Company and Bataan

Things got quiet after the initial bombing, but we remained on edge. After our first day of quiet we were loaded on trucks and moved to an area on the Bataan Peninsula. When we arrived all three machine gun platoons were assigned one platoon for each rifle company. My platoon was assigned to K Company and we were put under the command of the K Company commander. After receiving our assignment and positioning, we dug in.

Our squad leader told us where the mess truck was and had us go for chow, half a squad at a time. At that time there were about six or seven of us in the squad, including the squad leader. I was hungry and tired, and when it was time for my squad to go I was looking forward to getting a good meal. I was disappointed when I found out what we would be eating—white rice and something made with canned fish, along with an unripe pineapple that had been fried in some kind of fat. As bad as it was, I ate everything I could get; I was so hungry. I didn't know then that that meal was the beginning of a process of slow starvation on Bataan.

Despite the dismal food rations, that night I was to witness the only funny thing that I would see during my entire stay on Bataan. The mess sergeant for K Company had a pet monkey with a collar around its neck. He tied it to the back of the mess truck with a small chain, and the sergeant had his foxhole dug so that the monkey could reach it even if he was tied up. The monkey must have been close to some of the bombing before, because all of a sudden he started acting funny, jumping up and down on the mess truck, squealing and pulling on the sergeant's pant leg while running toward the foxhole. When the sergeant didn't go, he persisted, and we thought for sure that the monkey had gone crazy. However, just a short time later we heard the drone of airplane motors. When it became apparent that we might be bombed the mess sergeant jumped down off the mess truck and ran for the foxhole, but the monkey had already beaten him there! It knew what we didn't, and had heard the bombing coming before we did.

We had been on the move since the beginning of the war, and throughout all that time and throughout all that filth, I was still wearing the same canteen. I hadn't had a chance to bathe and we had been told not to use our canteen water, since the tropics were always very hot and humid and it was extremely important that you always have water in your canteen. Instead, we were told to drink just enough to keep our mouth moist. We kept a stone the size of a marble in our mouth to keep the saliva working.

Near where the mess truck was stationed we noticed a clean, pleasant stream running though. After we ate and things had quieted down, we requested and received permission to go and take a bath and wash our clothes. It felt great to feel my body submerged in the water. When I finished bathing I washed my clothes the way I had seen the women do it in the lagoon, and then I wrung them out and put them back on, wet and clean.

We moved by truck on that same day after dark, and we were repositioned in another jungle area. Once again we had to dig new foxholes and machine gun emplacements. On the morning after we had arrived, our platoon had just assembled when the sergeant said that he needed four men to volunteer for a dangerous mission, which would involve going back into Manila and bringing out some badly needed supplies. Being a young and inexperienced kid, I volunteered. One of the other three was Robert Travers. He wasn't in my squad and I didn't know him very well, but we would come to know each other quite well through that experience. With all the members of K Company, along with others from the regiment, there were about twenty of us.

After dark we were loaded on a truck and driven through the dark back to Manila. It was still dark when we reached the city, and all of us were quiet out of fear that the Japs might be there. We had left a city that was vibrant and full of life twenty-four hours a day, and it was a shock to return and find it so quiet that you wondered if it was even still inhabited. Manila was in constant blackout conditions by that point.

Just before daybreak we arrived at Pier #7, the same pier that *The Republic* had docked in just eight months before. When we were offloaded, the truck left and we were moved to the edge of the pier. As we walked I could see a small, inter-island freighter moored to a dock below. The hatches were opened and about half of us were placed in the hold of the ship to arrange the cargo as it was thrown into the ship from the deck above. I was in the group that remained topside. There were no cranes to lower the cargo into the ship, and when the truck returned with a load of mattresses and other material, those of us at the top were ordered to throw the mattresses down first. When we had thrown the mattresses in, the men in the hold laid them out to create a cushion for the next layer of material that we had received. As time went on more trucks arrived and we kept working as fast as we could. At about 11 a.m. the air raid alarm sounded, and the driver of the truck we were unloading immediately jumped in and drove out of there as fast as he could. We headed to the safest place available, which was on the lower deck of Pier #7, and once we had gotten there we tried to find the safest place to wait out the raid.

We could see the Jap planes coming from over the bay and heading straight toward the bay end of the pier. I was able to get in the back of a big steel anchor post just as the Japs started firing. The bullets were hitting the pier from one end to the other, and each of the three planes made two strafing runs each on the dock and the ship. The whole thing lasted only about fifteen minutes before it was over, but we remained where we were until the all-clear sounded. Once we heard that, we returned to the upper level, the trucks returned, and we went to work as fast as we could until we were finished.

To my knowledge, there were no injuries on that mission. I assume that the reason they did not bomb the docks and the ship was that they wanted to keep them intact to use them later. After we finished loading, the ship's crew put the hatches over the holds. We waited at the pier until it was completely dark, and only then were we told to get aboard; we were on our way to Corregidor to deliver the supplies that we had just loaded.

To Corregidor and back to Bataan for my first bombing

After the ship was free from the pier, we pulled away. As we moved, everything was quiet and I laid on the steel deck, so tired I could barely move and more hungry than I had ever been in my life. After we had gotten out into the bay we were given a can of salmon and some World War One hardtack crackers, but that was the only food we received in a twenty-four hour period. Luckily, though, we did have access to all the water we wanted. We ate and went promptly to sleep, and we were awakened during the process of docking at Corregidor. I think I may have had about two hours sleep, and that was all the sleep I had for the past twenty-four hours. The freighter docked and we offloaded our freight. At Corregidor we went no further than the dock, and during our time there we received no food or help of any kind.

After we had offloaded the steamer we boarded a launch and headed for Cabcaben, located at the southern end of the Bataan Peninsula, where we were let off. Once off the launch, Bob and I enquired about where the M Company was located and if anyone was coming to pick us up. We were told by an officer that we would have to start walking north and try to catch a ride, but he warned us that it was unlikely that we would catch a ride north, because everything was moving south. With that piece of information, Bob and I started our forty mile walk, already tired and hungry but with our canteens full of water.

We walked steady from about 4:30 a.m. until noon, and during all that time there was almost no one going the direction we were, and we were so tired and hungry that we were about to collapse. Then, we caught the aroma of cooking food, and started a serious hunt to find out where it was coming from. We came to a trail off the main road, just wide enough for a truck to travel, and about one hundred yards back in the jungle we found the 31st Infantry Mobile Bakery. Bob and I told the private that we were with M Company, 31st Infantry and why we were there and that we needed some food right away. He told us to wait while he asked the sergeant, and when he returned he told us that we could have something to eat. He told us to follow him and he took us to where the food was. He gave us each a small loaf of fresh bread and put three or four thick slices of meat in our mess kits with a big ladle of gravy. He also gave us a canteen cup full of coffee with condensed milk.

I tasted the meat and asked him, "Man! What kind of meat is this?" Even though he replied that it was mule, we didn't even care; Bob and I both agreed that it was very good. We ate every bite of it and cleaned all the gravy out with the good, small loaf of fresh bread. When we were finished and had washed and put away our mess kits, we asked if they knew where M or K Company was located. They answered, "All we know is that it is north of here." They gave us a loaf of bread to take with us, and we started walking again. We walked all day with short rests, and sometimes we would get off the road quite a ways so we could take a nap without the dust from the southbound Army trucks making it hard to breathe. After one of our short naps we were picked up by a truck going in our direction. We rode about ten miles in the truck, which took about three hours because of the heavy traffic.

When we arrived at the truck's destination we were fed and allowed to stay for the night, and early the next morning we were up and on our way. We had been told how to find M Company, and we spent most of the next day on the road. We finally got back with our company and were able to get something to eat, although it was not nearly as much as we would have liked, since food was short. We had only two small meals a day, usually rice and beans with some type of canned fish, and occasionally we had a vegetable. For beverages, the only thing that we had was what the Mess Sergeant could try to make from what was available, which wasn't always much.

The day Bob and I returned, we received our food and a canteen cup of sassafras tea with sugar, which tasted really good. After we ate we were assigned back to our original squads, and Bob and I weren't able to see each other for awhile. I returned to my squad and was shown where to dig my foxhole, and I had to dig it before I could rest. I started at once because I was so tired that I wanted to finish as soon as possible. The ground was soft and I was about half finished when I started to feel sick to my stomach and began throwing up. I emptied my stomach completely of all the food I had needed so badly. Seeing that I was so sick, two of my squad brothers, whose names I can't remember, finished digging my foxhole. To this day I am grateful to them, because I am sure that they were as tired and hungry as I was. The tea I had enjoyed so much must have been what made me sick.

As soon as my foxhole was finished I took some water and rinsed my mouth, then lay down and slept soundly. We were awakened just before daybreak and told to go fill our canteens with water and have breakfast. It was a very small breakfast that did not fill our empty stomachs. After we ate we were ordered to stay near our foxholes for further orders, and that suited me just fine. I was still worn out from all I had been through during the last few days and nights, and I went back to my foxhole, laid down beside it, and fell into a sound sleep.

When someone woke me shortly after, I heard the drone of airplane engines in the distance. A group of ten twin-engine bombers in staggered formation were headed in a direct line over our position. I lay on my back in my foxhole and saw as they opened the bomb bay doors and released the bombs. As I saw them begin to fall I knew that this was different; we were going to get hit hard. I had been attacked by strafing before, and had felt nervous then, but this was the first time I had been bombed.

The first bombs started hitting the ground quite a distance from where I was, but in short order they were exploding all around me. The power of the explosions made you feel as if you were being picked up and then slammed back to the ground. The raid lasted about five to ten minutes from beginning to end, but that time felt like an eternity to those of us who were experiencing our first air raid. When it was over I was like a skittish cat, and I witnessed a change in all those around me as well. We were at war now.

Outpost at Dinalupihan

Later on the night of the air raid, we were formed up and moved out to a new position. When we arrived we immediately began digging our foxholes. We were only there a few days, but during our time there we were all assigned various duties. They asked our platoon for two volunteers for outpost duty, and I volunteered.

When all the volunteers were together we had a weapons carrier assigned to us, with a .30 caliber machine gun mounted on cross bars over the top. We loaded the weapons carrier with our full field packs and extra water, hardtack and canned fish, and extra belts of ammunition.

When darkness fell we started driving north; there were about twelve of us, commanded by a sergeant and a corporal—the rest of us were privates. We took the only road running north to south the length of the peninsula; while we traveled north, all the rest of the traffic seemed to be only heading south. It eventually led us to Dinalupihan, a small town at the top of Bataan. We took the only road that led to the southern end of Bataan from our regiment, and at Dinalupihan this road was intersected by another, to form a T-shape. Directly across the other road, at the top of the T where our road ended, was a pump gas station. Prior to the war the proprietor and his family had lived about twelve feet behind the pumps. The house they had occupied was built of nepa, and it stood about ten feet off the ground. It was large enough to conceal our weapons carrier underneath so that it could not be seen from the air. When we arrived we were told to find another place close by that was under cover. About twenty feet away was another nepa house built off the ground, large enough for four of us to stay under and still maintain the required distance between us.

Twilight was just beginning to appear, and we could see that it would take some work to clean up where we were going to sleep. The Filipinos who had lived there had followed the custom of keeping the pigs, chickens and other animals under their house. We saw the work that needed to be done, and Corporal Wood went to ask the sergeant if he did, in fact, want us to dig in. The sergeant said no, because we were not going to be there long. Instead, we were told to look around and use whatever natural cover we could find, in case it was needed later. Instead of digging a foxhole, the four of us were left to start cleaning a place within all the animal feces so that we would have a place to lie down when we could.

Our duty while we were on the outpost mission was to go out in twos, on the road and to different parts of the town, and watch for any sign of the Japs. If we saw anything we were to rush back and tell the sergeant, who would take it from there. That was the only form of communication we had. During the time we were there, the traffic was almost non-existent and all of it non-military. We patrolled all that day, constantly on edge because we had no idea what to do if we did see the Japs. None of us had received even as much as fifteen minutes training for anything like this. We kept our eyes open for Jap airplanes and did see them quite frequently. Every time we spotted one we took cover, hoping that they had not seen us. The only firearms we had with us on this patrol were our .45 automatic pistols. We each pulled a two hour sentry duty each night. When it was time to sleep, we were allowed to open our field packs and lay our shelter halves on the dirty ground. I was so exhausted that any time I had the opportunity, I would immediately fall into a restful sleep.

I was awakened the first morning, and felt that I must have slept extra well; I just felt better for some reason. However, by the time we were issued our breakfast I was back to feeling the same old way: underfed and exhausted. Once again we received one number ten can of salmon and four hardtack crackers to be divided between the two of us. After eating, we filled our canteens with chlorinated water.

At about 8:00 a.m., Rufus Hunt and I were sent out to our area for patrol. We had been out about three hours when we heard airplane motors. We found ground cover and located the plane; it was a small plane, flying at about three or four thousand feet. As the plane flew over us we could see something fluttering to the ground, and after he had made three or four sweeps over the town and flown away, we went over to see what it had dropped. They were leaflets written in English, telling everyone in the town to leave before 2:00 p.m. the next day or they would be caught in a heavy bombing raid. When our tour of patrolling was over, we returned to the command post and showed the flyer to the sergeant. It turns out that one had been dropped by our command post and he had already seen it.

I was sure that once we were aware of what the Japs were threatening to do, we would be ordered to dig in. However, we received no change in orders and, just before dark, we were issued our salmon and hardtack as usual. As soon as I could I unrolled my backpack and laid down and went to sleep until the time came for my sentry duty. When I was relieved from duty I had about two more hours of rest before I was awakened for early patrol with Rufus. We had our salmon and hardtack and headed out.

Wounded

We patrolled until we were relieved around noon, and we arrived back at the command post by around 12:30 or 1:00 p.m. I was just starting to take my backpack off the weapons carrier and unroll my shelter half when the sergeant told me to leave it where it was. I went back to my resting area and laid down where I had previously made my bed, and I was almost asleep when I heard multiple airplane motors in the distance. Corporal Wood, who was about fifteen feet away, looked at me and said, "I guess those Japs are going to do what they said they would."

As the planes got closer, they started dropping bombs. The only cover we had was a piece of twelve by twelve timber about fourteen feet long. Corporal Wood told me to get as close to it as we could and as flat to the ground as possible. When the bombs got to where we were, one of them hit between our nepa hut and the hut that our weapons carrier was under, and about three others hit very close to where we were. The last one that hit lifted me completely off the ground and slammed me down again.

Within a few minutes it was all over in our area, and it was only after all the noise and excitement had died down that I was aware of a sharp pain in the left side of my chest. I looked down and saw that my left side was covered with blood. I didn't know how badly I was hurt, and before I could find out I heard Corporal Wood calling, "Help me. Please help me." He was still lying on his stomach, and when I got up and went closer to him I could see a hole the size of a golf ball near his shoulder blade. He was bleeding but had no heavy hemorrhaging. Once I saw that he was injured I started hollering for help, but it took awhile for anyone to come because we were all in the process of recovering from the pounding we had received.

The first one to show up to help us was a little redhead from Cuomo, Mississippi by the name of Morgan, who we called Red. He took one look at us and went looking for the sergeant, and he quickly returned with him. Wood was still lying in the same position I had found him in. The sergeant looked at the two of us and said, "We have to get you both to an aid station. Let me see if the weapons carrier will start."

By this time the dust had settled and I could see the sergeant running toward the nepa hut where we had parked our weapons carrier. The hut had been blown away by the explosion, and the weapons carrier was the only thing left; it was obvious that it was in no condition to be driven. The sergeant came back and got close to Wood's face, and he asked Wood if he could turn him over. Wood said yes, and the sergeant and Red turned him over as easy as they could. They got him on his back and put him in a sitting position. I don't know why he didn't pass out, because he was hit very badly, but he never showed much pain. Once he was in a sitting position, the sergeant said, "Red, if he can walk, I want you to help him get to an aid station."

Then, he asked me if I felt strong enough to help. I said, "I think so," and we started off.

We got Wood on his feet with Red taking his good arm and putting it over his shoulder. I took my right arm and put it around Wood's waist, and we started down the road to Bataan. While we were walking everything was quiet, and I thought the bombing was over. Although my side was hurt and I was bleeding, I felt some sense of relief.

There were no vehicles on the road except for a small truck that was parked in the middle of the road, about three hundred yards from where we were. We were about half way to it when we heard the drone of airplanes starting again. We started moving as fast as we could, but just before we reached the truck the Japs started bombing the town again. We approached the truck on the passenger's side and found that there was no one in it, although the motor was still running. Red asked me if I could hold Corporal Wood by myself and I said no, so we took him to the running board on the truck and sat him on it, with me beside him, holding him in sitting position.

There was a ditch on the side of the road by the truck, and Red went into it and found the Filipino driver. I heard Red say, "Joe, are you the driver of this truck?"

"Yes sir," he said.

Red said, "Well come out of there now, because I have two men that I have to get to an aid station."

The driver answered, "But sir, they are bombing."

Red took out his .45 and pointed it at the driver and said, "You son of a bitch, if you don't move now, I'll shoot you."

Upon hearing that, the driver was out of there in a flash. They both came over to where Wood and I were, Red still holding his .45 and the driver walking in front of him. They got to us and Red said to Wood, "Can you stand up?" Wood shook his head yes. Red then told the driver to help him up, and after the driver and I got Wood up and moved away far enough to open the truck door, Red asked me if I could get on the back of the truck by myself. I said I could, and he told me to go on and get up. I released my hold on Wood and Red put his .45 back in his holster, and he and the driver put Wood in the cab between the two of them. The whole process took about ten minutes, and during this time the Japs were still bombing the town.

Just as we started to move, the truck came to a stop. I looked around to see why, and I saw a motorcycle with a sidecar, with a staff sergeant in it. They were trying to give directions to the aid station, but with the noise of the bombs, the motorcycle and the truck, it was impossible for the driver to hear. Even though I was hurting, I got out of the truck to find out where to go, but just as I got off, they drove off and left me standing in the middle of the road. When the sergeant in the sidecar saw me he got out and came over and helped me into his place in the sidecar, telling the driver to take me to the aid station. We caught the truck and led it to the aid station, which was back in the jungle just off the road.

When we arrived there the driver of the motorcycle helped me out of the sidecar and we went to the truck as Red and Wood were getting out. I'm sure that Red didn't even realize that they had left me standing in the middle of the road. As soon as we were out, two orderlies came running with stretchers and put Wood on one, carrying him in for treatment. I was able to walk, and was treated too. Between the time we were injured and the time we arrived at the aid station, about an hour and a half or less had elapsed.

After Wood was placed on the stretcher and carried in, I never saw him again. I don't know how things turned out for him. As for me, they examined me, taking out two pieces of shrapnel to stop the bleeding. I would find, some years later, that they had left one piece of shrapnel in.

When they had finished, the doctor ordered one of the orderlies to get me a clean uniform. The one I had on was the same one that I had last washed just before we went on detail to clean the ship, and I hadn't had a bath or washed my clothes since. I threw away the old ones, putting clean clothes on my body that was only clean in the area of my wound; the rest of me was still filthy. I was given a folding cot under the trees and was told that I would be observed for twenty-four hours.

Morgan, the red-head from Mississippi, was just seventeen years-old when he was given the responsibility of getting two wounded men to treatment under very dangerous circumstances. He did it all calmly, and when force was needed he did not hesitate to use it. I didn't know him before the war, although I knew of him. He was in the heavy weapons platoon under Sergeant Burbank, who treated him like a son.

After some medication and a good night's sleep under the trees, the next morning they removed the bandages and checked me over. They said that they would like to keep me for a few days, but under the circumstances they wouldn't be able to. They treated my wound and gave me some medication to take with me, and I was returned to outpost duty.

When I arrived back at our post, I could not believe all the damage that the bombing had caused. It was also hard to believe, although a huge relief, that Corporal Wood and I had been the only ones wounded. The house that we had stayed under was completely blown away and the command post moved, but they were not far from where they had been before. The weapons carrier was full of shrapnel holes, and the machine gun had been removed from the mounting. I looked the weapons carrier over, and could see that it was no longer usable. After I was placed in my new position, I went back to the weapons carrier and retrieved my full field pack. Shrapnel had penetrated it in several places, and my mess kit also had several holes in it. When I unrolled my field pack I found that it had been ruined too. From that time on I would not have a full field pack again.

A few days later I found a sugarcane sack made of some kind of woven material. I cut it at the seams and made it into a pretty good blanket. The only time we used the shelter half was to put it on the ground; we didn't need shelter from the rain because it was the dry season the entire time we were on Bataan. As for the mess kit, it wasn't essential because it wasn't that often that we had anything to put on it. I was able to keep my mess kit knife and spoon and I also managed to salvage a pair of socks and my toothbrush and toothpaste. However, I had to improvise another method to carry them until I was able to get another sugarcane sack.

We were on outpost duty for another ten or twelve hours after I came back, and during that time I made no patrols because I was still in a lot of pain. The truck came to get us in the middle of the night, and we were all relieved to get out of there and back with our respective companies. We reached our company, and after daybreak and a very small breakfast I went to see the corpsman to change my bandage. When he finished he said that the bleeding had stopped and that I seemed to be okay.

Layac Junction

We had just gotten back to the company when we were told that we would be assigned by platoon to a rifle company, and my platoon was assigned to L Company. It took awhile to fit in with new people. We were told that L Company had a new Company Commander, a First Lieutenant who had previously been with the Military Police.

We were in the L Company bivouac area for about a day or two, and during that time I was able to take my second bath in about a month. It gave me an opportunity to clean my entire body as opposed to just the wound area, and it raised my spirits enormously. I am sure that it had some effect on my rapid recovery. However, I wouldn't be able to stay clean for long, because we received orders to move to a new defensive position, a place called Layac Junction.

Sometime during the night we were loaded on trucks and driven for about an hour before we were offloaded and marched the rest of the way to our new position. We arrived early in the morning and had our positions posted before we were ordered to dig, which meant that we had to dig in for our machine gun and for our foxhole. I found myself in quite a spot. I had no entrenching tool because I had left it on the weapons carrier where my backpack was destroyed. I started looking for a depression in the ground, no matter how small. Luckily, I found a small eroded area that was about three feet wide and six inches deeper than the surrounding area. I started in with my mess kit knife, spoon and canteen cup to try and enlarge and deepen the depression. However, the minute I began I knew I was in serious trouble. The ground was so hard I wasn't even able to push my mess kit knife into it. The only way I could penetrate it was to hold my mess kit knife and drive it in with a stone I had found. I couldn't hit the knife handle too hard for fear I would break it.

I wanted to dig the best foxhole possible, because I was aware of how important it would be if we were bombed. My side was hurting, but I worked as fast and as hard as I could with the tools I had. Blisters developed on my hands, some of which had broken and were bleeding. It was about 110 degrees, and the sun was beating down on me. I was drinking too fast and using up the little water I had in my canteen, and I was starting to wonder if I would have enough to last long enough to get this done. After working for awhile with what I had, I sat down to rest and saw LaDue working with his entrenching pick. I went over to him and asked him if I could use it while he was cleaning out what he had worked so hard to loosen. He was ready to clean out so he handed me the pick, and I went back to my hole and started swinging the pick as fast as I could. When I saw that he had finished cleaning out, I took the pick back to him and returned to my hole to clean it out with my canteen cup. When I was finished, I had a hole that was about three feet wide and three feet deep, and about six inches shorter than I was. I was so tired I could hardly move.

We were located in an open area near the top of a gradual hill, with large trees in back of us and a steep gully with more large trees to our right. After I finished my foxhole, I lay down on my back with my knees sticking up because my hole was too short. It was quiet, and there were no planes in the air. Suddenly, from the trees behind us there came a loud explosion, followed quickly by three more. Quickly, we were made aware that the trees in back of us were cover for a battery of .75mm artillery and the Filipino Scouts 26th Cavalry. The battery of .75mm had begun firing on the Japs.

Soon after, I experienced my first horrifying beating from Jap artillery. The first round went right over my head, and it sounded like nothing I had ever heard before. It was a loud rushing noise, followed by an explosion in the trees in back of me. Then came many more shells, getting closer and closer to where we were, and the explosions started in our area. Chunks of earth rained down on us and we were covered with dust. This was worse than taking the bombing from the air, because you didn't know where the rounds were coming from. When they hit very close, it gave you a feeling of being picked up and slammed back down. It felt like it went on forever, and some of the stuff falling near me was more than dust and chunks of dirt; there were also spent pieces of hot shrapnel raining down around us.

The first barrage lasted about an hour and a half and for about ten or fifteen minutes after it was over things were so quiet that I felt very apprehensive. I didn't know what was going to happen next. I stayed as low as I could and looked around the area of my foxhole, and I could see that quite a few of the holes made from the shells were already bigger than the foxhole I had worked on for hours. I started looking toward the foxholes of the other squad members and I could see that they were doing the same thing that I was. When I would rise up and look, I would see one of those old World War One helmets bob up. It was a little like watching prairie dogs in a prairie dog town. We were all hollering to each other to see if anyone was hurt, but luckily everyone in my squad was okay.

Unfortunately, it wasn't quiet for very long. The two gunners on our machine gun opened up firing six round bursts—six round bursts only, so that the barrel wouldn't get too hot and cause the water in the jacket to boil. Also, short bursts were less apt to give our position away. Shortly after our gun started firing, the Filipinos on the .75mm started firing too, and we were to go through the same thing for two hours. When all of that was over, I was hurting so bad from not being able to stretch out because my foxhole was so short, and during a lull I stood up and faced toward the trees in back of me.

There, I saw something that I would remember for the rest of my life. A large group of horses with riders came out of the trees in a fast gallop. I was so surprised that I ducked down in my hole and watched as they approached my foxhole. It was amazing the way that they were able to ride between the foxholes and shell craters. They were working toward the trees near the ravine in front of where we were, and they were about halfway to my foxhole when all hell broke loose once again—the Japs were giving us another pounding. I saw a few rounds hit inside the men on horses, but I saw no men or horses fall. The whole thing, from beginning to end, lasted no more than ten minutes. By then the whole group of riders were out of my sight and I was back in my hole, ready to take a beating from the Japs for another two hours.

The most wearing emotion was the constant fear that plagued me, realizing that at any moment one of those shells could hit directly on me and take my life. Although I am an older man reflecting back on that time, even as an eighteen year-old boy I was aware, because of those experiences, how precious life is. I was beginning to learn how to gauge when a time was right to be very afraid, versus when it was alright to relax some, when the shells were falling some distance from me. I was learning that I would not survive a life of constant fear. I was starting to become a seasoned soldier.

While I was sitting on the edge of my hole during some downtime, I saw a lone person walking in my direction, looking down as he walked. At times he reached down and picked something up before moving near the next hole and doing something near the ground with his hands once again. He finally worked his way up to where I was, and I saw that it was a young soldier, about twenty years old, who was repairing a telephone line that was laid through our position. He brought the line over to my position and was splicing the two ends, when the .75mm started firing in back of us. No sooner had that started than we began getting heavy return from the Japs. In no time, the lineman was in my hole with me. I discovered then that no matter how small the hole is, there is always room for one more when you are under artillery fire. We had to remain that tight for about an hour, with no chance at all to talk to each other. When we finally got a short lull, he got up and started running in the direction he had come from, and to my knowledge I never saw him again.

During this barrage the Jap artillery were able to zero in on the battery of .75mm's in the back of us. They must have hit the battery's ammunition dump, because during the barrage there was a large explosion followed by many smaller ones. As a result of the explosions, we were presented with another frightening situation. Shrapnel and other pieces from the exploding shells were falling all around us, and when you looked up you could see it raining down. Some of the pieces were large washers, or rings, and when one was in the air you could hear it spinning, and whenever one was falling toward me I wished I was somewhere else. One of them landed about a foot from my head, and after things had quieted down I found the piece and picked it up—it must have weighed about half a pound.

Leaving Layac

After the Japs knocked out the .75's there was only small arms fire to be heard, and when it got quiet we had the chance to check on each other. To this day I will never understand how we got so lucky, but everyone in my squad was okay. We didn't receive any more artillery fire that day, but for the first time we were starting to receive small arms and mortar fire. None of the mortar fire was reaching our area, but I could hear the bullets from the small arms as they went over my head. It was starting to get darker all the time, and our machine gun and other fire started dying down. Another hour or so after it was completely dark, a member of our squad came to my hole and told me in a low whisper that we were moving out, and to assemble at the gun.

When I got to the gun, we were told to quietly give our last name. It was so dark that it was hard to tell who was who, and I'm sure the corporal wanted to make as sure as possible that we were all there. When he had checked on us he had us all follow him. There were only six of us in the squad at that time, and the corporal wanted to keep us all together. He led us to the ravine in front of our position, and we went into the trees where it became darker still. When we got there I could hardly see anything, but I knew that there were a lot of people there—all of L company plus the entire M Company platoon.

A command was given and quietly passed on that each person was to grab the belt of the person in front of him and to follow him as he walked. I took the belt of the person in front of me, the person behind me took mine, and we stood that way for quite awhile. Then, the quiet was broken by a distant pop, followed by a loud explosion in the area that we had just left.

I felt the man in front of me start to move and I moved with him, and the one who was holding my belt did the same. We were walking in complete darkness, and after moving for about twenty minutes, we heard another distant pop and explosion from where we had previously been. Shortly after that explosion, word was passed back in whispers that we were to hang on and look forward for the lieutenant's light.

I looked for the lieutenant's light, all the while trying not to trip and fall on something in my path. Finally, I was able to see a soft glow in front of me. Those of us in back were to learn later that the light was a piece of phosphorous wood that Lieutenant Thompson had found; I suppose he was trying to give us a little encouragement. It gave me a feeling of hope and a little extra drive to continue moving forward. After stumbling around in the dark for about an hour, staying just ahead of mortar fire, Lieutenant Thompson finally led us to a road. We followed the road for about two miles to where some vehicles were waiting to take us out. The vehicle I was loaded into was an old bus with the top cut off so that the occupants could see the airplanes when they were moving during the day.

After we boarded and were on our way, some of the men from L Company began talking about who had been killed or wounded. They were concerned about whether any of them were left behind. Hearing that, I began to try and see if all of my squad was there, but I couldn't locate any of them at that time. We finally arrived at the bivouac area where we were offloaded and told to find a spot nearby to try and get some rest. As soon as I could, I found a spot in the dark that was big enough for me to lie down, and as soon as my eyes were closed I was fast asleep.

The next thing I knew it was daybreak. In short order I found my squad and it was good to know that they were all okay. All of us at Layac had a look of complete exhaustion. The entire time we were there we never had a bite of food, and the water in my canteen was almost gone. After daybreak I could see that we were in an area with good cover from the air. Our platoon leader was able to locate all of his squads, and to my memory we lost no one. In about two hours we received the first food we had eaten in forty-eight hours. It was the largest portion I had received since the beginning of the war. When I came to the first server he asked me where my mess kit was. I told him that it had been ruined by shrapnel, and he told me to step out of line and wait. Then he hollered for someone to take his place and, when someone had, he walked away. When he returned he gave me a mess kit and told me I could keep it. While I was waiting, and looking, and smelling that food, I was getting hungrier all the time, but as soon as he gave me the mess kit he motioned for me to get back in line. He filled my new mess kit with food, and I found a place on the ground where I could sit. I went through that mess kit full of food in no time, and I'm sure I could have finished off another.

On the Move

We were assigned to areas and posts in a way that would prevent a large number of men from being killed by one bomb or shell, and once that was done we were ordered to dig in. The ground was much looser here than it was in Layac, and I was able to borrow entrenching tools from a squad member near me. In a short time we had all dug our holes. I laid down in mine, using my sugar cane blanket as a pillow, and was able to stretch out and get semi-comfortable by removing my canteen belt. It gave me a sense of relief to feel my full canteen, and I was asleep almost as soon as my eyes closed.

When I awoke it was late in the afternoon and things were all quiet except for the occasional sound of airplane motors. We had been through so much hard work and stress since the beginning of the war that none of us were very talkative. We were greatly pleased to learn, however, that General MacArthur had informed us that help was on the way, with hundreds of ships and thousands of men.

It's amazing how fast news travels if someone has been wounded or killed. After I had talked to some of the other men, I learned that L Company had lost quite a few men at Layac, some injured and others killed. There was talk that they were going to get replacements from units that weren't infantry.

We remained at this place for two or three days, but we did not receive another issue of food that would equal even half of the amount that we received on the morning after our withdrawal from Layac. In fact, my canteen was about half filled twice a day.

Soon we received an order to move out, which for a machine gun squad takes some time because we had to get the belts and boxes of ammunition together and loaded on the vehicle, along with all the other equipment. When it was finally loaded, we rode for a short while before offloading again and walking for about two hours. The next morning we were posted and told to dig in, to set up our gun and to sandbag the tripod, which had to be done to keep it from moving when the machine gun was firing.

After about three hours we were finished, and I was sitting on the edge of my hole resting, when I looked over and saw a soldier about my age, just twenty feet from me. He had finished his hole, and when we noticed each other he came over to where I was and sat down by me. He told me that he was in a rear echelon unit and that he hadn't been exposed to bombing or any other close explosions. While we were talking, one of our .155mm canons fired close to where we were. It startled me for a moment, but I knew at once that it was outgoing and that it wasn't time to get into my foxhole. I looked over, and an expression came on that young man's face that was likely just like mine was at the time when the battery of .75s opened up at Layac.

He sat by me for awhile after that, and I tried to explain the difference in the sound of incoming and outgoing. He told me that he had no training with a rifle and that he was very nervous. Shortly after, the big guns fired again and he ran back to his foxhole, and I was never to see or talk to him again. I hope he made it okay.

In the Zero's Gun Sights

We were only in this position for one night and one day before we were ordered to prepare to move out. When it was time to move, one man carried the machine gun which weighed about forty pounds and the number one gunner usually carried the tripod weighing fifty pounds. The rest of us carried belts of ammunition, either in wooden boxes or draped around our necks or over our shoulders. The weight per man—with spare parts, canteen, pistol and other essentials—averaged about sixty pounds. All told, we carried about two thousand or more rounds of ammunition for the machine gun, which could fire six hundred rounds per minute.

When we were all assembled, Lieutenant Thompson told us that we were moving out. We would be going into battle that day, and we would have to march all the way. We were to form two columns and march in close formation until we came to the main road, then we would split and march single column on each side of the road. He also told us that we would be marching under fast march orders. Prior to our orders, we had been served a small breakfast and had been able to fill our canteen. When we started our march, most everyone was quiet, but there was some conversation to be heard, in quiet tones. I'm sure that, like me, most of the other men were feeling a good deal of apprehension. In my case, every move I made in the war against the Japs became dramatically more explosive and dangerous as time went on.

In spite of my apprehension, I was in the line with my squad, moving forward and doing the best I could along with everyone else. We walked for about two hours, stopping only for fifteen minutes rest before starting onward again. From time to time we would see flashes of light in the distance, but we didn't hear any explosions. We were still walking when the sun came up, and I had never been as tired in my life as I was at that time. Every step was a struggle to move forward, and at times I thought that I might never make it.

I was third in line in my squad, and the person in front of me was carrying the gun. I could see that he was staggering and having a hard time keeping the gun balanced on his shoulder, and I knew what he was going through and the fatigue he was experiencing. Our round water jackets made the gun the hardest thing to carry, especially in addition to our already heavy loads. I caught up to him and tapped him on the shoulder and asked him if he wanted to exchange loads. He said yes, and we fell out to quickly switch loads before rushing back into formation.

By this time we had left the main road and were marching on a farm road lined with sugarcane fields and other vegetation. Soon, someone spotted six or seven fighter planes several miles away, heading in our direction. I knew we were all getting nervous because we were all bumping into each other. We received an order from Lieutenant Thompson that no one was to disburse until he gave the order. At that time, the plane formation changed; they began preparing to fly over two at a time, one after the other, from the front of our column to the rear. The first two went over about a hundred feet off the ground without firing a shot, and then all the others did the same. Even though we were nervous, no one broke ranks. We were all thinking that this could be the end, but we continued marching until we could once again see the planes circling to make another run over us. As the first two approached again, I felt sure we would receive a disband order, but the order that came back through the ranks instead was to remain in formation. Once again, no shots were fired, and it was only as the Japs were forming for a third run, with the first two lined up and starting their dive, that we received the loud order to disburse. When we received that, we got off the road as fast as we could and put ourselves as flat to the ground as we could get. I was sure we were going to be shot up very badly and that I might be one of the ones shot, but all the Jap planes flew over us for a third time without firing a single shot. We remained down until the order was given to form ranks.

For thirty-six years after that terrifying experience, I asked myself the question: Why did Lieutenant Thompson issue the order to stay in rank and not disburse? Eventually, I received the answer from Lieutenant Thompson personally. I met with him during a reunion of the 31st Infantry at Fort Sill, Oklahoma in 1987. Lieutenant Thompson was Colonel Thompson by that point, having stayed in the service after the war and eventually retiring as a Colonel. It was a wonderful reunion, and I was able to ask Colonel Thompson about the order. He looked at me before asking me where we would have disbursed that would have given us any hope of cover. He told me that he had seen the same kind of action used by another officer, and he hoped it would work in our case. Although it had worked, I told him how it had scared the shit out of all of us, and I was surprised to hear that he had been scared too. However, he felt that our only chance was that they would not be able to make out if we were Americans or Japs from their place in the air, and his plan saved all our lives.

During that reunion I was also able to have other questions answered with Colonel Thompson or others, like Captain Bell, my commanding officer in M Company, who had retired at the rank of Major. For example, I asked Colonel Thompson about our withdrawal at Layac and about the phosphorous stick, and he told me that it was, in fact, to give us hope and motivation to move forward.

Abucay

After we were formed back on the road we marched for about half an hour before we left the farm road and were led through a sugarcane field. While marching, we crossed an irrigation ditch that was about three feet deep and four feet wide, and once we had crossed that, we were separated and each machine gun was assigned to a placement position. We were led to our position, which was just below the crest of a gradual declining hill. The area before us gave us a good line of fire, and the best part of all was that the machine gun position was already dug, as were all the holes for the squad. We learned that they weren't foxholes, but were called spider holes because they were dug as round holes and were only about four feet in diameter and about five feet deep. They were much safer than the long, shallow holes we had been using.

After we were assigned our position, we all went to work setting up our machine gun. We had been carrying empty sandbags which we started filling with dirt, and with sand if it was available. We placed the equipment so it was as accessible to the gun as possible, and while we were setting up we began hearing artillery fire to the right and left of us, as well as large shells going over our heads toward where the Japs were. They were very loud, and made that unique sound that the shells make as they go over your head.

When we finished our work setting up, the corporal took the position to fire the gun and the number two gunner was beside him, with the rest of the squad in our holes. I could hear small arms fire on both sides of me, and I heard our gun open up with six round bursts. At times I would hear a pop as a bullet went over my head, but as often as I could I raised my head and looked in the direction our gun was firing, to see if I could see a Jap soldier. I couldn't see anyone in our line of fire, but I was sure they were out there because someone was shooting at us.

At that time, the only Jap I had seen was the one who was waving to us from the cockpit of his fighter plane at Nichols field. However, after all we had been through I was sure they were around. I was looking in the direction of the Japs when all of a sudden I heard all the riflemen from L Company start firing. When the riflemen stopped, all the machine guns from M Company were working. Then, a signal was given and all the men in L Company were up and running in the direction of the Japs. They ran for about twenty or thirty feet and hit the ground, and as soon as they did our machine guns opened up and fired for about a minute. When the machine guns stopped, the riflemen were up and advancing again, and they repeated this move until they had advanced about one hundred and fifty yards, then they started returning to the positions they had just left, using the same procedure on their return.

I know that L Company lost some of their men, but I don't know if we did in M Company. I do know that I was completely worn out from the long, quick march, the buzzing by the Jap fighter planes, setting up our gun, and not having anything to eat. Even then, I can't imagine how tired those riflemen were after the action they had just performed.

After they returned, things became quiet for awhile, until I heard an airplane motor about an hour before dark. It turned out to be a small, slow, observation plane. He was flying about a hundred feet off the ground and looking out of the cockpit. He could see where all of our guns were placed, and after he made his observations we started receiving mortar fire, which was followed on our side by a barrage of artillery fire which landed in the area that we were receiving mortar fire from. After that, things became quiet again.

It was starting to get dark, and I was sitting in my hole with my knees next to my chest, starting to doze off, when I heard, "Hey Starky, we have to get some ammunition." It was LaDue.

I climbed out of my hole and he told me that we would be walking about forty-five minutes from where we were. It was on the other side of the farm road that we were on when the Jap planes had given us such a scare. Before we started, we were told that the password was lollipop, and if we were challenged we were to say it as loud and clear as we could, as quickly as possible. It was quite dark when we started, and not being familiar with the area, it was like the blind leading the blind. Finally, we crossed over the irrigation ditch and got to the farm road. As we were walking along, we were challenged, and you never heard two men holler lollipop as loud and fast and in unison as we did then.

We were told to come forward and be recognized, which we did immediately. When we had done that, we were escorted to the ammunition dump where we loaded ourselves with as many belts as we could carry. We made our way back to our gun, and again we were challenged. After we unloaded, we were told we could go in our hole and go to sleep.

Before I go to sleep, let me explain something. I am sure you have noticed that I haven't used a name for many sergeants or corporals. That is because I am not sure that the name I would give would be the right one, and many of our NCOs were transferred to other units and replaced with people that were promoted or came from another unit. When I use a name, I want to be sure it is correct, and if I don't know for sure I don't use it at all. Here at Abucay, the names are no different than at other places, except for the absence of Corporal Wood.

When I was told that I could go to sleep, I left as fast as I could. Quickly, I was in my hole with my knees to my chest, and in that position I fell fast asleep. I was awakened about an hour before daylight and was told that two of us from my squad could go to the farm road for something to eat. We found the mess station quite easily; it was just a small truck that pulled a trailer made to hang a lister bag on. The lister bag held about fifty or sixty gallons of water, and had several spigots at the bottom. We filled our canteens and drank all we could, and then refilled them. We were given two cans of salmon and some more hardtack.

We were also told that the quinine tablets that we had been issued in Bataan to take once a day as a prophylactic against malaria were no longer available. The supply had run out, but they would try to supply us with a liquid form, which was the bitterest tasting thing you could imagine. Eventually they ran out of that too. Further, we were informed that they had run out of chlorine for our water, and instead they gave us a small bottle of iodine and told us to put two drops in our canteen every time we filled it.

When we got back to our position we did what we were told to do. We found a way to open one of the cans of salmon, which was a chore in itself because we had no can opener, and we shared one can and kept the other for the next day. That was our only food for four days.

The heavy weapon bombing from airplanes was becoming more intense every day and extending into the night, along with the artillery and mortar fire. I'm sure the riflemen were very active, but our machine gun was especially active because it was set up for defense of and support for L

Company. When the machine gun is doing a lot of firing it will work the ammunition carrier to the point of exhaustion, especially when you are undermanned as we were. When we were low on ammunition and were ordered to go for re-supply, we had to go no matter what time of day it was and whether it was light or dark out. The majority of the time, however, it was after dark, which was much safer.

I remember one time in particular when LaDue and I were ordered to go for ammunition in the middle of the day. We were receiving extremely heavy fire from the Japs, and when we came out of our spider holes I wasn't confident that I would even survive long enough to make the trip. Fortunately, just as we were getting out, the small arms fire stopped long enough for us to get to an area where we wouldn't be hit by it. The only fire we could have been hit by was from the air or from mortars, making our trip a bit safer.

We proceeded to the area where the ammunition dump had been, but it wasn't there. That really put the pressure on us. The area had previously had some cover, but it had been blown away by the bombing and artillery. Things were fairly quiet and we were wondering what to do when we heard one of the machine guns firing. We went to find it, to see if perhaps whoever was firing knew where the ammunition dump was moved to. As we got near the gun, I heard someone holler, "Hey Stark!" I looked over, and there was Bob Travers.

I stood there, asking Bob if he knew where the ammunition dump had been moved to. No sooner had he told me no when he yelled, "Get down! Those sons-of-bitches are shooting at you!" LaDue and I got down into a prone position for quite sometime, until it was safe for us to move on. We started back to our gun without what we had worked so hard for.

On our way back, as we were passing the irrigation ditch, we saw three fighter planes in the distance, flying toward us—it was clear that we were their target. The only cover we had was in the dry irrigation ditch, so we jumped in and laid down as close to the ground as we could, hoping for the best. My head faced the approaching planes and watched them coming in. LaDue was facing me and couldn't see them, and as one would start his dive LaDue would say, "Where is he?" and I would answer, "Coming straight at us." We were both doing everything we could to be as small as possible, but the cover we had wasn't much and the planes approached in such a way that they could fire straight down in the ditch. The bullets were whizzing all around us, but when the three finished their strafing runs, neither of us received any kind of wound.

When it was all over LaDue said, "I will never get in the same hole with you again."

"Why?" I asked.

He answered, "Because, when I asked you 'Where are they?' you told me they were coming straight at us, and that scared the shit out of me."

After all we had already gone through, we had to report back, under fire, that we couldn't locate the ammunition. The corporal told us to go back to our foxholes and wait. I, as a private, was used to not being aware of what was going on, even five feet away from me. The only communication we had was delivered by a runner. However, someone eventually received the information that ammunition would be on the farm road after dark.

We all had short turns on the gun to give the number one crew a break, and at night we were assigned a time that we could sleep. However, as our time there grew longer, and we felt the daily pressure of the heavy increase of violence from the Japs, and we continued having almost nothing to eat, it is hard to even describe the type of pressure and strain that put on me as an eighteen year-old boy. In time, however, I began to become acclimatized to the conditions that I was in. I was at the point where it took close and prolonged pressure or violence to make me really frightened and, the moment that was over, I could quickly settle back and become calm again. It seems that is the mind's way of adjusting to the pressure we were under during that time.

After being in Abucay for three or four days, I was looking in the direction of our gun when I was surprised to see two of our men walking in our direction and stopping at every hole. When they stopped, the soldiers in the hole would stand for awhile until the men moved on to the next hole. As they got closer, I saw that one of them was Captain Bell and the other was Lieutenant Thompson. When they arrived at my hole I stood at attention, but Captain Bell told me, "At ease, and don't salute." Then he asked me, "How are you doing Private Stark?"

I said, "Okay sir."

They both told me, "Good luck," before moving on to the next spider hole.

During the time that they were making their visits, they were both fully exposed to enemy fire in order to give us some encouragement. Both of them looked just as tired and dirty as any private, and their clothes were in the same shape as ours. These two men were men that I held in high regard, and they gave me, as well as the others, the only type of visual or verbal expressions of courage that we were receiving at the time. Not long after their visit we received information that an artillery shell had hit at M Company Command Center, killing First Sergeant Fountain and seriously wounding Captain Bell, who lost a leg. It wasn't until the end of the war that I would even find out that he had survived.

Every day that passed was becoming more difficult. In addition to a lack of food, we were having great difficulty getting the most essential thing—water. When you are in a hole in the ground, with the sun beating down on your steel helmet for twelve to fourteen hours, holding a stone in your mouth trying to gather some moisture from a body that doesn't have any, and trying to conserve what you know is limited water, you are in serious trouble. It got so bad that the ammunition carriers were sent to the sugarcane field to bring back cane stalks to peel and chew to get moisture and nourishment. We were swarmed by mosquitoes all night and big flies all day, and we were beginning to experience the stink of decaying human bodies.

After we were at Abucay about six days, the ammunition carriers were issued World War One British-made Infield Rifles with a bayonet. Not one of us had ever seen one before, and we had no instructions but could only figure out how to use them on our own. All we knew was that the bayonet would have come in handy earlier when we were cutting sugarcane with our mess kit knives, but it was too late for that when we received them, as the fields had pretty much been flattened by artillery bombing and small arms fire.

A few days after we heard that First Sergeant Fountain had been killed and Captain Bell wounded, we heard that Sergeant Burbank had been killed also. That greatly upset me, because he was one of the most respected men in our company. I was also concerned if Red Morgan had been wounded. We heard that the others were wounded from a Jap mortar shell that hit our .81mm mortar. We were later told that our mortar had been firing for an extended period and his gunner had requested permission to move; if he was firing in one place too long, the Japs could locate his position. He was told to stay where he was until five o'clock which would have been about a half an hour, but before they began their move the Japs located where they were.

One bit of information did give us great encouragement and pride at Abucay in the midst of all the news of destruction. We heard that a full blooded Indian by the name of Joseph Longknife, a man in K Company, had asked permission to set his air-cooled machine gun in a camouflaged position in the middle of the farm road where he would have a good field of fire. He was granted permission and he went to work when it was dark, and by daylight he had his position so well camouflaged that you would have a hard time spotting it even from ten feet away.

Once he had done that, he was very smart about the way he used his gun and cover. He would watch for a Jap to start across the road, then when they were in the middle he would fire a short burst intended to wound. When the others came to help their wounded comrade, he would shoot some more.

We had been at Abucay about a week, and I was manning the gun when we started receiving heavy mortar fire. The next thing I knew, I had someone helping me. I didn't know what had happened, but I couldn't hear anything, my nose was bleeding and I had blood on the side of my face. There was no way for me to get to an aid station with so much firing going on, so they moved me to my foxhole and went back to the gun. I stayed there in that condition, deaf and confused, but out of total exhaustion I either passed out or went sound asleep. I don't know how long I was in that condition, but I do know it was a day or two before I could hear anything and finally regained the hearing in my left ear.

During the time I was unable to hear, I could feel the vibrations of the explosions. When there were no flashes of light I would look up from my hole and see the sky full of stars, and I would think of Mother and Daddy and my brothers and sister. I wondered how things in the heavens could appear so clean and beautiful while at my spot on earth my comrades and I were so insignificant that we had to endure slow starvation, a constant state of anxiety and a deep feeling of being abandoned. In spite of these thoughts I continued on, trying to be a good soldier and to fulfill every order that I was given.

Withdrawal

I believe that we were in Abucay for eleven days, and every day that we were there the Japs were hitting us with more and more, while we had less and less with which to hold them back. When the withdrawal order was finally given, I didn't even know about it until I heard someone hollering at me. He was mad and nervous because the Japs were shelling very heavily, and he told me, "Get your ass up here now. We are withdrawing."

As soon as I was out he was on his way, with me following as close as I could because it was dark. We arrived where the others were assembled and checked to see if everyone was there. They were one short from L

Company, but because of the heavy incoming fire they decided not to go back for him.

We were withdrawing straight back from where our guns had been set up—about three hundred yards from the rim of a ravine, unfamiliar ground to us. We began our descent to the bottom of the ravine, which was about fifty or sixty feet deep. The grade was steep and it was hard to keep from falling, but there was some vegetation that we could hold on to. It also helped that we were leaving Abucay with a much lighter load then we had arrived with.

Before we started our descent, we could see the Jap artillery hitting heavily right along the rim that we were heading for. I was sure that many of us would be lost if we had to climb out of the ravine under all that artillery fire. However, shortly after we got to the bottom and had started across the six or seven hundred feet we had to go before we began our hard climb to the rim, the Japs began shelling where we had just left, leaving the other rim free of artillery fire. Consequently, we were able to reach the ridge safely, as well as the farm road beyond. From there we began our long walk back to where we had come from eleven days before.

I don't know how much I weighed when we arrived at Abucay, but I am sure I lost quite a lot of weight while we were there. For the eleven days we were there, I had received about five or six cans of fish and ten or twelve hardtack biscuits. When coming out of the ravine, I was so weak from lack of nourishment that I wanted to throw my Enfield rifle away, just to have less to carry, but I hung on to it. I don't know if they brought the machine gun out or not, nor am I sure how many of my squad finally finished the withdrawal. At the end of the war, thanks to a record that Colonel Jasper Bradley, our 31st Infantry Commander and others had compiled while POWs, we knew that seven men from M Company were killed during that time period.

We reached the farm road and I found myself with people I didn't know. I did not know who had come to get me when I was asleep, but I assumed it was one of the men from my squad. For all these years since that time I have wondered who it was, and I have felt extremely grateful toward him and have hoped that he made it okay. By the time of the withdrawal I was in a state of total physical and mental exhaustion, and I could see the same in the other men around me.

Once we had reached the farm road I went in the direction that the others were going. After walking for an hour or more, we were packed into some busses with the tops cut off, and we started driving south. As soon as I sat down I was asleep, and I slept until I was awakened.

A Peaceful Area and Death in a Different Form

When we got off the bus someone told us to find a place to lie down and go to sleep; as soon as I heard that I found a place and the next thing I knew I could see rays of sun shining through the huge trees. When I woke up there were a lot of men still sleeping. I looked around to try to find someone from my company, but at that time I wasn't able to locate anyone. I was so tired and weak from hunger that it wasn't very important to me at that moment.

What I wanted most was food and water, but I wasn't to receive any of that for quite awhile. Things seemed to be in a state of confusion after such a disorderly withdrawal, and it would be three or four hours before any type of order was restored. Everyone was so tired, though, that I suppose they had the same thoughts that I did—I was just content to be in a place where it was quiet, with the exception of the occasional plane flying overhead. As time went by we all became restless and people started asking when we were going to receive food and water. First, we were assembled by company, and I stood along with a few others when they called for M Company.

Soon, we were led to an area where there were about fifty or sixty of us from M Company. We were dirty and haggard from starvation, and those old enough had grown beards that covered their faces. When the war had started two months earlier, M Company had one hundred and fifty-five men. Now, I saw men that I knew but could barely recognize, due to the extreme circumstances we had lived through in that short time. It was just another example of growing accustomed to a situation that was increasingly out of my control.

After we were assembled as a company, I started to find a few men that I knew. However, I was unable to find Bob Travers and Red Morgan, and I was worried about what had happened to my friends. I still hadn't seen them when we were organized and taken to a river a short distance away, where we were told that we would be able to take a bath and wash our clothes. As soon as I heard that, I was in that running water with all my clothes on, and I wasn't the first one. The clothes I was wearing were the ones I had been issued at the aid station in Dinalupihan, and this was my first bath in over two weeks.

130

After we were in the water for awhile, we took our clothes off to wash them. With my clothes off, I could see how much weight I had lost; I could count every rib and my legs had very little flesh on them. I noticed that all the others around me were in the same condition. At the beginning of the war I had weighed 170 pounds and by that point, I'm sure, I did not weigh more than 130.

I finished my bath and went back to our area, and within an hour we were told where to find the mess truck that had brought more food. We arrived at the truck and found a Lister bag for us to fill our canteens. We were told not to drink the water from the river because it might be contaminated from the dead bodies upstream from where we had taken our bath. Fortunately, I had not yet filled my canteen from the river.

I filled my canteen and then went for my first hot meal in two weeks. It consisted of half a mess kit of rice, a heaping tablespoon of corn beef and a canteen cup of colored water, which may have been intended as coffee, but only resembled coffee in that it was liquid and hot. However, it was better than nothing, which was about what we had been receiving for the last eleven days. After I finished eating, I washed my mess kit and went back to my piece of ground to lie down and rest some more.

It was finally quiet, with no explosions, airplanes or small arms fire for the first time in weeks. There was little conversation among us because we were all anticipating what was to come next. Would we get more food? Were we going to receive help as we had been promised by General MacArthur? I didn't talk to anyone because I was too worn out and weak that I wouldn't have even known what to say. At that point, there was nothing to say; things were bad and we were near exhaustion. I knew that no one there could offer me anything that would make life any better. With a little distance from the war and a bit of quiet, I was realizing just how bleak our situation was.

We were in this area for a few weeks, and after the first few days the murmurs of talk began, none of it optimistic. We saw some of the propaganda fliers that the Japs had been dropping, trying to get us to surrender. I was a young man and I wouldn't say much, but I did listen, and there was a lot of talk that we had been abandoned, or that we were in a struggle that we could not win. However, I never heard anyone mention what would happen if we lost. During all the time we were there, as our morale sunk lower, I was just trying to stay alive on two meager meals a day. I was in a constant state of anxiety about what the next order would be, and my state of mind was unstable at best.

It was with all of these pressures weighing on my mind that I went through the chow line one night, where Filipino men worked as mess boys serving our food. One of them who was serving the rice was a little Filipino who weighed only about one hundred pounds. He was as skinny as we were, and he was working just to get a little bit of food to stay alive. I went through the chow line, and when he served me my small portion I said to him, "Hey, Joe. You gave me less than you gave the person in front of me. I want a little more."

He said, "No sir, I can't."

I said, "Yes you can," and he replied, "No sir," once again.

I was starving, and I did something that I would never have done under normal conditions. I said, "Stick it up your ass, you gook son-of-a-bitch."

He never said a word, and after I got what I was given I went over and sat down on the ground with a group that was eating. I had just sat down with my legs bent and folded and my mess kit on top of them, about to get my first bite of food, when I saw two small, brown, bare feet just in front of where my legs were. I heard a soft voice say, "Sir."

I looked up to see the little Filipino mess boy holding a bolo knife in his hand. It was about two feet long and very sharp. Holding it near me he said, "Do you wish to challenge me, sir?"

Before I could say or do anything, I heard one of our men pull out his .45 and jack a round into the chamber. Just as softly, he said to the mess boy, "Put the bolo down or I will shoot you."

The mess boy hesitated for a second, then lowered the bolo, turned, and walked away. When he was gone, I turned around and said thank you to the other soldier.

"That's okay," he replied, and we both continued eating our meals.

I wish I could tell you his name, but I can't, perhaps because of the dangerous and deplorable conditions we lived in during that time.

About an hour after the incident, I was told to report to the company commander. I think I was more nervous reporting to him than I had been thinking that the mess boy might kill me. I knew what the mess boy was going to do, but I didn't know what the captain might do, and I didn't want to be separated from my company.

It was the first time I had met this commander personally. He was about twenty-five or twenty-six years-old and a replacement for Captain Bell. I reported as ordered and he said, "At ease."

I relaxed a little, and he asked me what had happened. I told him everything about how the situation had unfolded and he said, "Private

Stark, I could punish you for your actions as they are unsatisfactory, but I won't do so unless you have a similar violation in the future. We are all equally hungry, and getting angry won't help us." Then, he told me that the mess boy had been dismissed, told to leave the company area and not return. Then he dismissed me to return to duty. I said, "Yes sir," gave a salute, and left his piece of ground to go lie down and rest.

Later, some of my friends came over and asked what had happened, and they were pleased with the outcome. However, as I am writing this and reflecting back sixty-four years, I do not have any animosity toward the Filipino. What I said to him was wrong, and his reaction to being insulted in front of everyone was probably the same as mine would have been. I can only express my appreciation to the soldier who saved my life, and hope that he made it through the war. At the same time, I hope the little mess boy did too, and that both had good lives after it was all over.

We remained in that area for ten days after my near-death incident with the Filipino mess boy, and there were fewer and fewer of us as a recent hit of malaria and dysentery was decreasing our ranks. I never got dysentery, and in fact had a problem with severe constipation, due mainly to the lack of food. When I did relieve myself, it was difficult and painful, and the conditions were never good. We had what is called straddle trenches to defecate in, and they were located over ditches that were open to big blue flies. The flies fed on our waste and carried it to our food that they also fed on as we ate. When we first arrived the trenches there had been sanitized to a degree, and were covered with some sort of white powder. The flies eventually increased to such a degree that, when I did use the latrine, the maggots made the human waste look like it was boiling. I'm sure that if a healthy person suddenly appeared to witness the conditions we were in, he would have gotten sick from the smell alone.

Malaria

I had my first malaria attack about a week before our next battle order. I was running a high fever and had a bad chill before finally breaking into the sweat and going to the aid station for help. They took my temperature and told me that I had malaria, but that they had no more quinine. The hospital couldn't help me either, as they were also out, so I had nothing to do but lie on the ground and wait for the malaria attack to be over. When it was over it left me much weaker than before, and I was often unaware of what was even happening around me. In fact, I hardly even cared what was happening and I remained in that apathetic state for several days.

Just when I was beginning to feel better, I had another attack, and this one was more severe and lasted longer than the previous one. After it was over, I was left once again feeling ambivalent about my future or about what was happening around me; the disease had left me entirely wiped out. Although I remained weak, in a few days I once again began to take an interest in my well-being and what was happening around me.

While we waited for our next battle orders, we lost more and more men to illness; I think there were only three or four of us left in my squad. When we were told that we would be moving to the front line soon, we were also told that the chaplain would be having a religious service before we moved out. One of my friends asked me if I was going, saying that I should accompany him. He told me it was like going to church back at home, but I wasn't interested in accompanying him. He said, "Come with me. I want you to go."

He was so sincere that I said okay and went with him. There were about twelve or thirteen people there, and although we had no singing, Chaplain Taylor gave us a sermon and we all prayed together. The whole thing lasted only fifteen or twenty minutes, and afterwards we returned to the other troops and waited for our impending orders.

Our Last Battle

When I arrived back at our spot, I felt the strongest sense of apprehension that I had felt since the beginning of the war. When the order came for us to move out I was so weak that I could hardly walk, but I was able to make it to Mt. Samat and the last battle for the 31st Infantry in Bataan. However, I wasn't able to see it through until the finish because just after we arrived I started my third malaria attack. It started while we were being exposed to heavy shelling, bombing and strafing, and I knew that I was totally useless in the shape I was in. I started looking for a superior in order to find out what I should do.

I was told where I could find an officer and a medic, and when I located them I must have looked sick enough, because when I asked what I should do the medic replied, "We can't do anything for you here and we can't help get you to a hospital. But you are released from duty, and if you can make it to the road in our rear, go to your right and about half a mile down. There you will see a small building in a shallow depression. If you are able to get there, sit and wait for the ambulance that will be coming by. When you see it, be at the road so they can see you. If you aren't there when they come, they won't stop." Then he said, "I hope you can make it."

I started off as fast as I could to where he had directed me and shortly after I left I could see the road about a half a mile below me. The view was clear to the road because all the foliage had been burned and blown away by bombing before we had reached Mt. Samat. I was fortunate one more time during this part of my journey, because I was leaving an explosive area for an area that was much safer. I reached the road safely and went to my right as instructed, but I doubted that I would find any type of building because everything had been burned down. However, after a half mile I came to a gradual depression on my right, and when I looked down I could see that there was a small building with no roof. It was built out of stone and was about twelve by fourteen feet, with a door and one window opening with no glass remaining. It was located about one hundred feet from the road.

I was overjoyed to see it; I had been beginning to think that I might not find it or that it would collapse before I could reach it. I walked through the door opening and found nothing but four stone walls. I looked around before taking a seat in a corner on the dirt floor. It was covered with ashes from when the roof had burned. I sat there, in the burned out building in the middle of a war zone, when suddenly I became overcome with the most helpless and lonely feeling that I had ever experienced. That feeling overtook me for a few minutes, but soon I stood up, realizing I should stand for as long as I was able and watch for the ambulance to come.

I stood there, fighting malaria and a high fever, for about forty-five minutes. I was about to give up when I suddenly saw the ambulance coming very slowly down the mountain road. When I saw it I started up the small hill to the edge of the road, and I was waiting there when it pulled up by me. There were two soldiers in the front and when they stopped the passenger told me to open the back door and get in. I opened the door, and I was shocked by what I saw. The ambulance was filled with what I though were the wounded, with four stretchers on top of each other on each side, filled with soldiers in each stretcher. There was so little space for me that I could barely even close the door.

I got the door closed and the ambulance started moving, but there was no place for me to sit down. I was so sick that I thought I was going to pass out. I was holding on to the edge of the stretcher on each side of me to try and keep from falling when the coreman hollered back, telling me to move the feet of one of the wounded soldiers to make room to sit down. I moved one of the soldier's feet, saying, "I hope I don't hurt you."

There was no response, so I made just enough room to sit down. When I was seated, the arm of the soldier on the top stretcher dropped down and his hand was dangling a few inches from my face. I got up to put it back on his chest and to see if I could help him, but when I looked at his face I knew he was dead; soon, I realized that they were all dead. I silently said a prayer for them and sat back down.

I tried to make myself as comfortable as I could until we got to Hospital #2. When we got there the corpsman came and opened the back door and told me where I was to go. I don't remember seeing any buildings, but a member of the medical staff came to look at me and said that I had malaria, and then someone took me to the folding cots in an area out in the jungle. He showed me to my folding cot and told me that someone would come see me soon. I lay down, and even though there was no blanket or pillow, it was still the first bed that I had laid my body on in four months. I needed the bed at that time; the malaria was worsening and my body hurt all over.

I must have passed out or collapsed from total exhaustion, because when I became aware of my surroundings again it was nighttime. Someone had put a blanket over me and it sure felt good. I was so tired that I made no effort to move, even though I was also very thirsty. It was an unbelievable quiet compared to all the loud and violent explosions I was used to hearing around me. I'm sure that I was given food and water at some point during the night, but I don't remember it.

I vaguely remember an officer and a corpsman coming to my cot to examine me and giving me a spoon full of liquid quinine and a full canteen of water. The water was the most important thing for me at that time due to my extreme dehydration. I remember them coming back late in the afternoon to refill my canteen and give me another spoon full of the quinine. As bitter as it was, I am certain that the quinine I received is what saved my life.

At the beginning of the second full day, my fever had subsided and I was starting to feel better; I could feel that I was regaining some of my strength. I was sitting on my cot with my eyes on the ground when I heard someone say, "Hey, Stark."

I looked up and saw Bob Travers. He had a smile on his face, and it was the first smile I had seen in a long time. It made me feel good and, as tired as I was, I had to smile back at him. The smile was short-lived, however; the more we looked at one another the more we each realized how much the other had changed. We saw the drastic changes we had been through, and they were all the more jarring because of the short time that had passed. He had been in the hospital under the trees for awhile before I arrived, and he was also being treated for malaria. He didn't stay and visit long, but he pointed me to where his cot was. He left and I lay back down to sleep.

I'm sure we must have received some food while I was there, but I can't remember it to tell how it was served. I do remember that, while I was there, Bob and I were together quite a bit, and a friendship was developing between us. I am eternally grateful to him for his friendship and strength during that time.

Part Three

Prisoner of the Japanese

Surrender and the Death March

Many of my memories of the death march are hazy at best, but I have tried to incorporate them here to the best of my memory. I do remember hearing that we were being forced to surrender by General King and that if we had any weapons we must dissemble them and throw away the parts. At that time I didn't know what day it was, but I learned later that it was April 9, 1942—exactly four months and ten days after the beginning of the war. I remembered the prediction that the young soldier had made four months and ten days earlier, that we would whip their asses in two weeks. I'm sure that if that young man was still alive when we were forced to surrender, he had aged years after all that we had been through. Everyone on Bataan had aged years in that short time.

I can't remember my thoughts upon hearing the order; I was still very sick and weak, and I have very little recollection from that time. I do vaguely remember the expression on some of the men's faces who were close to me when I received the word, but I was so sick that I didn't dwell on what was happening. I just went back to my cot and lay back down.

I remember Bob and I going to a river near the hospital. We had crossed it looking for food but couldn't find any, so we were on our way back to our area when there was a sudden, large explosion several hundred yards down the river. I was just about to step from one stone in the river to another when a large piece of shrapnel hit the stone I was going to step on. If my foot had been on that rock when the shrapnel hit, I would have surely lost my foot. Smaller pieces of shrapnel splashed the water around us and we could hear smaller explosions some distance away, but neither of us was hurt. We found out later that the artillery fire was from the big guns on Corregidor and that some of our men had been killed, but I still don't know how long this was after we had received the surrender orders. The explosions did make the severity of the situation more clear to me, but I was still very weak from the malaria and we were still getting very little to eat.

I was sitting in my bunk later on that afternoon when I heard a noise in the distance, coming in our direction. It got louder and louder, and when it finally came into view we were surprised to see that it was a Jap tank. It went by us and then stopped just up the road. When it stopped, I saw the first Jap soldier I had seen up-close throughout the entire war. I was still uncertain what would happen next. They walked up to a flagpole that I hadn't noticed before, and one of them lowered our flag, took it off and stepped on it, then replaced it with the Jap flag. We still didn't know what to expect, but we soon received another surprise. They made no move at all toward any of us and only boarded the tank and drove off.

After they were gone it all became quiet again. Sometime later, I remember being on a truck loaded with POWs and hearing someone say, "We are at Cabcaben." Soon, we were offloaded, and that is the last thing that I remember for a long time. This was at the beginning of the Death March, and at this point, as well as during my time at Camp O'Donnell, my memories remain only in flashes and are very incomplete. For the last sixty-three years, I have dealt with these memories in flashes and small segments; at times I can remember being at certain places, but will not remember how I got there. The malaria had put me in a state of delirium, not uncommon for malaria patients, so my memories are spotty and come and go at different times. I do remember, very vividly, some of the atrocities that were committed along the way. I'm sure that I did not walk the entire distance of the Death March, but with all the information I've received since and the other stories I've collaborated with, I feel strongly that I was on it for some length of time.

There is one memory in particular that haunts me vividly. We were being marched into a building that was fenced in with open walls on all sides. As we were walking in, there were Jap guards lined up so that we had to walk in between them to enter the building. As I was walking, I turned my head to the right and my eyes met the eyes of a Jap guard with a rifle and a fixed bayonet. When our eyes met, he yelled something to me in Japanese, and as he yelled he lowered his rifle to make a thrust toward me. I never took my eyes off his, and he stopped just inches before his bayonet would have entered my abdomen. I have struggled with that memory all my life, wondering why he stopped, and I believe it was because I never made a move or a sound, but just kept my eyes on his. Like so many of my memories and the atrocities of war, it cannot be explained.

A POW at Cabanatuan

I don't know how many weeks my memory loss caused me to lose, but when my memory came back from the malaria, I was at Clark Field. I am still not sure how I got there; I was as sick as a dog, but was still managing to function on a basic physical level. I had a high fever and chills every day, and I knew that if I didn't get some quinine I was going to die.

One of my friends told me that someone in camp had some quinine, and even though I was very weak I was able to locate that soldier. I told him that I was sure I was dying, and if he could give me any quinine it might save my life, although I admitted I had nothing to give him. We talked for awhile and he took some quinine tablets from his meager belongings and gave me a few. I wish I could tell you what his name was, but I can't remember it. I do know that he saved my life, perhaps at the expense of his own. I am eternally grateful to him for what is certainly the most generous gift I have ever received.

Before the quinine had a chance to cure my malaria, the Japs sent the sickest among us to the Cabanatuan Hospital. However, since my fever had broken, I was sent to the main camp instead. It was the largest camp in the Philippines and had a population of a few thousand, although I don't know the exact number. When I got there, I was assigned to a barracks built of nepa and split bamboo. I was informed that I had been made one of a group of ten, and if one of us escaped the other nine would be executed.

After I got there I was unable to move around much; I was still too weak. I was able to go and get my food, which was served twice a day, and to take five of the ten canteens and stand in line for several hours, enduring the tropical sun and rain, in order to fill them with water. There was just one spigot for several hundred people, and so it was always someone's job to wait to get water for the entire group. On one occasion I was only ten men away from the spigot when it was turned off, and we sat or lay on the ground for hours, waiting, before they turned it back on.

I was at Cabanatuan for about ten days before I was able to move around a little more. One day, as I was going by one of the barracks on one of my infrequent trips to the latrine, I turned the corner and saw Bob Travers opening up a can of salmon. He saw me and a pronounced look of disappointment came over his face. He said, "Oh you son-of-a-bitch!

You would show up now! Where the hell have you been?" Before I could answer he exclaimed, "Go get your mess kit and I'll give you some of the fish." When I came back he gave me two heaping spoons full of salmon, and I have been grateful to him for my whole life for sharing that food with me; just like me, and everyone else, he was certainly starving too.

In camp, we were always trying to locate a friend or to find out what had happened to one of our fellow soldiers. As I went through chow line I would inquire about my friend Ray Pierce. After about three weeks at Cabanatuan I was talking to a POW and asked him if he knew Ray. He told me yes, that he had been sent to the hospital with malaria. The next day I got a pass to go to the hospital to try to find Ray.

I left the main camp and crossed a dirt road to an enclosure that was fenced in like the main camp. This was where the so-called hospital was. I inquired about Ray and was told where he was and where to find him in another building. I proceeded as I had been told, but quickly realized that the building I had entered was the morgue. There were about thirty POWs laid out on the floor, naked. I felt a deep sense of sorrow looking at their bodies, and I said a prayer before I left.

Later that day, I did find Ray Pierce. He was delirious and never knew I was there to visit him. It hurt me to see him in that condition, but I took one of his hands in mine and said a prayer, and I sat with him for about ten or fifteen minutes before I left, back to my own camp and my own misery.

The next morning I witnessed the dead being carried out on makeshift stretchers from the morgue to the cemetery, a common practice that I saw often in Cabanatuan, and on one day I counted as many as thirty-two bodies. I feel very strongly that Ray was one of the dead that day, although I don't know for sure.

One morning, while waiting in line to fill the canteens, I heard a column of Japs coming up the road. I watched them march by the camp in the rain and the mud in two double columns of about twenty Japs each. There was a distance of about twenty feet between the lead column and the second column and in that space two Japs marched alone. One Jap carried a Japanese flag and the other a human head tied by its hair to a bamboo pole. They paraded it to the main gate, where they hung the head and put a sign under it that said, "If you try to escape, the same thing will happen to you."

The sanitary conditions at Cabanatuan were the worst that I remember at any camp. The flies hovered around you in droves, constantly in your face and around your head, reminding you of your situation. The stink was awful: the smell of death hung over the entire camp and was impossible to escape. I felt more and more alone and isolated, but managed to maintain my will to live and my desire to survive by any means possible.

Leaving Cabanatuan

One day, while sitting with two of my new friends, I learned that the Japs were looking for healthy men to sign up at the American Headquarters for detail. It seems that by healthy they meant only willing and able to walk, because I was accepted for the detail as soon as I walked in. I could walk, and that put me at an advantage to many of the others, and I suppose at that point I looked about as healthy as anyone else, even at a mere 120 pounds. I was still wearing the same clothes that I had received at Dinalupihan when I was wounded, although by now they were no more than rags. The only bath I had at Cabanatuan was when it rained and I stood under the eaves of the roof and let the water fall on me and my clothes. I had no soap and nothing to dry myself off with, but since it was always hot in the tropics I didn't feel uncomfortable while drying off.

Two or three days after I signed up we were told to report to an assembly area to be moved out, and when we reported we were told that we were being sent to Davao, on the island of Mindanao, which was the second largest island in the Philippines. I was surprised to see how many of us were being sent—there must have been at least a thousand men.

We were assembled and ordered by our American commander to form in a column of twos, and thus we began the six mile march to Cabanatuan City. It was very early in the morning, and as we went out of the gate on October 22, 1942, it occurred to me that I had reached my nineteenth birthday in that hell hole. I was leaving, unsure of what I was going to, but I was sure it couldn't be any worse than Cabanatuan.

As we walked out in the early morning, past a small nepa hut, we all smelled the wonderful aroma of bacon cooking. Sixty-five years later, the smell of bacon cooking outside still takes me back to that time and the six mile march. We stopped one time for a fifteen minute break, but we weren't allowed to sit down. As we walked, I made every effort to stay as far away from the Japs as I could.

We arrived in Cabanatuan City where we were packed into freight cars. We had to stand or sit for quite awhile before we started to move. Eventually we made enough room for all of us to sit down with our knees pulled up to our chest. I don't recall how long it was before we got to Manila, nor do I recall if we were trucked to the pier or if we walked. Further, I am not sure whether we stayed in Bilibid Prison overnight or not, although I think that we did. We were fed there after we arrived and we were also fed there the next morning, October 28, 1942. After we had eaten, we were all moved to the pier where the ship was docked to take us to Davao. It was a freighter and we were put in the hold while we were in the harbor. After we got underway we were allowed to come topside for the trip to Davao, which took about ten days.

We were fed very well on our way down; in fact, it was the best treatment I received the entire time I was a prisoner. We were very crowded, but it was a wonderful feeling to sit on the hard steel deck and smell the clean fresh air instead of the stink that we had left at Cabanatuan.

It was also wonderful at night, when most of the POWs were asleep and everything was quiet, to hear and feel the pulsing of the ship and to feel the warm, clean breeze as we moved through the sea. It gave me quiet time to reflect without being distracted by all the pain and misery around me, and I thought about my mother and father and brothers and sister. I missed all of them very much. It had been seventeen months since I had said goodbye to Daddy and it is amazing how much had happened to me in that short time. When daybreak came, it meant another day and another struggle just to stay alive.

On our way down, we stopped in Cebu City for a very short while before proceeding to our destination on Mindanao. When we arrived we were offloaded and put on trucks for our trek to the Davao Penal Colony. I don't recall how far it was, although I think it was about thirty miles. It was on a one lane road that allowed for two vehicles to pass one another at frequent intervals.

Davao Penal Colony

The distance from the coast to the penal colony was traveled entirely through a large, dense jungle. I had been in jungle before, on Bataan, but it was not as impressive or as dense as what we were traveling through now. We were crowded on the truck, but it wasn't as bad as it could have been because we were shielded from the sun by the jungle. When we finally came out of the jungle and arrived at the penal colony, I saw right away that this place was much better than the one we had left behind twelve days before. The buildings were more permanent than any of the other camps I had been in.

When we arrived we were all assembled on the parade ground in front of the camp, where the Jap camp commander gave us a speech about what was expected of us. From there, we were moved inside the fenced enclosure. There were eight barracks, a hospital, a kitchen, a building for eating, and other buildings. The best thing was that there was an unlimited water supply from three wells, with a platform by each of them where we could take water from the well and pour it on our body to bathe every day.

After we were assigned our barracks, I found that the accommodations were also much better than they were at Cabanatuan. Shortly after we were assigned to our quarters we were told to report to the mess hall for our first meal. When I saw it, I was very surprised by the portion of green vegetables and a small portion of fish. We were also served a canteen cup of coffee that I would later learn came from the farm that we would work on.

This farm was enormous, and only a short distance from our camp. As I recall, there was about a thousand acres of rice and six hundred of vegetables. In addition, they had a pig farm, a fishery and a place where they grew hemp to make rope. The camp I was held in had previously been used as a penal colony for the Philippine government to hold their prisoners, and it could accommodate up to two thousand prisoners. By the time I arrived, there were already a thousand there. We saw right away that they were much healthier than the ones we had left behind, because on Mindanao they hadn't had the same hardships that we had endured on Bataan and Luzon. Also, the camp had much more sanitary conditions. It smelled clean, and when we ate our first meal we weren't bothered by flies.

When we had been there for about a week, our barracks leader had us stand in front of our sleeping area, and he went down the two rows and gave us each a piece of white cloth about twelve inches wide and three feet long, with a strap of about forty-eight inches. These, we were told, were called g-strings. Then we were shown how to wear them: you tied the belt in front of you, reached between your legs, and brought the wide piece of white cloth up to be tucked under the belt. The excess hung down in front. We were told that this was the only clothing we would receive, but if the clothes that we were wearing were good enough we could continue to wear them. The next morning there were only about ten men in the whole barracks that weren't in a g-string. When I put mine on, it was the only thing on my body; I hadn't worn shoes in quite a long time, as I had completely worn through them awhile ago.

We were given a grass mat and one blanket for sleeping, and we laid these on the floor to sleep. When I exchanged the rags for the g-string, I washed the rags and rolled them into a pillow. I was fortunate that I was able to sleep; every night I would be glad when night came, and the darker the night was, the more secure I felt. The night was much quieter, and then I didn't have to see all the skeletons in g-strings who had once been my fellow soldiers and strong, able-bodied men.

I always liked the breakfast meal the most, even though it was mostly the same food as the evening meal, because on some occasions I was able to get a bit more food. When all the rice had been taken out of the cast iron caldrons, the cooks would use a large, flat scraper to get all the rice that was stuck to the sides. It came out in flat brown or black pieces and I just loved it, and sometimes I was able to get it in addition to my other ration. I was never able to get it at the evening meal because there was always a bunch of people there before me.

I was given my first detail a few days after we arrived. In most cases, we were all lined up at about 5:30 or 6am, before breakfast, to be assigned detail. My first detail was on the fruit and vegetable farm. It was a ten acre squash field about a mile from the main camp. When we arrived, under the eyes of one Jap guard, the twenty of us were issued a long, thin stick with some type of soft object on one end. For the next eight hours we were told to walk all over the field, going from flower to flower and placing the soft end in each of them for pollination. We had a different name for it; we called it, "breeding the flowers." After our days work, we would start our walk back to camp. Along the way there were large papaya trees on one side and mango trees on the other, with full, ripe fruit on each, but we weren't allowed to pick any of them. It seemed that every day on the way back from work it would pour down rain, but it never happened while we were at work. That upset us, because if it had they would have moved us back to camp and our day would have been shorter.

Jaundice and the Medical Treatment

After about six weeks at Davao I was *hit* with dysentery; despite the good sanitary conditions, I had it bad, worse than I had before. When I reported to the aid station I was put in the hospital, where I remained for about a week. They were able to get it under control, and I was released back to the barracks where I was given light duty. When you were on light duty, if you were unable to do field work you received half rations (which was still almost as much as full rations at Cabanatuan). I was in the barracks for light duty for about ten days before I went back to the farm. Even though I went to work every day I was still weak, and after I was back to work for about two weeks I was so weak I went to sick call, and they told me that they were sending me back to the hospital.

When I arrived at the hospital I was told that I had yellow jaundice and that I would be isolated. They put me outside under the trees on a folding cot, but I was only there about six hours when I was escorted out of the camp with a corpsman. We took a seat on a little flat car on a small railroad that traveled to the rice fields a few miles from our camp. The little train was on its way to pick up the workers at the rice fields, but after we had ridden for about a mile we got off the train, and I found that we were standing in the jungle. I looked down the tracks and saw a small road. We walked on the road a short distance before we came to a fenced in area with a building inside, and here I was isolated with other POWs. I don't recall exactly how long I was there, but I believe it was about three weeks. While I was there, I received the first dental examination that I had ever had. When it was time for me to leave there my jaundice was gone, although I'm not sure what it was that they treated me with.

The doctors and the corpsman that we had at Davao were much more efficient and thorough than the others had been, and I can say nothing but good things about them. The death rate dropped drastically at Davao, as a result not only of the sanitary conditions but also of the work of these men. I saw the doctors do things that were absolutely amazing, especially under the circumstances.

While I was in isolation under the trees, there was another POW occupying the cot next to me. They had done a spinal tap on him and removed spinal fluid. They also conducted autopsies at this location. The most impressive thing that I remember, however, was the work that they did on one of us from Bataan, from the Tank Company, who had been seriously burned on his neck. The wound was quite large, and shortly after we got there he went to sick call and was put in the hospital. The American doctors made two parallel incisions in his leg, about six inches each, and lifted the flesh up before suturing the incision back together, thus leaving the strip of flesh attached at one end. The wound and the strip of flesh would be allowed to heal, and the strip of flesh would grow longer and longer. After it reached a certain length they attached the loose end up higher and severed the lower end. In this end-over-end process they moved the strip of flesh from his leg to his neck and used it for a skin graft over the raw wound, and it worked great. During most of this process the soldier was able to work and get his full ration of food. Although the entire process was performed under conditions that were much better than they were on Luzon, they were still very crude.

The only other medical problem I had at Davao was an infection in the big toe of my left foot, caused by an ingrown toenail. I went to sick call and was sent to the hospital, where they cut it out without any type of pain killer, which was very painful. Also, all of us from Luzon began to suffer from beriberi. My feet were swollen, burning and tender all the time, but beriberi never kept us from working, because we all wanted and needed the full ration of food.

Christmas

After I was released from the hospital and was assigned to a different barracks I went through a period where I just wanted to be alone. I was thinking of Ray Pierce and the others I had known who had died or been killed since the war began. Also, I had left the last person that I knew, Bob Travers, behind at Cabanatuan, and I didn't have the energy or desire to try to get in with the groups of friends that had already formed at Davao.

However, at Christmas time that year I came out of this slump, and began wanting to make friends again. The Japs gave us three days off, and we all went to bed on Christmas Eve looking forward to the time to rest, but not realizing yet how wonderful that Christmas was going to be. I laid my head on my pillow and went into a sound sleep, and the next thing I knew it was barely morning. In the distance I could hear the most beautiful voices singing Christmas carols. It made me think of Mother, Daddy and my brothers and sister, and I felt the most intense desire to be with them that I had felt the entire time I had been overseas. When the singers got to our barracks we all got up and went outside so that we could hear and see them. It was the most beautiful sound that I have ever heard, and it was all coming from ten POWs, tired and underfed, nothing but skin and bones in the g-strings. When they were finished we all applauded them enthusiastically, and with big smiles on their faces they moved on to the next barracks. That wasn't the only surprise we would receive that day. When we went to breakfast we found larger portions of food, even though we had the day off. Christmas that year was one of the most memorable I have ever had, because of those simple gifts.

We also received our first Red Cross package that Christmas, which warmed all of our personalities despite the hard times we were going through. The carols and the Red Cross packages initiated a change, and we all began to interact and trade goodies with one another. All the activity helped me to reach out to others, and I began to make friends again. In a few of the packages were notes that had been included by the packers, and these notes always gave me encouragement. When we found one, we would pass it around so that everyone could see it. It made us feel that we weren't abandoned and that someone did care about us. The nourishment from those packages helped us unbelievably.

Camp, Caribou, Rice Paddies and Snakes

About two weeks after Christmas, I was put on rice field detail. My job was to plow the rice paddies to get them ready for the next planting. Before we were able to start plowing, we had to catch our caribou or water buffalo from a herd of about fifty or sixty and that, in some cases, could take an hour or more. After we were ready to catch one by the ring in its nose, we were still a long way from finishing our days work. I don't recall how many of us were assigned to a paddy, although I think it was determined according to the size of the paddy. We were assigned to one before we were released to catch our caribou, when we would all be set free to do so at the same time. As soon as we were released it became a mad rush to catch a caribou and go to work. The Japs gave us an incentive, saying that if your crew finished first you would receive a stalk of bananas and have the rest of the day off. To make things more interesting, there was one caribou in the herd that had only one eye, and if you could locate him you were able to just go up on his blind side and catch him by the ring in his nose, making things pretty easy.

Even if your crew was the first one to start plowing it didn't mean that you would be the first to finish, because there was always a control problem with the caribou. They were trained in a Filipino language, and no matter what we said in English they always did whatever they wanted. They were also prone to laying down in the water or mud if they felt too hot, so your team would be in the lead and almost ready to finish first when one would suddenly stop and just lie down in the mud. When that happened, there was no way that you could get it up against its will, and we saw our bananas slipping away.

We plowed in black mud that was almost up to our knees, and there was some type of small insect that lived in the mud and was constantly biting our legs. After working at plowing for awhile, we would start to get sores on our legs. When that happened we were put on another detail for awhile. While we were at Davao, everyone worked, regardless of rank. You couldn't tell a private from an officer, as we all did the same work.

I have a vivid memory of being on a detail that controlled the flow of water for the rice paddies. I always tried to stay as far away from the Jap guards as I could, but this particular day, while we were sitting down for our two hour break in the heat of the day, one of the guards motioned for me to come with him. I was a little nervous, but I got up from where I was and walked to where he was standing with his rifle and bayonet, which was longer than he was tall. As soon as I got over to him he started walking, and I followed. We had walked on the dyke for about three hundred yards when he suddenly stopped and began to scream, jumping into one of the flooded rice paddies and dropping his rifle in the mud. I didn't understand what was happening and it gave me quite a shock to see him behaving this way. I kept my eyes on him for a few seconds before looking down into the dyke, when I realized why he was so scared. About three feet in front of me was a cobra, standing about three feet high with his hood spread. I didn't know whether I should jump in the paddy with the Jap or jump in the paddy on the other side, so I just remained where I was and stayed very, very still. After staring each other down briefly, the cobra went in the paddy on the other side of the dyke, away from the Jap. After the Jap regained some of his composure, he retrieved his rifle and came back on the dyke, very muddy and without his dignity.

After this experience I understood why the Filipinos always worked on a paddy from the inside out, in order to drive the snakes away. On one occasion, I was with an American crew that had finished our allotted work for the day and had only one paddy left, and we all surrounded the paddy and started cutting from the outside in. When we got close to the center the snakes started coming out all over the place, and we were fortunate that we got out of there without anyone being bitten. On another occasion there was a sixteen foot python near the camp, and a POW was able to kill it to be cleaned and cooked for us to eat. I was able to try a bit and it tasted like chicken.

We had a Jap interpreter at the camp, Mr. Wada, and he was a very unusual and mean person. He was difficult to understand, and we had the feeling that he was hated by the other Japs as much as he was by us. Whenever the other Jap guards would play catch or hit balls to one another, he would never be with them, and only when they finished would he start playing by himself. He would take a ball and bat, toss the ball up and hit it, and run as fast as he could. Then he would hit it back and start the whole thing over again, sometimes for an hour or more. We could hear him talking to himself the whole time he was out there, but he never had another friend to play with.

One of the few things we enjoyed during our time there was the variety show that the POWs put on once a week. It included little skits and music that they made without any instruments. The singing was always very good, but the thing we enjoyed most was the act of a POW named Yeager, who would sing and whistle. He was very good at both, but he was a master at whistling especially; he could do it with a cigarette in his mouth and not miss a beat.

Escapees and Those Who Wished They Were

In March of 1943 we had ten men escape. Immediately upon hearing this, all of us from Luzon immediately assumed that the Japs would execute one hundred of us, following the rule of ten deaths for every man who escaped. We hadn't been placed in the ten men death squads, but we still felt sure that there must be some type of retaliation. However, the Japs only doubled up the guards and set out searching the entire camp. When the men did not show up, they moved all the men out of the barracks the escaped men had lived in and into the isolation compound, where they put them under heavy guard for a few weeks. We were all very concerned about what would happen to these men and we lived in a constant state of tension as we waited to see how they would respond but, again, nothing happened.

No one was executed, but we were all kept in the camp for the next few weeks. They cut our rations in half, and the only the essential details were sent out. Then, just as suddenly, everything returned to normal. However, it was clear that the Japs had become more apprehensive because they set to work completely improving the fence around the camp. They even put in new fence posts, about twenty feet long and sunk into the ground about eight feet. They came from trees that were about twenty inches in diameter, and we were surprised when they all began to sprout branches. A friend of mine told me that they were made from Kapok trees, which grew so fast that the branches had to be cut every five to six weeks.

About the time that the prisoners escaped, we received a few pesos from the Japs and were told that we were being paid one hundred and fifty pesos a month, although we only saw about ten of them; we were told that the rest was for room and board. It made many of us mad, including me, and I used the ten pesos to wipe my ass. We were also told to report to a station where we would fill out cards to be sent home. POWs sat at typewriters asking us questions and telling us what the answers should be, although it didn't even matter what I said because Mother and Daddy didn't receive the card until after I was already liberated and back in the states.

We were always looking for ways to make our bland diet taste a bit better and to try to find food that we could eat while we were at work, but we had to do it when the Japs weren't looking. One of the plans that worked was to watch the larger birds while we were working and try to locate their nests. When we found a nest we would steal the eggs and eat them. Also, near the jungle there were always wild lemons around, and if we were able to get a few of these without getting caught it was a big bonus. The lemons were about the size of a grapefruit, but after it was peeled the flesh was only the size of a regular lemon. We ate the skins and all. However, the things we really cherished were the small red peppers that loaded the six foot bushes that they grew on. When we found these we put them in a community bottle with homemade vinegar, and the concoction sure fired up the rice. When we were on detail and wanted to steal food for a "quan," which in the Philippine language meant to pool our food resources, we knew that there were some guards that would look the other way. At the same time, there were others who would surely beat you if they caught you. One of the things I enjoyed was watching the large fruit bats that flew by the camp every day just before sunset; there were hundreds of them, and I would wish that I were one of them so that I could fly away too.

In March or April, at the urging of the American camp commander, the Japs had some books brought in to start a small library. As soon as it was ready I started checking out books. I have always loved to read, and one of the books that I read while I was a prisoner was *Devil's Island*, which told the story of British prisoners who were sent to a remote island by the British government. While I was reading I felt a deep sorrow for the prisoners, and I began to cry softly to myself. As I looked around at the starving and sick men around me, I realized that we were much worse off than the men in my story.

In the fall of 1943, around the time of my twentieth birthday on October 2nd and twenty-three months after the start of the war, two more men escaped from our camp. The Japs told us that they had captured and executed them, although we never had proof of this. Nonetheless, we had our rations cut again, which meant that our rice portion was cut and instead we were given a portion of small, green beans, which were called mungo beans. As it turned out, the Japs were doing us a favor because these small beans had more nutrients in them than the rice they replaced.

Even with all the hardships that we had gone through on Davao and despite the fact that we were all skin and bones, the death rate had dropped off to almost none. By this time we had a will to survive and make it to the end of the war, and we also had more sanitary conditions and better doctors than we had previously. However, we still had lice at Davao, which caused us all a good deal of aggravation. We would spend hours trying to find and kill them between our thumbnails, and they stuck with us all for quite awhile. When we were finally rid of the lice, they were replaced by something much more irritating—bedbugs. Although it seemed that the bedbugs had run the lice away, the bedbugs were much worse because no matter what we did they remained with us the rest of our time at Davao.

During this time, a prisoner tried to escape by overpowering a Jap guard at the main gate. The Japs stopped him and took him to the guardhouse where he was kept overnight and executed the next morning. The man was a Major who had graduated from West Point, but that was the only information we were able to gather about him. Another tragedy came when two young men, on duty at the edge of the jungle, found some fruit that looked edible ate it, only to die of food poisoning. I later learned that they had eaten poisonous caster beans.

We had gone a long time without anyone having a malaria attack, but it started to hit some of our men again. This made me very apprehensive, because it had almost taken my life the first time. However, we did not lose anyone during this bout because the doctors had a large enough supply of quinine. Whenever someone had it he was sent to the quarantine hospital and it was taken care of. I was lucky, however, and did not come down with it again the entire time I was a POW.

For a short time I was on rice planting detail. I am grateful it was only for a short time, because we had to work bent over all day, standing in mud and with bugs biting your legs. During all of this we were constantly going hungry, and we were forced to load tons of food on trucks for the Japs to take to Davao to feed their own troops.

The only thing that kept us going was the news that we were able to collect from the English language newspaper in our library, which told us that the Americans were on their way to the Philippines. I am sure the Japs were not aware that this is what we were being sent to read, but this information gave me the motivation to keep fighting to stay alive. We were also able to glean information from a shortwave radio that one of the POWs had built. He was able to occasionally pick up a station from San Francisco, and the news from home would get us fired up and give us the hope that we needed.

In March of 1944 the American commander told us that the Japs were asking for five hundred volunteers for ship detail, but although I was eager to go I wasn't healthy enough. Most of the men who were healthy enough were those who had surrendered on Mindanao and thus were in better shape than those of us who had come from Cabanatuan. At the end of the war I learned that the ship had been sunk by an American submarine, and only forty-three of the five hundred men survived.

One of the men who left had slept next to me, and he was the only one of us who wasn't sleeping on a mat. He had scrounged enough material to build a frame like a folding cot, and he had stretched a shelter half over it. As he was leaving I asked him if I could have it, and he told me that I could. I laid down on it immediately after he had left, and it felt good to my body of skin and bones. I slept on that frame until we left Davao.

After the first of the year in 1944, things went from bad to worse; even those Jap soldiers who had once looked the other way when we took a few peppers or some fruit were starting to watch us a lot more closely now. Although fruit was rotting on the ground in the orchard, we did not dare take any because getting caught meant a serious beating. Things stayed that way until early June 1944, when the Japs doubled the guards around the camp and stopped all work detail besides the essentials. We wondered why things had changed so quickly and eventually our American camp commander told us that we were all being moved. That was all the information that we received.

The night before we moved, I was alerted to the wonderful aroma of food cooking. I followed my nose, and when I walked out of my barracks I found a group of six or eight men gathered around a small fire. I walked over and saw a five-gallon can with the top cut out, full of some kind of stew. I asked one of the men what it was and he told me that it was puppy stew. They had been able to catch and butcher a dog that had wandered into the camp. A veterinarian had examined it to be sure that it was okay to eat, and once they had gotten the okay each man had contributed something to add to the stew. When we had finished talking, he told me that I could taste some of the stew, and they filled up half of my canteen cup. I ate it slowly, savoring every delicious bite, and when I had finished eating I thanked them, and returned to my barracks to sleep on the homemade bed for the last time.

Life on the Hell Ships

The next day, at about four in the morning, we were awakened and sent to have our last meal at Davao. At about five o'clock the first group of sixty was loaded onto a two and a half ton truck. When twelve trucks were loaded they drove away and returned empty at noon.

At noon, my group was called. We were able to take a few things with us when we left, although that wasn't much of a problem as we didn't have much to bring. We were packed into the trucks, and after we were seated the Japs tied a long rope around all of us. Those of us who had shoes on were asked to take them off, but it made no difference to me as I had none. We were blindfolded and instructed by Mr. Wada that we were to keep our hands in the air.

A guard sat on the cab of the truck with a long bamboo pole, and if you dropped your hands he would hit you on the head. The ride from the camp to Davao took about an hour and a half—an impossible length of time to keep your hands in the air, even for someone in good health. I was so tired that I couldn't hold mine up any longer, but the moment I put them down I received a hard whack on my head. I found that I had more strength than I thought I had and kept them up for awhile longer, but eventually I was so completely worn out that I couldn't possibly hold them up any more. At that point I lowered them on the top of my head and locked my fingers together. I guess that was okay with the Jap because he never hit me again. When we arrived in Davao we were told to remove our blindfolds and they untied the rope.

At that point we were allowed to free ourselves and were offloaded to walk down the pier and board a barge that took us out to a freighter. There were several rope ladders hanging over the side, and we were forced to climb them to get on the ship. It was very difficult for most of us to do so in our weak condition, and I struggled just to get onboard. Once we made it on the ship, we were packed in like sardines; there was so little room that we had to take turns sitting down.

Once approximately one thousand of us were loaded, the ship got underway. We moved away from the main island to a small, nearby island where we remained for several days. While we were there, we were allowed to go topside in shifts, but it was just plain hot no matter where you were, with no relief from the heat. Topside was hell because of our limited clothing and no shoes, and it was nearly impossible to sit or stand on the hot deck without something to guard your body from it. When it was my turn to go topside I tried to stay near the rope ladder in the hopes that I could find a place on one of the large timbers or near some shady spot. At night topside offered some relief, and if we were lucky enough to be topside when it rained it gave us a chance to wash some of the filth off our bodies and to feel an ocean breeze.

We were fed twice a day, which took some planning to feed all of us our small ration of wormy rice and our equally small portion of fish or vegetables. Water was scarce once again, as bad as it had been back in Cabanatuan, and when we had a rain storm we used our canteen cups to catch any dripping water. If we could catch enough, we would use it to fill a canteen. The water often tasted suspect, but if that was the case we would drink as little as possible and hope to try to find a new, cleaner source soon.

The Japs must have been nervous about us escaping, because they had machine guns set up on the superstructure as well as riflemen posted all over the ship. They kept things well lit at all times so that they could keep an eye on us.

After a few days at anchor under these conditions, we heard the anchor being lifted early one morning. I was fortunate enough to be topside as we went underway, and after we were moving for awhile I noticed that we were part of a small convoy being escorted by a couple of small gun boats. We moved all day in sight of land, and just before dark we stopped just offshore. We dropped anchor once again and remained there until early the next morning, when we were on our way again. We continued to hug the coast of Mindanao all day, and just before dark we pulled in close to the shore at Zambourango and laid anchor for the night.

Just after dark the machine gun opened up, firing over our heads. When the firing was over the Japs ordered those of us topside to go below, and as soon as we were below they closed the hatch above us. Approximately one thousand of us were crammed in an area so small that there was no room for us to sit down. We remained that way in the hold all night long, and we were starting to use all the oxygen when sometime before dawn the Japs opened the hatch, finally allowing us to get some air. However, it was too late for some of us and we lost men that night. We later learned that one POW had escaped overboard, and we all rooted for him, hoping that he had made it. We later learned that his name was Lieutenant Colonel McGee, that he had been stationed on Mindanao during the war, and that his escape was successful.

We started moving again, and the next morning the Japs removed the hatch and began to allow some of us to go topside. As the day went by things became more routine again. They rotated groups for topside and my turn came just after dark. I had just found a place to lie down and make myself comfortable when I heard the machine guns start firing and all hell broke loose once again. We were all made to go into the hold of the ship where we were suffocated again; another escapee had gone over the side.

Later, I learned that his name was Donald H. Wills and his escape had also been successful. After the war I discovered his book about it entitled, *The Sea Was My Last Chance.* I was able to get in touch with him and we had a long conversation about our experiences; he sent me a copy of his book with a note inside. I was happy to know that he had survived the four and a half mile swim and that he later became a guerilla fighter.

Following his escape, we were ordered back to the hold and our food and water were reduced. The Japs were getting meaner in light of the recent escapes; they would hit us with a rifle butt or kick us for no reason whatsoever. We were subject to that abuse for the rest of the trip, and finally we arrived at Cebu City where we were offloaded and moved to a metal warehouse. We were pushed in because there wasn't room for all of us, and eventually they put some of us in a fenced area outside where we remained for two or three days. From there we were loaded on another ship, which was even worse than the one we had just left a few days before. There was almost no food or water, and we lived in those conditions for about a week before we arrived at Pier #7 in Manila.

Thinking back on it now, I realize that when I left Cabanatuan for Davao I likely weighed about one hundred and ten pounds, and after the eighteen months at Davao I'm sure my weight was about the same. However, despite all the hardships that we went through at Davao, I feel that the move from Cabanatuan to Davao is likely what saved my life. At Davao I had good doctors with more resources to work with, more food (even if we had to steal it), a renewed will to survive, and, most importantly, ample water. Not only was there water for drinking, but also enough water to allow for improved sanitation.

Return to Manila

When we arrived back in Manila we had lost fifty-seven men on the two hell ships. When we were offloaded and being marched to Bilibid prison from Pier #7, there were Filipino people watching us march, and some of them tried to get food to us. The thing I remember most was hearing a record played over and over again, as loud as possible, playing

"There's a Great Day Coming Mañana." This actually gave us a great deal of encouragement.

We were at Bilibid for only a week when we were informed that we were being moved again, and the very next day we were marched back to Pier #7 and loaded on another freighter, *The Canadian Inventor.* There were about a thousand of us on this ship—six hundred in the forward hold and four hundred in the aft hold. When we had all climbed down we were so cramped that once again we had to pull in our legs to our chest just to sit down. I was one of the first ones down and so I immediately went searching for the best place to sit, which turned out to be in a corner by the back wall. In this spot I was able to have something to lean against and I was also free from the hot sun.

The hold we were kept in was an open space of about sixty by sixty feet, which the Japs had built from lumber. In the center of the hold was a hatch of about twenty square feet, with a rope ladder leading down into it. There was also a hatch going to the lower deck, but it was closed off, and they had put a wooden floor around the lower hatch with a wooden lid over it.

It turns out that my spot in the back corner was not only a bit more comfortable than most, but it was also a lucky choice because I was surrounded by people that all supported one another through this difficult ordeal. I met one of my most trusted friends on that ship, a Mexican by the name of Alexander Moreanos, from Colorado. I spent the rest of the war with him, and no matter what we had we shared with each other.

After we were loaded onto the boat we were served our first meal, and we were pleased with the portion. It took some organization to feed and give water to so many people in such a small space, and it was done by assigning sections. When your section was called you would stand and congregate by the bottom hatch, which was covered. Those closest to the hatch were fed last, to keep people from climbing over each other with food in their hands.

We pulled away from the pier out into Manila Bay before dropping anchor. At that time the rope ladder was pulled down and we were told that some of us could come topside in groups. My group was called just before sunset, and when I walked up onto the top deck I was surprised to see that some of the Jap ships had been damaged. I looked out at the city of Manila, and was also surprised by the sense of nostalgia that washed over me. My time in Manila, before the war, had been wonderful, and I hadn't even realized it at the time. I thought about the time I was invited to eat with our bunk boys and how much I would enjoy having some of their white rice and fish-heads now. I wondered how all my family was, and I thought about how Bilon might be doing since the war had started.

We stayed all night docked in the bay and the next morning we started moving with a convoy. After we reached Corregidor those of us who were topside were all marched back to the hold, except for those whose job it was to pass food down in buckets tied to a rope. Once underway we found that our rations had been reduced drastically from the amount we had received prior to the beginning of our journey. Our journey turned out to be very short because on the first day we were out of Manila Bay, our ship broke down and our convoy left us. Eventually we got our ship moving and we started back toward Manila Bay, where we were to remain for the next week and a half. While we were there, we were once again allowed to go topside in groups.

My group was topside one evening at about 10:00 p.m. when we realized there were ships all around us. Things were quiet for a few minutes, and then all of a sudden one of the anchored ships was blown up within three or four hundred yards of ours. It was a tanker, and the huge explosion it made lit up the entire night sky. The Japs became very excited and began rushing us back to the hold, and we remained there with no idea what might happen next. For the next few days we were all kept below deck, except for those few who prepared our meager issue of wormy rice and soup that was made from stinky fish. The soup was beneficial in that it provided us with liquid, since our water supply had once again been cut drastically.

Eventually we felt the anchor lift and we began moving, once again attempting our trip to Formosa. However, the ship soon began having engine problems again, and once again the convoy pulled away and left us behind. This started the most unpleasant experience of the entire trip.

After we had been left alone for a few days, the ocean started to become very rough. It was so rough that when the ship would roll to its side we could see, from our hold, the next wave coming. The waves were forty to fifty feet high, and it got so bad that the Japs had to lower the hatch in order to avoid our being swamped. After the hatch was closed again, all hell broke loose. It was dark and the oxygen level was falling fast. There were six hundred of us in the hold, and men were panicking all around me. We could hear the commotion getting louder and more frantic all around us, but one of the men in our group calmly and quietly reminded us that to survive we would need to move as little as possible and remain calm.

His calming voice soothed us a bit, and our corner got quiet and remained calm; we felt that we could survive this ordeal.

We could still hear crying, screaming and sheer panic unfolding around us though. During this time, I started experiencing hearing loss in my good ear for the first time. I'm not sure why it happened, although I think that it may have been due to the mortar shell wound I had received during combat.

The next day the typhoon had ended and the ocean was calm once again. The Japs opened the hatch for us and we were able to see daylight and breathe fresh air again. We received our first meal in thirty-six hours, and it was a decent portion which included some type of meat that was much better than the stinky fish soup. After we had finished eating and were waiting for the rope ladder to be dropped, I was sitting talking to Moreanos when someone hollered something that I couldn't hear. Moreanos said to me, "Darrell, you was in the 31st Infantry. They want to know if anyone in this hold was from the 31st."

I don't know why I responded, but I did. I had no idea what I was getting myself into, but by that point it was too late to change my mind. I started climbing over people, trying not to step on anyone, and I made it to the rope ladder where I was told to come up. After I reached topside, I was met by one of our POWs who told me to follow him. I didn't know what was going on, and I was starting to feel more nervous. Shortly after, we came to a spot along the rail where there were four of five POWs stationed around what appeared to be a board, attached to the railing so that it could be tipped up while still attached to the railing. When I arrived I was informed that I was to be on the Honor Guard for Corporal Raymond Cunningham, who was a member of my company and who had just made Corporal before the war began.

I had a chance to see his face briefly, and then one of the men who was there said a touching, beautiful prayer. The order to attention was given, followed by the present arms command. As we were told to present arms, the whistle on the ship started blowing, and the board with the body on it was lifted, and we watched it slip away. I will always remember the sound of the weight that was tied to his feet and the sight of his nude body slipping peacefully into the sea. As I watched him sink I was so overcome by how clean he looked that I had the urge to follow him in. Since that day, I have always felt that I would be proud to be buried at sea. Whenever I go to the West Coast I always make a visit to the ocean in order to put my hands on the water and feel him and others who are buried there. Although I do not know the names of all the men who made up the honor guard, I am quite sure that one of them was Captain Thompson, the commander of L Company.

I was the only one there from my hold, the corporal that we buried along with the other men present all came from the other hold. Even the Jap captain paid his respects before we were released, and I returned to the filth, stink and starvation of our hold, a contrast to the clean and peaceful ceremony I had just witnessed. I wondered why we continued to fight; the alternative seemed a welcome respite from the life we were living in the hold of the death ship. I made my way back to my corner, stepping on a few people on the way, and I told Moreanos about what I had just witnessed. With that I was back in the fight, willing myself forward in the struggle to live that had become our daily routine.

The next day the Japs took away the buckets we had been using as toilets and hung straddle boards over the side of the ship. I had a need to relieve myself, and I hollered "Banjo," meaning toilet, up to the guard. If you were given permission, you could climb the ladder and go relieve yourself. I was given permission, and made my way to the deck, which was boiling in the hot afternoon sun. I had no shoes and my feet were blistered as I scurried to find a cooler spot; it was a relief to finally arrive at the split boards hanging over the edge, but I spent the entire time dreading the trip back to the hold. The entire time we were in prison camp, we never had any toilet paper, (a thought that still remains with me when people talk about appreciating the smaller things in life). When I had finished relieving myself, I re-tucked my g-string and made my way back to the rope ladder next to another POW who was lucky enough to have shoes. As I walked, I tried to find any way I could to relieve the pain in my feet. When I reached the rope ladder, I noticed that a Jap guard was laughing at me. He stopped me on the hot steel deck and made me kneel down on my bare knees, which immediately began blistering as well. To try to relieve the pain in my knees I balanced my weight on the balls on my feet, which also became blistered. The Jap made me kneel for nearly five minutes, laughing at me the entire time. When he allowed me to get up, the skin from my knees stuck to the scorching steel deck. I finally made my way back to my corner where Moreanos asked what had happened. I told him what I thought of the Jap who had done that to me and he agreed with me, saying, "That dirty little Jap son-of-a-bitch."

Shortly after the incident on the deck, Moreanos discovered a small door in the wooden wall in back of us and was able to open it. He told me about it and we both went through to investigate. On the other side we were surprised to discover a light, and even though it was only a forty-watt bulb it was enough for us to look around. As soon as we stepped on the other side it felt like we had stepped on white crushed stone. We could see the steel hull of the ship only about six or eight feet from the back of our wall, and after we were there for a short while we discovered that the crushed stone was actually rock salt.

Even though it made us nervous, we continued to explore, becoming more confident with every passing moment. We found a small, sealed, wooden keg, which we broke into with a sharp object. Inside, we found the most beautiful purple plums. We couldn't wait to start eating; we each grabbed one and took a bite at the same time, only to spit them out together—they were preserved in salt brine! They weren't wasted, however, because we used them to improve the taste of our rice. Furthermore, we were able to use the hidden room to relieve ourselves, and it was no longer necessary to go up to the scorching hot top deck.

Finally, the Japs were able to get the ship running again and we proceeded to Formosa. I suppose it was because of the constant stink from the hold, but the Japs allowed us to take salt water baths in groups. It was a cloudy day and I knew the deck would be cool, so I decided that I would go. A POW would spray us with salt water, and we were allowed to wash ourselves while he sprayed us. If you had soap you could use that as well, and Moreanos was generous enough to share his with me. It wasn't salt water soap, but it did fine to clean our bodies. However, when we put it in our hair we found that we couldn't get it out. The more it dried the more discomfort we felt. However, just before we were about to go back down into the hold the clouds gathered and delivered a downpour, and I was able to get all the soap out of my hair.

After the Japs got the ship moving we finally made it to Formosa. We were told we would join a convoy there, but when it moved out, we weren't with it. Instead, we were broken down for another week and a half before finally moving onward to Okinawa. While we were in Okinawa we were issued clothing, because the weather was colder. It was made from some type of fabric that was woven so loosely that you could see through it when it was held up to the light, even though it was dyed a dark green. Upon leaving, the ship broke down once again, and we had to return to port to wait for another convoy.

We were parked in the harbor and being held in the hold of the ship when it was jarred by a violent explosion, followed quickly by several more brutal explosions. The whole ship became quiet as we all waited to be struck, but we were luckier than the ships around us. We were never struck, but I found out that the ship next to us, which had all Jap citizens and mostly women and children, was struck and sunk by an American submarine. Over fifteen hundred Japanese lost their lives on that ship, which was right next to ours.

We were finally able to resume our voyage to Japan, and we arrived at Moji at the beginning of September 1944. The POWs had named *The Canadian Inventor* the "Mati, Mati, Maru" which in Japanese means: *wait, wait ship*.

When we were offloaded at Moji, I had a chance to reflect back on the two ships we had been on between Davao and Manila. On those two ships we lost approximately fifty men, while on the "Mati, Mati, Maru," over a period of sixty-two days, we only lost ten. The conditions on all of the ships were about the same, except for one thing which I believe was able to save so many lives on our ship—the rock salt. Many of the men were able to defecate into the rock salt instead of going topside, which was especially beneficial for those with dysentery. In addition, I feel that the salt, in such a quantity, had a sterilizing effect.

I also think that our ship lost fewer men because of a sense of camaraderie which fostered a will to fight in us. On the other two ships, it seems that the men just gave up the fight and chose to die, as I had seen so many do at Cabanatuan. There is no way to know for sure, of course, but I attribute my survival and the survival of those I was with to the three reasons I have mentioned. Much of our survival, however, I credit to the way that the groups on the "Mati, Mati, Maru" looked after one another, and in my case I credit Moreanos in particular.

As I left the last hell ship and climbed the rope ladder, I found myself wishing that some of the salt on the ship would be used to pickle plums, and that the little Jap son-of-a-bitch that made me kneel on the hot steel deck would eat all of them. I especially hoped that the salt where I defecated would be the salt that pickled them.

Japan

When we were offloaded at Moji we were moved to an area near a train station, where we were dusted with something to get rid of the lice that covered us from head to toe. It was applied to our whole body and our clothing; they even made us cover our eyes, nose and mouth as they applied it to our face. We were then loaded on a passenger train, instead of a boxcar like we had traveled in while in the Philippines, and we rode on the train still covered with the dust.

After being held in a seat with two others for about an hour, the train finally started. We had two Jap guards for our car, as I'm sure the others cars did as well. After we had been moving for awhile a cart was wheeled in, loaded with little boxes. Two Jap civilians gave each POW a box, and when I got mine I was very pleased at what I saw inside. There were three compartments, two that were about four inches square and one that was four by eight inches, and the whole box was four inches deep. The large one contained the most beautiful white rice that I had seen in quite awhile, and the smaller boxes had a vegetable and a portion of meat. It was the best meal we had received in a long time.

We didn't know what our destination would be, but we went through Hiroshima. I don't recall how long we were on the train, but I do know that it was at least several hours. Even though we were still covered in insecticide, we had a good meal and we were safe from the hold of a ship. Instead, we were on a moving train and able to watch the changing scenery out the window. This, to me, was a different and much more pleasant world. I felt a renewed sense of freedom; finally my eyes were able to focus on something other than a bunch of starving men.

Yokkaichi

We finally reached our destination and were informed that it was Yokkaichi. When we pulled into the train station we were moved to a secure area and loaded on a truck, which took us to a barracks no more than five miles away. We were surprised to find that our new location was built on a black sand beach on the ocean side of a twenty foot earth retaining wall with a road on top. The buildings were built with rough cut lumber stained black, with no windows, and I can remember four different buildings. The longest building was where the POWs were to be housed, and the second longest was the hospital. There was a small building attached to the main housing building which had a bath house and latrine. All of the buildings were surrounded by a solid board fence of about ten feet high, which was also stained black. There was an opening for two solid doors, each about five feet wide. Just inside these doors was the American and Jap Camp Commander quarters. The last building, near the entrance to the POW quarters, was the kitchen.

We arrived and were offloaded and marched, in formation, through the gate. Inside, we were halted, formed into groups, and led to our sleeping quarters. When we went inside we had to wait for our eyes to adjust to our poorly lit quarters. On the way through the building to our bay I noticed a Jap guard station to our right.

I was surprised to see that our bay was about twenty by twenty feet and would sleep about forty men. Our bunks were arranged on platforms that sat up off the floor; there were two on each side of the bay with a space of about six feet between them. For a mattress we had a woven straw pad that was about an inch thick, as well as two thin blankets. There were no interior walls and the floor was the black sandy beach. The only light we had was one forty-watt bulb for each bay, and there was no heat except for a small charcoal pit in the open pit between the two sleeping platforms. All of our meals were brought to each bay in five gallon cans and distributed by the POWs there. While the food was the best we had had in a long time, it was still very inadequate.

When we had to use the latrine we were forced to go to the guard station and stand at attention, facing him and asking permission in Japanese to use the banjo. When he granted you permission you had to thank him, again in Japanese. When you returned from the latrine you had to use the same procedure again. This was very difficult when you had to go several times during the night, as we did due to our poor diet and a poorly functioning urinary system. If there was a mean guard on duty that was asleep or pretending to be and you woke him up or used the latrines without permission, you were apt to get slapped around or issued a severe beating.

The thing I did enjoy, however, was being allowed to go for a bath. This was a new experience for all of us. There was a long tub, filled with hot water that would hold about twenty of us. Before we went in we had to soak for twenty minutes and wash our entire body. If it wasn't too cold in the barracks we could wash our single set of green clothes and put them back on after we had finished our hot water soak, letting them dry on our body. When the weather turned really cold we didn't wash our clothes because the only heat was generated from the small charcoal fire pit and about one thousand POWs.

We used the fire for making green tea or heating hot water to drink with our morning and evening meals. That was the only time we were allowed to have a fire, and we had to use charcoal because it didn't smoke and we had no chimney or windows.

Shortly after we arrived at Yokkaichi we were all issued our first pair of shoes, which were made of rubber and canvas and were one-size-fits-all. They were open in the back for sliding your feet in, and when you slid your foot forward your big toe was separated from the other four. They closed with a hook in the back. We were given the shoes because the weather was starting to get cold, and receiving these shoes was not the only good luck I received in Yokkaichi. The POW that slept next to me was a big Polish POW from Pennsylvania. It was a good thing that the shoes were made to fit all sizes because my newly acquired best friend, Ted Schwarczynski, had very large feet, a fact that I know well because of the way that we had to sleep. In such tight quarters we slept with my feet to his head and his to mine. On some occasions it was down near zero degrees, and we would put one blanket on the bottom and use our three remaining blankets to cover both of us. Then, we would hold each other's feet for warmth; all of us in the camp used that method to survive the extreme cold.

After a few days we were moved by groups outside the camp to an area on the beach, and we were made to learn close order drills in Japanese. I am not sure exactly why they did this, except that it was a very degrading and difficult exercise. Some of the POWs were slapped on the face or kicked in the shins by the Jap's hobnail shoes. I was able to avoid this abuse, but now, years later, I wonder why. After about a week of drills we were marched to the factory and given our work assignments.

The factory where we were moved was about a half a mile from our camp, on the land side of the dyke. From our camp we could see what I was told was the tallest chimney in the Orient, which was about four hundred feet high and built with mortar and bricks. After we worked there for awhile we found out why it was so high: it served to vent the toxins the factory created.

The factory's primary product was copper, and to manufacture pure copper it was necessary to use vats of sulfuric acid. Therefore, in addition to the copper, they also manufactured sulfuric acid in huge quantities. I was put to work in a group with about five other men, and we were lucky to receive a Jap civilian as our boss. He was a man in his late forties who turned out to be very compassionate. It took me several weeks to put even a reserved trust in him, because of the mistreatment I had received from the Japs, but eventually I did come to trust him. I was fortunate to have Mr. Nakahara as my boss because he tried to make our work as light as possible, and he would give us a little food when he could, even though it was hard and dangerous for him. Every day we went into the factory we had to stop at the large brass Buddha and say a prayer, and on the way out we had to do the same. If the Japs had known the prayers we were making, they probably wouldn't have wanted us to pray.

One of our jobs was filling a hopper with a mixture of various materials which were all put into a compressor and discharged as round solid objects of about four inches in diameter. We would break them off in twelve inch bits and store them for removal.

While the work was hard and we still didn't have enough food, one of the most wonderful things that happened the entire time I was a POW happened in Yokkaichi. About a month after we arrived, near my twentieth birthday, I received my first and only letter from my family along with my only gift package. It wasn't a large package, but I remember that there was cod-liver oil, pills, and chocolate candy. I ate them all the first day. When we received Red Cross packages there was a lot of trading, but when we got packages from our family there was very little trading, and I felt that this package was so personal that I didn't trade anything. However, I did share it with Ted because he didn't receive anything.

While we were in Yokkaichi the weather was getting colder, and we started looking for anything we could find to wrap around our feet to keep them warm. We were issued large wool overcoats to wear to work, but we had to turn them in again when we returned to camp at night. While we were at Yokkaichi we were always on the watch for anything useful that we could steal, and with the large overcoat this became easier because we could conceal things in our clothing. Occasionally, when we were lined up in columns of four for dismissal, the guard would start a shakedown. When that happened, the contraband was passed from the first column to the forth and dispersed along the wall of the barracks. After the dismissal order was given and we were all going inside, we could see all kinds of stuff, from firewood to rags, along the wall.

One of the things that we smuggled in was a chemical that tasted like salt, which we used to spice up our bland diet. When you put it on your food it would turn red. I don't know what it was, but all of us used it.

When my first and only Christmas in Japan came we were all issued Red Cross packages, and that is when the wheeling and dealing began. It would have made the New York Stock Exchange look like a training school. We had no Christmas carols or performances of any kind; except for the trading it was very quiet. After the call to bed I laid there for awhile and thought about my family. That Christmas we had two days off from work, and it felt good not to have to go to the factory. We were all in bad shape from the extended shortage of food, poor clothing, and exposure to the cold temperature after coming from the tropics. There were a lot of us who were starting to get sick from colds, and when you went to bed you could hear men coughing all night long. The next morning, however, almost all of them would go to work because the half rations for no work rule was still in effect.

Wheeling and Dealing for Survival

Around the end of January or beginning of February, one of the pipes that went to the tall chimney was starting to have a problem and had to be cleaned out. It was so large that it had a door large enough for a man to go through, and two of us were assigned to clean it. When we were inside we had just enough room to stand bent over.

The flow of air had been shut off at its source and we were to clean away the accumulation of white dust that ran about ten to twelve inches thick around the flue. After we were inside, our Jap boss gave us the tools we needed and opened some vents at the top. As careful as we were to keep the dust down and cover our nose and mouth with a cloth, we were still covered in acrid dust that we were forced to breathe in. When we finished we had no way of washing our clothes until the end of our workday, when we were allowed to go to the bathhouse to wash our clothes and soak in the hot tub.

I'm sure that the dust was bad for our long-term health, but the cleaning of the flue almost caused me to lose my life then and there. About a week after we cleaned it out, Ted and the others found that I hadn't moved after wake-up call. Ted said, "Hey! Starky! It's time to get up!" When I didn't answer or move, he got close to my face and started asking me what was wrong. I told him that I couldn't move, and he sent someone to get a medic. When the medic came he checked me over and sent someone to the hospital to bring me up a stretcher, and I was taken to the hospital.

At the hospital I was examined by an American doctor who told me that I had pleurisy, and that he thought I would be okay because they had just received some sulfa drugs from the International Red Cross. I was so sick and had been fighting to live for so long, and now I was afflicted with this. I was starting to give up my fight. After the work detail returned that evening, Ted and Moreanos came over to see me. I told them that I had experienced all that I could take, and they got angry with me. "Like hell, you son-of-a-bitch," they said. "We aren't going to let you give up after all this time."

After they left I began to think again about trying to survive, and shortly thereafter I had another visitor. I don't want to give his name, but he was a camp wheeler and dealer, and he said, "I heard you were sick so I thought I would come over and see how you were doing." I told him I was not too good, and he asked me how my appetite was. Once again, I told him not good. Then he said, "I have a deal for you. If you give me your half ration, when you are able to eat I will give you one and one-half rations for every meal I get." I agreed.

About three days after my treatments I began to have an appetite and started eating my half ration. The dealer came over every evening to see how I was doing. When I reached the point where I could eat one and a half rations, plus my own half ration, he brought them to me every evening for six evenings. He was completely honest in everything he said, and the extra food got me back on my feet. Most of the POWs didn't like the wheelers and dealers, but that is the only dealing I ever had with one and he was very honest and forthright with his deal. I will always be grateful for what he did for me when my survival was at stake.

Earthquake!

One morning after I had almost recovered from my illness, I was sitting on the edge of the bed platform against one of the support beams, facing another POW on the opposite platform. We were eating our morning meal when he asked me "Did you feel that? The post just shook." Before I could say that no, I hadn't felt it, there was a violent shaking and we both realized that we were experiencing an earthquake. We got up and ran for the door as fast as we could, but it was shaking so hard it was difficult to even stand. We got to the door and were going to step out when we saw a crevice in the black sand about a foot wide. We didn't know which side of it we should be on, because we had heard that when there was a break and you saw another one a short distance away, the earth could fall in between them. I jumped over the crevice and went to a clothesline post and held on.

As I was holding on tight I heard someone yell: "Look at that!" I looked in the direction he was pointing, which was toward the factory, and I saw the tallest chimney in the Orient swaying like a snake. It started to fall and crumbled into a huge pile of bricks and mortar. Shortly after we saw it fall, we could see water coming up from the crevice on the beach. The entire thing only lasted a few minutes, but the water continued to rise and the Japs had us all moved to the road on top of the dyke, where we remained for several hours.

The Japs ordered out a detail which went back through a foot of water to move all the food they could salvage up to dry land. We remained on the high ground for several hours until the ocean water receded and they were able to move us back to the camp. We returned, but were very apprehensive about what was going to happen next. Surprisingly, the damage was minimal and we were happy to hear that even our men at the factory had not been hurt. We all felt a sense of joy that Mother Nature had been able to destroy, in just a few minutes, what we had wanted to destroy ourselves.

Shortly after we were returned to the hospital I was released and sent back to my barracks. It was sure good to be back in my bed, relatively healthy again and with Ted and the others. After the earthquake we still went to work in the factory, doing clean-up or repairs. However, the earthquake made some of the guards become even meaner. On one occasion there were two POWs caught with contraband, and they were used as examples to the rest of us. They were tied up and hung by their arms just above the ground, just close enough that they could extend their toes and take some of the weight off. They hung that way for a couple of hours before they were cut down. That was enough to make the rest of us a lot more careful about not stealing anything.

The earthquake put the factory out of production, and as a result about three weeks after we heard that two hundred of us were to be moved to a new camp. When the list was made I was happy to find that I was on it, along with Moreanos and Ted.

As I remember, it was near the end of March and the weather was starting to warm up before we moved. Even with all the hardships of short food, poor housing, cold temperatures and hard work that faced us at Yokkaichi, we did not lose a single POW there. Before I left, I had the chance to see Mr. Nakahara, the man who had helped us and made our stay there a bit easier. He asked me for my address and I gave him the last one I knew of, but I was surprised to receive a letter from him about five years after the war ended. He had someone write it, because he could not speak English, and his letter is included in the index.

Toyama

The day we began our move from Yokkaichi was warm and sunny. I remember that detail well because when I got on the truck and waited to start moving, I could feel the sun's warmth. The ride to the train station was as interesting as it had been from it, and I took some joy in watching the scenery go by. When we boarded, we found the accommodations about the same as they had been from Moji, with the exception of the insecticide dust. We were being moved to Toyama, about four hundred miles away and approximately the same distance as Moji to Yokkaichi. When we arrived we were loaded on trucks and moved to our last camp as POWs.

We arrived to see a black-stained, high board fence around a camp whose buildings were also stained black. There was a double-hung large gate and four buildings which made up the quarters for the POWs. The headquarters had a kitchen, a latrine and showers, the first I had seen as a POW. There was a courtyard of about one hundred by two hundred feet. It was clear that our new quarters at Toyama were much better than those at Yokkaichi. We had wooden floors and there were two sleeping platforms, one over the other. The mattresses were still made of woven straw, and we received about the same amount of food, but there was one big change for the better—we had two working shifts. Each shift consisted of about half of the population, and we would change shifts at regulated intervals. Each POW now had his own bed, with more room to sleep in. Our new Camp Commander was Captain Thompson, who was formerly the commander of L Company.

The camp was about half a mile from the factory and by a river, or some type of body of water, with a fairly long bridge over it. The distance from the bridge to the factory was farmland with only one road. The factory was a steel mill which produced war materials, and it was much larger than the factory at Yokkaichi. It was the Nagoya PW Branch Camp #7, operated by Tateyama Heavy Industries, Toyama Steel station.

When we were assigned our sleeping arrangements, Moreanos, Ted and I had one pallet of other prisoners between each of us, and they worked opposite shifts than we did. That worked out just fine, because we were all working the same shift, and that is how we wanted it. We were in the camp a few days before the first details were sent to work, and the three of us were all put on the day shift. We were under forced labor at Toyama to produce war materials for the Japs to fight against our troops, and we all hated this thought. However, after having been through so much torture and pain from the Japs, fighting every day for three years just to stay alive, those of us who had survived to this point weren't going to give up. When we were at work, we just tried to slow down production in any way we could.

After we were marched from the camp to the factory, we were assigned to our jobs. Moreanos and I were put to work as stokers for a large furnace, and our job was to keep the hopper filled with coal. Air was blown into the furnace and coal was fed to it by an auger. We had to make sure that the air flow wasn't restricted, and when the clinchers would build up they would have to be cleaned out of the furnace several times a day. It was hot and the work was very hard, and we worked a twelve hour day. Moreanos and I had this job most of the time we were there, and although I don't recall the work that Ted was doing, I'm sure it was dusty and hard.

Our boss on the day shift was a civilian of about sixty years old. He turned out to be a kind and caring Jap, one of the two that I met in my forty-two months as a POW. When we worked the night shift we had a Jap soldier who only checked us a couple of times a night. It might have been easy to escape, but where would we have gone?

As usual, we were always hungry. We only received a small meal every twelve hours, and as a result we did something very stupid, that could have cost us a severe beating or even our lives. After we had been there about six or eight weeks, we stole the lunch that belonged to our day boss. He knew who the thieves were, but he didn't report us. After that day, he always brought two lunches, and he told us: "One for you and one for me." I am sure he brought us food that his family could have used, because the Japs were feeling the effects of the war as well, but he knew that we needed it and he did this for us the rest of the time we were there.

To explain a bit more about the factory: the furnace we fired was one of several used to heat steel igniters that weighed several tons, and when they were heated to a certain temperature they were removed by a large overhead crane to a hammer mill, where they were shaped into the finished product. One of the ways that Moreanos and I found to slow production was to put a piece of trash in the hopper with the coal which we were supposed to be searching for impurities. This would cause the auger to freeze up and break. We always did this on the night shift, usually once every two weeks but some weeks even more often.

There were a lot of ways that we worked to survive and make our lives a bit better. The weather was beginning to get warmer, and weeds were starting to grow along the side of the road. You will always find, in large groups of men, one or two that have a helpful specialty, and in ours there was one who knew how to identify an edible weed. He would pick one and bring it to camp, and we would plant it in the courtyard in a little three by four foot garden that he had hilled up. He had a variety of them which created a big interest among us. We started making little gardens of weeds all over the place, and these were a big supplement to our food supply.

At the factory, we had to go outside to use the latrines. Next to us was a Jap farmer who had planted a garden of twenty by thirty feet filled with carrots and a long, white radish. The Japs used these foods to pickle, but we continued watching them all the time, looking for an opening. After they had been growing for quite awhile I noticed that there were a few being pulled during the night shift. As the radishes and carrots got larger they began disappearing faster, until one night every carrot and radish was pulled and consumed by the POWs. Looking back, I believe that perhaps they had been planted by Koreans for our consumption, not by a Jap, because there was no effort to find out who was stealing them and none of us were ever punished.

We were starting to see a change in the Japs; they were shaking us down every day and would slap us around for the smallest infraction. One incident I remember was when one of the POWs was caught with a newspaper, written in Japanese, that he wanted to use as toilet paper. None of us could even read a word of it, but the Jap guard that found it became very angry, hitting the POW with the butt of his rifle and kicking him on the ground. I am sure all of us POWs wanted to kill the little son-of-a-bitch but, when he finished beating on him, two of the POWs picked up their unconscious buddy and carried him back to camp. Even with the severe beating he had taken, he was back to work in a few days in order to get his full rations again.

Hope and Destruction

It was a real clear day around the end of June when a POW looking at the sky pointed and said to me, "Look at that!" I looked and saw what I thought, at first, was a small plane. However, the vapor stream was wide and large, and as it got closer I realized it was a large plane. After it passed us we could see puffs of anti-aircraft fire, much lower than the plane. We all realized it was one of our planes, and it was the first morale booster we had seen since the war began.

We were to see one of our planes about three times a week for the next three weeks. It kept us looking at the sky whenever we could, to try and see some hope. Near the end of July, 1945, we experienced more than just vapor streams. I had just returned to camp from the night shift, and I was in the shower room with my clothes off, ready to get in the shower. At that moment, I heard a sound that I had heard many times before—a bomb falling. I ran for the door as fast as I could and flattened out in between two of the weed gardens. Just as I landed, a huge bomb exploded near the factory. It missed the main part, but hit the outer edge, the part that was closest to our camp. It was a big bomb and when it exploded the concussion was so great that the air blew the wooden fence and the shower wall in. It was the only bomb that was dropped, but we were all very concerned to find out about our fellow POWs. However, they had all returned early, and not one of them was even hurt. After the bombing, we were all kept in camp for a couple days before being sent back to our regular details.

The bomb caused a lot of damage to some of the buildings, but not enough to stop production. The ones that were damaged were all made of sheet metal and were repaired quickly. However, we knew that there would be more bombs coming, and we were all nervous. At the same time, we were also happy because it meant that the war was going in our favor.

After the bombing the Japs increased the blackout rules and started sounding air warnings when a plane was spotted. We could hear them at the factory and in the city of Toyama when we were in camp. At this time the Japs had us destroy our weed gardens and had POWs dig three open pits that were large enough to hold all the POWs in air raid shelters. The pits were about three feet deep, but the dirt that was removed was also piled up around the pit, making the wall about four and a half or five feet around us.

Sometime during all of this, Moreanos and I were on the night shift, all alone in the furnace room at about 2 a.m. Suddenly, the blackout curtain was pulled back and an Asian man came in, set a lunch box on the floor, and made a gesture that it was for us. Then he left, as fast as he could. When he was gone we looked at each other and picked up the box. Inside was rice, a bean paste and a vegetable. We looked at one another, wondering out loud if we should eat it; we didn't trust the Japs and wasn't sure if it was some kind of trick. Finally, we said to hell with it and started eating. Afterward we found out that the man was Korean and that it was likely one of the Koreans that had planted the carrots and radishes we were able to steal in the night.

There was another interesting encounter that occurred, this time during the day shift. Our Jap boss told us that the war would be over in a short time because the Americans were using an electric bomb. Whether he meant incendiary bombs, which were being dropped on Tokyo and other cities, or if the first atomic bomb had been dropped, I do not know.

Near the end of July, about three days after we had been told about the impending end of the war, I was lying on my straw mat just after dark after having worked the day shift. I was almost asleep when I heard the sirens start, and we headed for our assigned air raid shelter. Ted, Moreanos and I were near the door and were among the first to reach the shelter. We sat down at the back of the hold, facing toward the city of Toyama. We chose that spot because we felt it was safer than if we faced the factory, which we assumed was the target. After we were all in, sitting close to one another, there was a Jap guard posted on each corner of the shelter with fixed bayonets. In about a half an hour we heard the drone of multiple airplanes. As they approached us they grew louder and louder, and as they flew low over us we could see one from the Jap's searchlights. The Japs were firing anti-aircraft at them, and although I don't know how many of them were in the air I am sure there were at least fifty in the first wave. They flew over and returned for a second time, and the second time they started dropping bombs.

The first ones fell on a fuel dump containing highly explosive material, and the whole sky lit up upon the impact. Even though it was after dark we could see each other very clearly. When the first wave came over there was another one just behind it, and it remained like that for several hours. As I recall it ended at about 4 or 4:30 a.m. We never heard an all-clear because the entire city of Toyama was in flames along with the factory.

During the bombings I was experiencing two simultaneous feelings—fear and a great sense of satisfaction. The greatest sense of fear came after the bombing was over and a high speed, cold wind began pushing flaming timbers, both large and small, into the air. We felt totally surrounded by fire, but our distance from the factory and the city probably saved our lives. During the whole ordeal we never lost a man at the camp or the factory. After the fire storm was over we found that only one bomb had landed in our camp—a dud, which was safely removed. We also found one at the factory. Unfortunately, a POW was ordered to remove it and in the process it exploded and killed him.

After the bombing we were all kept inside the camp for a couple of days. Then we were marched to the factory and put to work cleaning up.

One of the buildings that had been destroyed by fire was a potato shed with at least three or four hundred bushels of potatoes in it. I'm not sure why they were stored at the factory, but during the fire that destroyed the building, it burned all the potatoes on the top foot of the pile, and baked all the ones below. As hungry men, our sense of smell for food was unbelievably sharp, and one of us who had an even better nose than the others started crawling under debris that had cooled to find the source of the smell. He located the potatoes, coming up with a few, and soon we all started looking for our own. I got mine, and they tasted as good as any food that I have ever eaten.

Later in the day I found myself close to the potatoes once again. There were no Jap guards around and I was still so hungry, so I crawled through the debris to get some more potatoes. As I was coming out I was hit with something that almost knocked me unconscious. After my head started to clear, I could see a little Jap boy of about fourteen or fifteen years-old, holding a club and hollering for a Jap guard. One showed up and marched me to a small sheet metal building that had been put together after the bombing and had no top. Inside were about ten or twelve POWs standing at attention in the hot sun. I was ordered to join them.

I don't know how long they had been there. A Jap guard stood in back of them holding a small chain in his hand, and soon I would find out what the chain was for. After I began to stand at attention I could hear the Jap sergeant, who was standing in the shade, stirring some sort of liquid that sounded as if it had ice in it. After I had stood for about an hour, my head was really pounding from the clubbing I had received and the hot sun. I put my hand up to where I was hit and felt the large bump that had formed. Immediately after, I felt a severe pain in my back. The Jap in back of us hit me with the chain he was carrying, twice, and although I felt like I was going to collapse I found the strength to keep standing.

Victory!

In the first part of August, 1945, the Jap commander informed our commander that there would be no work because it was a Jap holiday. Then the next day was declared a Jap holiday, and the next. I was told later that Captain Thompson, our American Commander, pointed out to the Jap that he had never heard of three Jap holidays in a row, and that he wanted to know what was going on. The Jap commander then told Captain Thompson that the war was over.

Our American commander assembled all of us in front of the barracks for an announcement, and he told us that he had some good news for us. When he told us that the war was over there was silence for a moment, then we began to cheer. I felt immediate joy, but soon fear crept in as well. After all I had fought for had finally arrived, I was afraid that the Japs would find a way to take it all away somehow.

After everyone had settled down we were told that no one would be permitted to leave the camp and that our commander had assigned a POW to guard the gate to ensure that everyone stayed inside, for our protection. He said that he didn't want anything to happen to us and that he had ordered more food to be brought in. He asked us to be patient until we were freed by our troops.

We were dismissed and immediately began talking about when and how we would be liberated. We were hoping it would be soon, and as time passed we became more and more anxious. In two or three days our officers were able to get some white paint and about three or four of us went up on the roof and painted a big POW on it. The next day a fighter plane flew over us at about one thousand feet. We all saw him and began cheering, and after he was past us he turned and came back. This time he went no more than a hundred feet off the ground, wagging his wings and waving at us as he went over. He did this two or three times, with us cheering and waving the entire time. After he flew away I felt a sense of immediate loss, but I got over it quickly as I saw all the smiling, happy faces around me—something we hadn't seen in quite awhile.

The Japs had a truckload of food brought in, along with some Red Cross packages. This meal was the first time in three years when we were able to go back for seconds, and it was a great feeling to have as much food as you wanted. However, it made us madder at the Japs that they had given us this Red Cross food only after the war had ended. The Japs were also ordered to bring us some clothing, and a short time later a truck drove in the gate with a load of clothing and shoes. One of the two Japs on the truck was one that was especially hated by the POWs. One of the X-POWs, whose nickname was Gunner and whose last name, I believe, was Hoyt, ran toward the little Jap guard that he hated so much. He jumped on the truck and started hitting him and stuffing a shoe in his mouth. I am sure Gunner would have killed him if three or four other POWs hadn't pulled him off. The clothes were Jap uniforms, and although we hated to have to put them on, our clothes were so ripped that we had no other choice. That night we built a campfire outside the barracks and sat around it talking, waiting to see what the next day would bring.

The next day a fighter plane flew over once again, and this time he had something special for us. He flew over the camp a couple of times, and on the last pass he dropped a small parachute that floated down and landed in the camp. Everyone was anxious to see what he had dropped and we retrieved it immediately. A note and a few magazines were tied to it. The note said that there was much more on the way, and he wished us good luck and signed his name which was, as I remember, Lt. Hugh Batten, U.S.S. Aircraft Carrier Saratoga. The magazines were distributed one to a group, and as they were finished we switched so everyone could know what was said. Several different people would read a different article out loud, and it was like story time for little children. We were so hungry for news and to find out what was happening in a world we had known nothing about for the last four years. The more I heard the more anxious I was to go home.

A day or two after the parachute was dropped a larger plane flew over the camp two or three more times. On its last pass, three objects appeared in the sky. There were three parachutes and we could se the three men who hung in the harnesses. They landed in a field close to the camp and a detail was sent out to meet them. When they came in the camp we all began cheering. I wasn't expecting to see three men who looked so clean and well-clothed and healthy. For the last forty-two months I had been living with men in rags that were severely underfed and in poor health. When they were inside the camp our Camp Commander met them, and we all formed around them. It got very quiet as he introduced the three who had come to help us, and we soon found that they were very compassionate and capable.

The first one spoke to let us know that there would be many more supplies arriving, and he asked if there was anything he could do to help us. One of the POWs said yes; he had seen two hogs and a steer near the factory and he asked, if they were still there, if he could have them to butcher. The one in command said okay, and they put together a detail of POWs. All of the new arrivals were armed with .45 automatics, and after about two hours the detail returned, leading the steer and carrying two cleaned and dressed hogs. Shortly after they came back, the steer was shot and cleaned and the cooks started cooking. We were all delighted with the aroma and it was hard to wait for our first meal of fresh meat in years.

About a day after we received those wonderful gifts from the sky, we were to receive thousands more. It began when we heard a large plane, which flew over our camp once before making a large turn and heading back. We saw the bombay doors open, big objects falling, and parachutes opening. Some of them landed close to the camp and we all rushed out to see what they were. A group of us found a canister that was made with two fifty-five gallon barrels. They had cut both ends out and welded the two together and the finished canister was full of crates of food. The one I had the most taste for was peaches, but after I had consumed all I could hold I became sick to my stomach and started throwing up. When I had finished throwing up I just started eating more, eager and excited to be able to eat all that I could.

As a result of us getting all of the food we could eat, food that was much richer than we were used to, most of us had diarrhea. Food continued to fall from the sky at the rate of one or two plane loads per day for about three days. Just about every day we would have one or two carrier fighters fly over us and wag their wings. One day one of them had a malfunction and the plane crashed, killing the pilot. We were saddened because we felt a special closeness to these pilots who were the first to put us in contact with the outside world.

Despite the joy of being liberated, we experienced more sadness during this time. Two of our X-POWs violated the orders to stay in camp, and they went out of camp looking for alcohol to go with their food. They found some saki, but after a few drinks they were poisoned by it and died.

A day or so after their deaths I was outside the gate, looking at the bridge, and I saw that there was a group of Jap civilians walking to the factory. I was surprised and happy when I saw our old Jap boss among them, the one who had shared his food with us and had given us hope when he gave us information about the war being near the end. As soon as I saw him I approached him and motioned him to follow me into the camp. I could see he was nervous and because I wasn't fluent in Japanese I couldn't tell him why I was bringing him in. Once he was inside, however, and Moreanos also showed him the happiness he had to see him, our old Jap boss became happy and a smile came over his face. It was our turn to do something for him.

We took two blankets and laid them on top of each other and started piling on as much food as we could, so much that we were barely able to carry it. He folded the blankets and put a knot in them and we helped him carry the bundle halfway across the bridge. I wish I could share the name of this good, caring man, but we only called him boss in Japanese.

The next day we received the order that some of us would be flown out. I was surprised and euphoric to discover my name on the list, but I realized that it might have been the decision of the group leaders. Although we were all in bad shape, they might have though I should go first because my weight at the time was only one hundred and twenty pounds. I had gained some weight, however, from the food we received those two weeks. I was disappointed that Ted wasn't on the list, but when I laid down that night I still felt happy to know that the next day I would be on my way home.

Going Home

The next morning, when it was time to load on to a truck for our trip to the runway, I was glad I was leaving. However, it was still hard to say goodbye to my best friend, who I had been through so much with. Each of us said we would see each other again, but I now know that our goodbye would be the last time I would ever see Ted Schwarczynski.

We arrived at a short dirt runway that was very wet from the rain, and we were loaded onto what one of the POWs told us was a C-46. The planes that had bombed Toyama and the factory had all been B-29 bombers.

Shortly after we were on the plane it began to move; it was raining hard and I was sitting where I could see out of a small window in the direction that we were moving. All of a sudden I could see that we were approaching a fence, getting closer and closer. I thought we were going to hit it, but just before we got to it the pilot picked us up, and we just barely went over the top. We were flying for a little while when one of the crew told us that we were on our way to Tokyo.

After we had flown for awhile, we were out of the rain and I could see the ground. I don't recall seeing a single city that wasn't destroyed, nor do I recall how long it took us to make the trip. When we landed and taxied to a steel building we began to unload, in our Jap pants and hobnail shoes. We were walking to the hangar and several men in the Cavalry—I don't recall which unit—stood along the way. One of them was a brother to one of our X-POWs, and they had a very emotional meeting; I was touched by it and I knew that others were too.

We were in Tokyo for just a couple hours before we were boarded on a C-54 and flown to Okinawa, where we stayed for about three days. While we were there we were examined by a doctor and issued new American uniforms. The smallest size that they had was still too large for me, but it felt good to be back in an American uniform nonetheless. I was going to throw the Jap uniform away, but one of the men asked, "Why don't you keep them?" For some reason I did, and I still have them today.

We were there for about three days, and the mess hall was open to us twenty-four hours a day. We were told by the doctor that we could eat as often as we wanted but that we shouldn't eat too much at one time. When we left there I was carrying my things in a barracks bag, and it felt good to have more clothing than just what was on my back.

Our final flight was to Manila on a C-47. On our way I walked up to the cabin and was surprised at all the instruments that I saw. I was quietly standing there when the co-pilot looked around and saw me. He and the pilot and I all started talking to each other, and after about fifteen minutes I saw the pilot say something to the co-pilot. After they had finished talking, the co-pilot got out of his seat and asked me if I wanted to sit down while he went to relieve himself. I wasn't sure I should, but the pilot motioned for me to go ahead and sit down. After I was seated he asked me a few questions and I started asking him about all the instruments. About fifteen minutes later he told me to put on the headphones; I did, and I could hear conversations going on between other planes. After listening for a few minutes I took them off, and the pilot asked me if I wanted to fly the plane for a little while. I said sure, and he told me what I should do. When he told me I was flying the plane, I could feel it at once. I had difficulty maintaining level altitude; I would try to correct it, but fly too high, and we were up and down for about twenty minutes before he took over again. I turned around and saw one of the POWs standing behind me. With a smile he said, "No wonder all of us are sick."

When we arrived for our landing at Nichols Field, the pilot made the landing too hard. The plane bounced up and when it came down it hit hard a second time. We taxied to the hangar where we saw a bunch of pilots, all giving our pilot the thumbs down sign.

As soon as we were off the plane we were loaded on trucks and moved to a tent city near Manila. It was a very big one, and after we were assigned our tent we were shown where everything else was located. We received another physical and were told that the mess tent would be open twenty-four hours a day and that we could ask for anything that we wanted. If they had it, they would cook it for us. I only ate a couple of times other than at regular meals.

After having been there for about three days, I was talking to one of the X-POWs in the chow line and asked him if he knew a man by the name of Bob Travers. To my surprise he replied that he did; they were both in the same tent. He gave me the row number and the tent number, and as soon as I was finished eating I was on my way to see him. At his tent there was another X-POW sitting and listening to a record he was playing on a crank victrola. I will never forget it because he played it over and over, "Drinking Rum and Coca-Cola," by Frank Sinatra. I asked him if Bob was there and he said he wasn't, but he took me to his bunk where I sat down and waited for him.

When Bob came into the tent about half an hour later and saw me sitting on his bunk, he stopped and stared at me for a moment before asking, "Where did you come from? I heard you was dead." Then we started talking about what had happened to each of us since we had last seen one another, and we enjoyed our time talking and catching up.

Shortly after I had arrived in Manila, I learned that I was no longer Private Stark but Corporal Stark. Instead of making thirty dollars a month I was now making forty-five. I received a partial pay of about two hundred dollars, which was the first American money I had held since December of 1941, and it sure felt good.

We were in the tent camp for about two weeks, and every day I felt my clothes fitting me better and better as I slowly gained weight. I was getting very restless to go home and every day I waited, hoping to hear my name called. Finally I was told that I would be leaving on September 26, giving me about four days to wait, each one longer than the one before. When the day finally came and it was time to get on the truck I was excited and anxious to get moving toward home.

As we were driving through the city I was amazed at the amount of devastation. What surprised me the most was seeing how the Old Walled City had been destroyed. When we arrived at the pier and I saw the ship with the American flag flying it gave me a great feeling. We boarded and were assigned our quarters, and I found them completely full and clean, nothing like the hell ship "Mati, Mati, Maru" that I had been on only fourteen months before. We were now on a luxury liner. We got underway and were all excited until we passed between Bataan and Corregidor, which was a very sad time for me.

As I recall, the name of our ship was *The Joseph T. Dickman*. Onboard the ship we had the same freedom for food that we had had everywhere else, and after awhile I was able to start enjoying myself. I don't remember stopping in Hawaii, but the trip from Manila to the Golden Gate Bridge was eighteen days. Just before we arrived we were told that we would have to wait for awhile because there was no pier open. At first we were disappointed, but not for long, because soon we could see a small boat coming toward our ship. When it arrived we saw that it was about seventy-five feet long, loaded with a big band and performers. We were entertained for the next two hours while the band spent an hour playing on each side of the ship. When they were finished they circled the ship, waving as they pulled away.

Not long after they had gone we saw another ship approaching. As it went by we were all waving to each other, and it was only two and a half years later, through a conversation with him, that I learned that one of the waving men was likely my brother Bill, who was on his way to Japan as part of the Occupational Forces.

DARRELL D. STARK

OSAKA - OCTOBER 6, 1944

DEAR FAMILY,

I AM IN A NEW CAMP NOW, AND I LIKE
IT MUCH BETTER THAN THE LAST CAMP
WELL DAD I HAVE MY 21ST BIRTHDAY AND I HAVENT
FORGOT OUR BET, I WAS VERRY GLAD TO
RECEVE THE PACKAGE, AND LETTERS, TELL
ALL THE KIDS AND MY RELATIVES I STILL LOVE
THEM, AND, THANK OF THEAM AL THE TIME
. TELL EDD I WILL GET HIS BIRTHDAY
PRESENT WHEN I GET BACK. WELL I HOPE
YOU A VERRY MARRY XMAS AND A HAPPIER
NEW YEAR HOPE TO BE HOME SOON

LOVE TO ALL
DARRELL

This is an aerial
photograph of
Yokkaichi, Japan
prison camp taken
at the end of World
War II. This picture
was given to me by
Harold Vick, also
a former POW.

This is me and
Sergeant Emil
Crone in San
Francisco at the
end of the war.

Major Bell is standing
between two enlisted
service men. He was M
Company Commander
during the war. Colonel
Thompson is at the
far right in civilian
clothing. He was the
Commanding Officer
of L Company, and
I fought with him in
every battle. We were
prisoners together until
the end of the war.

These are the pants that were issued to me in Toyama,
Japan, prior to being granted my freedom.

These Japanese military shoes were also issued to me at that time.

TOP PANEL

DEAR SON HOPE YOU
WELL AND CAN SEE
YOU SOON BE GOOD
AND PRAY AND I WILL
LOVE FROM MOTHER
AND ALL

Loyd E. Wool
Medford Oregon

John N. Brown
Dixon Okla.

FRANK HARDY STARK
BAKERSFIELD CALIFORNIA
ROUTE 6 BOX 428

FROM (Sender's full name and address):

郵 俘
便 虜

PRISONER OF WAR POST
KRIEGSGEFANGENENPOST
SERVICE DES PRISONNIRS DE GUERRE

BAKERSFIELD
LAMONT
1945
4

POSTAGE FREE
GEBÜHRENFREI
FRANC DE PORT

INDICATE NATIONALITY OF PRISONER OF WAR | U.S. ☑ | BRITISH ☐ | CANADIAN ☐ | OTHER (Specify) ☐

NAME AND GRADE OF PRISONER OF WAR

PVT DARRELL D STARK

PRISONER OF WAR No.

ADDRESS

C-2 OSAKA

JAPAN

12328
U.S. CENSOR

VIA NEW YORK, N. Y.

#559 Skwarczynski, Ted | #563 Stark, Darrell D. Co. M 31st. Inf. Regt. | #267 Holly, | #510 Gregory, Romie Co. D. 31st. Inf. Regt.

All the names are below the pictures and they were
all in Prison Camp with me at Yokkaichi

#271 Johnson, Earl Hq. Co. 31st. Inf.Regt. | #255 Dunigan, Jim | #336 Van Brocklyn, | #352 Bond, Richard W. Co.L 31st. Inf. Regt.

All photographs were given to me by Wayne Lewis who is on this contact sheet.

#325 Gerlitz, Harry Co. H 31st. Inf. Regt. | #313 Cravitz | #319 Lewis, Wayne B. Co. D 31st. Inf. Regt. | Love, William R. . 31st. Inf. Regt.

WAR DEPARTMENT

THE ADJUTANT GENERAL'S OFFICE

IN REPLY
REFER TO
AG 201 Stark, Darrell D.

WASHINGTON

(1-6-43)PC-G

January 7, 1943.

Mrs. F.H.Stark,
    710 Menlo Avenue,
      Hantharne, California.

Dear Mrs. Stark:

    Reference is made to your letter of recent date, requesting information relative to your son, Private Darrell D. Stark, 18,050,363, who is being carried on the records of the War Department as missing in action in the Philippine Islands since May 7, 1942.

    The desire for news concerning your son is fully understood and I regret that no report has been received regarding his whereabouts. The War Department is receiving partial lists of prisoners of war through the International Red Cross, but to date the name of this soldier has not been found on any of the lists. I assure you that everything possible is being done to obtain information relative to the whereabouts and condition of United States Army personnel who were serving in the Philippines at the time of the surrender and when a report is received concerning Private Stark, you will be notified immediately.

    It is understood that the American Red Cross is accepting messages for delivery to persons who are carried as missing in action in the Philippines and that these messages must be submitted on forms furnished by the Red Cross. For further information relative to sending a message to your son, it is suggested that you contact your local chapter of the Red Cross giving grace, full name and Army serial number.

               Very truly yours,

               J.A.ULIO,
               Major General,
               The Adjutant General.

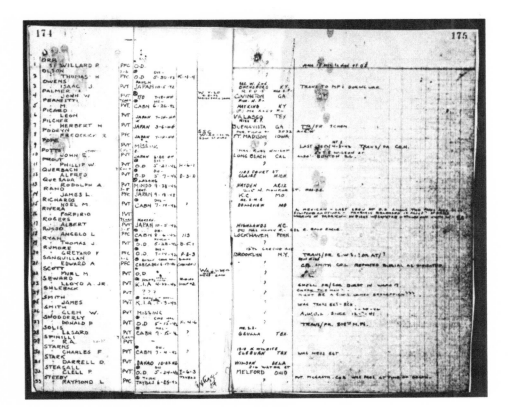

This Document was compiled by Col. Brady and other members of the 31st Infantry Regiment in secret, with a threat of death if they were discovered doing it. As to how they acquired the information to compile the document in detail as much as they did, I do not know. In attesting to the accuracy of this document, you will find my name third from the bottom, and I can certify that the information is absolutely correct. The document was preserved and buried at Cabanatuan prison camp before Col. Brady was killed being shipped to Japan. There is more detail to it, as the story will tell.

Below is a guide to reading the document

⊗	= Death
O.D.	= Camp O'Donnell
CABN	= Cabanatuan
KIA	= Killed in Action
W	= Wounded

As you will note the number of people listed on this document was 33, and of the number 20 had died just on this one page.

WAR CLAIMS COMMISSION
WASHINGTON 25, D. C.

Mr. Darrell D. Stark
Tolland, Conn.

AUG 4 1950

WCC Claim No. _P-11806_

Dear Sir:

    Your claim for benefits under Section __6__ of the War Claims Act of 1948, (Public Law 896, 80th Congress July 3, 1948), as amended, has been adjudicated, and an award in the sum of $__1247.00__ has been made to you ~~xxx~~ _____ to cover the period of imprisonment and/or internment, etc., of __yourself__ from _____9 April 1942_____ to _____6 Sept. 1945_____. These dates were determined after comparing the statements contained in your application and supporting evidence with official records on file in the War Claims Commission. A check for the amount of this award will be mailed to you by the Treasury Department.

    Pursuant to the War Claims Act of 1948, as amended, and regulations issued thereunder, a claimant may appeal the disallowance of a claim, in whole or in part, within six months from the date of the award letter. Persons desiring to appeal should request, in writing War Claims Commission Form 1105, which should be filled out, signed and returned promptly. Address all communications to the War Claims Commission, Washington 25, D. C.

                        Very truly yours,

                        Frank W. Barton

                        Frank W. Barton
                        Director, Claims Service

WCC Form 307
Revised Apr. 27, 1950

The Governor of the

STATE OF OKLAHOMA

In recognition of military service in defense of our Country and in profound acknowledgment of the privation of the birthright of freedom endured as a prisoner of war, the People of the State of Oklahoma have decreed that the

OKLAHOMA CROSS OF VALOR

be awarded to

Darrell D. Hark

Now therefore, as Governor of the State of Oklahoma, by virtue of the authority vested in me by the laws of the State of Oklahoma do hereby make this award in meritorious acclaim and recognition of valiant service rendered, as a member of the Armed Services, to our State and Nation that our people may remain free.

IN WITNESS WHEREOF, I have hereunto set my hand and caused the Great Seal of the State of Oklahoma to be affixed, on this *first* day of *March*, in the year of our Lord Nineteen Hundred and *Eightyfour* and the Independence of the United States of America.

BY THE GOVERNOR OF THE STATE OF OKLAHOMA

George Nigh

ATTEST

Jeannette B. Edmondson
Secretary of State

My dear Mr. Stark.

It has five years passed since
I saw you last. Now and then
recollecting at that time,
I feel yearning for you so much.
I am living the dreary life
since. I have lost my older
child last summer.
I have long wanted to write to
you, but please excuse me for
my long silence.
I future Japan existe on your
Kind helps. I am sure that
you will give me your Kind
guidance and friendship and
I hope they will be lasting
forever.
Wishing you many happyness
heartily yours affectionately.

8th march 1950
                    N. Nakahara.

              8. Suehiro cho
              yokkaichi city
                    Japan.

N. NAKAHARA.
8. SUEHIROCHO
YOKKAICHI JAPAN.

          MR. DARRELL D. STARK.
          c/o MRS. HARRY S. STARK
           660 EAST REGENT ST.
          INGLEWOOD CALIFORNIA

               U. S. A.

56 Saint Charles St
West Hartford Ct 06119
10-5-98

Dear Darrell,

Due to the circumstances surrounding our tour of duty in the Philippines. I thought that I should write to you and try to shed some light on the time we were confined at the prisoner of war compound located at Clark Air Field in the Philippines. I was in this POW camp about three months before you arrived there. We were housed in buildings erected just prior to the start of the war for new troop arrivals. These buildings were constructed of tar paper roofs, woven bamboo sides, and wood floors. No windows doors or screens. The buildings were standing about 4 feet above the ground on concrete posts. We slept on the bare wooden floors in rows 20 inches of space per each individual. If you happened to be so lucky to have a army blanket so much the better. Our diet was very meager at Clark. We received the amount of cooked rice you could put in a tea cup twice a day. The American doctors stated that our diet amounted to 800 calories per day. Definitely causing slow starvation.

Clark Field POW camp was a work camp. If a individual was to sick to work, he was transferred back to the main POW compound, Cabanatuan. In your case Darrell, you were being consumed by malaria fever. I recall some of your buddies from the 31st Infantry, sitting beside you all night putting wet cloths on you head to try to keep the high fever down. Well Darrell, we survived this ordeal, but not without recurring physical problems. Our only alternative available then was extinction. Take care, your friend.

Sincerely Yours

Everett Green

This picture was presented to Judy and I on our
sixtieth wedding anniversary in 2006.

PL   3 May 1949

TO WHOM IT MAY CONCERN:

                It has come to my attention that Mr.
Darrell D. Stark of Tolland is seeking appointment to a position
of trust and responsibility at the Tolland County Jail.

                I wish to make a brief statement in his behalf
as his friend and as a resident of Tolland County for the past 35 years.

                Mr. Stark first came to my notice as a veteran
of World War II when he visited the Manchester Service Center of which
I was Director for two and one-half years. He was a frequent visitor
there, and because of the nature of his problems we became well-acquainted.
I know him to be a mature, sensible young man, ready and able to take on
responsibilities of a serious nature. His war experience was especially
harrowing and the fact that he survived with a sense of humor and a
minimum of bitterness is much to his credit. It is my belief that he
possesses the qualities of leadership, devotion to duty, and stability
which will render him a good public servant in the position for which he
is being considered.

                Although he has not lived long in Tolland County, Mr.
Stark married Miss Julia Ridson of Tolland and with their two children plans
to remain there permanently. If his appointment is approved, I feel that
we can say without fear of contradiction that we are giving this position
to a worthy resident of our county.

                It is a pleasure to make this statement in his
behalf. He served his country well; we can do no less for him.

                                NATHAN B. GATCHELL,
                                Lt Colonel, 169th Inf.
                                G-3, State of Connecticut.

The staff at the
Tolland County Jail
in Tolland, Ct.

Me and Pop
Schofield
bird hunting
in Nebraska,
with my two
bird dogs.

Our home that I built
fifty years ago.

My mother-in-law
and father-in-law
Andrew and Mary
Ridzon.

Our wedding picture
in 1946.

Our home in winter.

United States Department Of Justice
BUREAU OF PRISONS

Jail Management Institute

This is to certify that

DARRELL STARK

has satisfactorily completed the

Jail Management Course

conducted at

Hartford, Connecticut

January 17-21, 1966

JAIL INSPECTION SERVICE

ASSISTANT DIRECTOR

DIRECTOR, BUREAU OF PRISONS

Part Four

Leaving the Military and Joining Family Life

Finally! Back on American Soil

Approaching the Golden Gate Bridge made me realize how close I was to finally being home. As we were sailing under it, one of my friends looked up and said, "With our luck, let's just hope the bridge doesn't collapse on us."

When the ship reached Pier #7 we sat, docked, waiting for all the preparations to be made for us to go ashore. Bob Travers, Ladue and I were standing by the rail when I heard Bob say, "Look! There's Captain Bell." He pointed him out, saying, "He's the one on crutches."

When I spotted him, I was as excited as Bob and Ladue were. We started yelling to get his attention, and when he heard us he looked up and waved, yelling that he would see us when we got off the ship.

The three of us stayed together, and when we got off the gangplank we got out of line and went to him, saluting. He put his hand out and we all shook hands, and we were able to talk for a short while. He told us how he tried to be dockside for every ship that came in with X-POWs on it. He said that he had only met with eleven of us from M Company thus far. We had to cut our conversation short in order to get our transportation to our first stop in the good old U.S. of A.

As we moved toward Letterman General Hospital, I felt happiness mixed with a lot of anxiety. We arrived at the hospital and were housed in large barracks as we awaited various examinations. Shortly after we arrived we were put in contact with the American Red Cross who helped me get in touch with Mother and Daddy through Uncle Hawley and Aunt Evelyn's phone number. When they contacted them I was handed the phone, and when I put it to my right ear I discovered I was deaf. When I couldn't hear I handed the phone to the Red Cross person, who told me to try it in my other ear. I did, and finally I could hear Aunt Evelyn.

During our short conversation she was able to tell me that Mother and Daddy had moved to California and that they lived in Shafter. She gave me their address and told me that they didn't have a phone. The lady who was helping me said, "You stay here, because I am going to get someone from your family on a phone." She made a few phone calls and told me to just be patient, that someone would call back as soon as they could get a member of my family. I was told it would take about an hour, and I was very impatient to talk to Mother and Daddy. I was also a little nervous because so many years had gone by without any communication between us.

When the phone rang I was startled. The woman from Red Cross answered it and talked for a moment before giving me the phone. I heard a voice on the other end say that my Mother was there, waiting to speak to me. I felt my pulse quicken as I waited to hear from a member of my family.

When Mother came to the phone, I could tell that she was having a hard time controlling her emotions, and I was too. It was so nice just to hear her soft voice and to know that I was safe again. We talked about how scary it had been, and she told me that Bill had gone into the Army now. She said she wanted to come and see me, but I told her no, not now, because I was going to be moved to a hospital closer to home. After we hung up, I became more and more anxious to be home and see my family again. When I got back to quarters, I told my friend Dotson, a friend for four years, about my conversation with Mother and about how she wanted to come and see me. He asked, "Why don't we go see her?" but I told him no, that I was going to wait until I was moved closer to home.

While we were at Letterman we were issued passes to go out and enjoy ourselves. With our first pass we went out to hit a few bars, where I saw beautiful American women and listened to live bands playing music we had never heard before. It was a completely different world to me, a stark contrast to the world I had been living in, and I enjoyed every minute of it.

At the same time, there were things that had happened that gave me a deep sense of loss. Friends I had been with for years were being sent closer to home, and as each one left I felt that I was never going to be able to see them again. I remained at Letterman for another ten days, and I was able to talk to Mother a couple of times during my stay. While I was there, waiting to leave, I had to say goodbye to Dotson and other friends.

Finally, it was my turn to leave. I was put on a train with other soldiers and a nurse and transferred to Van Nuys Army Hospital. I was there for two days when I was issued a seven day pass. As soon as I was issued the pass I called Uncle Hawley. He heard my voice and said, "Darrell! God damn boy, where are you?" I told him I was at Van Nuys Army Hospital with a seven day pass, and before I could say anything else he said, "Me and Evelyn and Hank and Ora will be out there to pick you up as soon as we can!"

Two or three hours later, they arrived, and I saw the first members of my family. It was a feeling of complete and pure joy to be reunited with them once again. After everyone had settled down we went to the car for the upcoming three hour drive. We all had a lot of questions for each other, and they all told me I looked good, which I guess I did by then—I had regained sixty or sixty-five pounds.

The closer we got to Shafter, California, the more nervous I became. We arrived after dark and had a hard time finding the right address. We stopped at a house to ask directions, and when I got out I was confronted by a large, vicious-looking dog on the way to the door. The dog held me at bay until a man came to the door, but when I told him what I wanted he went with me to the car to point out where the house was. We were at Mother and Daddy's in about five minutes.

My uncles and aunts stayed in the car while I went to the door. I knocked, and Daddy opened the door and hollered, "Darrell!" I went in to find my whole family, except for Bill, inside. They smothered me with hugs and kisses. After the joyous reunion with hugs and kisses all around we sat and talked after the young kids had gone to bed. My uncles and aunts stayed and visited for awhile too, but after they left the situation became more difficult. My family and I had been away from each other for so long and everyone had changed so much in the years since I had been gone; it was like I didn't recognize my family. My sister Jean, who was a fifteen year-old girl when I left, had matured into a woman of twenty. Ray, only an eleven year-old boy of about four and a half feet, had grown into a sixteen year-old young man, six feet tall. Ed and Pat had grown, but my little brother Bud, only three when I left, had changed the most. He was eight, and no longer the baby I had left behind but a tall, tow-headed boy. The biggest surprise of all was that I now had a baby sister who was three and a half years-old; this was the first I knew of my little sister Carol June. Mother and Daddy had also aged, but they still had the same loving look in their eyes that I had left behind.

None of us knew what to say. We had endured such pain being apart that it was hard to know how to put it into words. As we were sitting quietly, I found myself looking at them and thinking of all that had happened and all that had changed. Suddenly I was engulfed by my emotions and I broke down; I started to cry there at the table, and it took me awhile to control myself. When I was able to look up, I could see that all of them were standing around me, crying as well. After that, it became easier to talk to one another, as though some invisible barrier had been lifted.

The next morning I awoke to find Mother making biscuits and gravy with fried salt pork. We were all eating and enjoying each other's company, and I felt things loosen up so that we were able to have a more relaxed conversation. Mother and Daddy never asked me about my war experiences for the rest of their lives. After we had finished eating Daddy and Jean went to work and the rest of the kids went off to school, leaving just Mother, Carol June and I. I hated to see all the others leave for the day, but it gave me a chance to get acquainted with my little sister and to talk to my mother. While I was there for seven days I had a chance to use Daddy's old car and drive around the area. It was a desert that had been turned into farmland with irrigation. It was wonderful to get in a car and start driving again, and instead of driving alone I liked to take Carol and Bud with me. By the time my seven days were up we were all starting to get to know each other a lot better, and I enjoyed the fun times I was able to have with my family during that week.

I returned to the hospital, where I was treated for internal parasites. While I was at Letterman or Van Nuys I received a psychological examination that consisted of these four words: "How do you feel?" My answer was "good," and that was the end of my psychological examination.

"Good," was the only answer I could give. After what I had endured for so long, the medical treatment and kindness that I was receiving was good, and a welcome change. However, I would later realize that I should have been examined in more depth.

I was at Van Nuys for awhile, but I would get weekend passes and Uncle Hawley would pick me up so I could visit with them, as well as Uncle Odd and Aunt Ivy, Uncle Cleatus and Aunt Eva and Uncle Carl and Aunt Myrte. It was near Christmas time, so I spent some of my money buying presents for the family and storing them at Uncle Hawley and Aunt Evelyn's home. They were there when I was released from the hospital to temporary duty at home.

I also received most of my back pay at this time, and when I returned to Mother and Daddy's house I went shopping for a car. I bought a 1936 Ford convertible—my first car and a beauty in my eyes. The money I had left over went into a bank account at Uncle Henry's urging, and this was another first for me.

Not long after I bought my car it was Christmas, and Daddy, my brother Ray and I were on our way to Uncle Hawley's when one of the most wonderful things in my life happened, albeit in a most unlikely fashion.

The lights on my car went out, and I pulled over off the road to see if we could try and get them working again. I checked to see if anyone was coming before stepping out of the car, but I couldn't see any headlights approaching. I was just closing the door when I was hit by a drunk driver, driving in a car with no headlights. I wasn't knocked unconscious, but I could tell right away that I had been seriously hurt. In a few minutes a car stopped and the driver asked what he could do to help. Daddy instructed him to go to a phone and call the Van Nuys Army Hospital to tell them that a soldier had been hurt and needed an ambulance. We were just a short distance from the hospital, and it wasn't long before an ambulance arrived. I was able to walk to the ambulance on my own, where I laid down in the stretcher, but by the time we got to the hospital I was unable to get up, so they carried me in. I was examined, and they found that I had broken my arm along with other internal injuries.

It seems a story that is unlikely to have the wonderful ending that I claim, but it does. I remember little from my time in Van Nuys, although I do have vague memories of Mother and Jean coming to visit me. During my recovery Van Nuys was closed, and all of us were moved to Dibble General Hospital in Palo Alto, California, where my unfortunate accident took a turn for the better. In the Dibble General Hospital I met my wife, Julia Ridzon, a nurse's aid in the Army. She was only going to be in California for a few more weeks before she returned home to Tolland, Connecticut. In that time we got to know one another, and before she went home she accepted my marriage proposal. We agreed that I would meet her in Connecticut as soon as I could.

Prior to my release from the hospital, I sold my '36 Ford and bought a 1941 Ford Convertible as well as four brand new tires. As soon as I was released from the hospital I was on my way to Connecticut to be with Judy.

On my way I stopped in Oklahoma to visit with Mammy, Uncle Tom and Uncle Pete. I also stopped in Asher and had a nice visit with some of my friends. When I left Asher I drove out to Tulsa, and just after getting on Route 66 I saw a soldier on the side of the road, thumbing for a ride.

I stopped to pick him up and he told me he was going to St. Louis. I told him that I was going to Connecticut.

He then told me that he was actually going to New York City. He had put his wife and his baby on a bus in San Francisco but he was hitchhiking because he didn't have enough money for a ticket for himself. After his wife and baby boarded he had gotten to the highway, where he waited only five minutes before a man picked him up and brought him all the way to Tulsa. He and the man he had ridden with had just finished eating when I came by to pick him up. I dropped him off at his apartment in New York and he told me how to get to the Merritt Parkway, which would take me almost all the way to Hartford. I was on my way to Judy on a four lane highway, only the second one that I had traveled on all the way across the United States—the other was the Pennsylvania Turnpike.

After driving for awhile, the day was so pleasant that I stopped and put the top down in order to see more of the beautiful scenery. The further north I drove the more I loved it. By the time I arrived in Tolland, Connecticut, the town where Judy had been born, I had completely fallen in love with the fall foliage, the stone walls and the beautiful green landscape.

I stopped at a house to get directions, asking if they knew where Andrew Ridzon lived. I was told that it was the next house up, on the left, so I drove the three hundred yards and I was at the house. I drove up the driveway and up to the front door to knock. A lady came to the door and I introduced myself, asking if this was where Andrew Ridzon lived. Before she could answer me, Judy appeared at the door. When I saw her, I was as happy as I have ever been in my life. After we got over the joy of seeing each other again she introduced me to her sister-in-law, Jane, who was her brother Andy's wife. After a short visit with her, Judy and I got in my car and drove up to her father's dairy farm.

I don't recall who was there, although I think it was her mother, grandmother and younger brothers, Mick and Danny. After we were there for awhile her father came in, and I was introduced to him. We talked for awhile and he asked me, "You know anything about cows?" I told him that I knew just a little, and he replied, "You come with me."

In my clean clothes, I followed him into the barn. When we got inside I was surprised to see the size of the barn. He took me to a pen where I saw a cow lying down, and he walked around to the back of her, putting his hand inside as far as he could reach. He was working as hard and as fast as he could, and he told me that the calf was breached. Finally, he was able to pull two of its feet out far enough to tie a rope to the two legs. He gave me the rope and said, "When I say pull, you pull." He knelt down and put his arms back in again before telling me to pull. I started pulling, but not too hard because I was afraid I would pull the legs off. He looked up at me and asked, "Is that as hard as you can pull? Pull as hard as you can!" Shortly after, we were able to get the calf out. It was dead, but we were able to save the cow. After the birthing was done, Judy's father, a man of only 5'2", looked up at me, smiled, and stuck out his short, stubby hand. I took it in mine and he looked up at me and said, "You a good boy." From that time on, we loved one another.

Judy's mother and father were called Ma and Pop, and her grandmother was Mamo. The three of them had come over from Czechoslovakia in 1916, Ma and Mamo through Ellis Island and Pop and his father through Canada. Pop and Ma were married in Youngstown, Ohio shortly after they arrived, and Pop worked as a coal miner and a steel mill worker. In Ohio they had their two oldest children, Andy and Mary. Pop had always wanted to be a dairy farmer, and when he heard about a 114 acre farm in Connecticut with a good house and a barn for $1,400.00, he purchased it and realized his dream; the year was 1919. That is where Sue, Helen, Julia, Edie, Bill, Edward and Danny were born. Pop started his herd of purebred Ashure cows with only one cow, and with hard work he was able to build a herd of about fifty.

A Discharge, a Wedding, a Career

Judy and I were married on Christmas Day, 1946, and by then I had received my order to report to Fort Dix, New Jersey, which was what forced the quick wedding. I was to report for discharge, and we thought the trip would be a chance to have our honeymoon. After we were married at the Lutheran Church in Stafford Springs we had one night at home, and the next morning we boarded the train in Hartford for our ride to Trenton, New Jersey, then on to Ft. Dix. When we arrived Judy was put in a guesthouse and I was assigned to the barracks. When I went to see her we weren't allowed to be alone, so it wasn't really the honeymoon we had hoped for.

We were there long enough for our money to get short, and I was starting to get a little worried when luck played in my favor again. The barracks I was in were heated with coal, and they had new recruits that took care of them. On a very cold night they let the fire go out and everyone was covering their heads, trying to stay warm. During the night someone went through the barracks and stole every dollar he could get his hands on. I had my pants on the foot of my bed with my billfold in the pocket, and I was awakened by someone I didn't know who shoved me my billfold and said, "this is yours."

I asked him, "What the hell are you doing with it?"

He replied, "Don't get mad at me. We all got ripped off last night."

In the mess hall the next morning I was talking about what had happened and the poor financial situation I was in, being a newly-wed to boot. To make matters worse, I found out that I wasn't even on the roster to be discharged. Someone told me that I should try to go to the Red Cross to see if they could help me. After breakfast I located the Red Cross and told them my problem, asking if I could possibly get a loan. They said that they couldn't give me a loan, but they could see to it that I was discharged that day. After a few phone calls and a note saying that I could go to the front of every line, I was discharged in time for Judy and I to catch the last bus to Trenton. From there we were able to catch a train back home to Connecticut.

We lived with Ma and Pop for awhile while I worked at Pratt and Whitney on the night shift for seventy-five cents an hour and during the day for an old lady who owned a gas station. When I had time I would help Pop on the farm. One morning when Pop was having his coffee he asked me, "D, do you know anything about building?" I responded, "No, why?" He told me that he needed an addition built on the old barn to store the wood shavings that he used as bedding for the cows. He wanted me to build it, and he would help me out when he had the time. When I told him that I had never built anything in my life, he said, "It's okay, D, you learn." With that, I set to work building a cinderblock storage room, about eight by eighteen feet, which took about three months of part time work. I didn't do the best job in the world, but when I had finished I had a new kind of confidence that would stay with me for the rest of my life.

Shortly after I had finished, Pop said, "I am going to give you and Judy an acre of land to build a house on." I was grateful for his offer, and excited by it. I felt that this was about the best thing I could receive, because all I had ever owned in my life was two cars; the thought of owning a house was a great feeling. I knew everything would be okay, and I never had another doubt about it.

After Pop had given us the land, I went to work laying out where I wanted to put our little three-room home, which would grow into five rooms. I was anxious to get it finished because Judy was pregnant with our first child, and with the help of my brother-in-law Andy, we were able to finish it before our son, Darrell Wayne, was born on June 24, 1947. He was born premature and stayed in an incubator for six weeks before he came home. During that time I had to quit my job at Pratt and Whitney; for some reason, which at the time I couldn't understand, whenever I walked into a building I felt trapped and confined.

As soon as I quit I went to work for the New York, New Haven and Hartford Railroad as a brakeman. I worked there for about eighteen months before being laid off, at which time I tried selling Watkins products for a short while. That ended up costing me money, so I had to find a new job once again. I didn't want to work in a factory again because I couldn't bear the thought of experiencing the feelings of confinement that had caused me to leave Pratt and Whitney. The only job I could find to pay the bills was at the American Screw Company in Willimantic, but I was able to cope with the conditions there, perhaps because of the work I was doing. I was working in the tool and die department, which was very challenging work, and it made it easier for me to ignore the feelings that had caused me to leave Pratt and Whitney.

During the early part of my married life, I also had a lot of Army records that had to be straightened out. At that time there were a lot of World War II veterans that were in the same condition, and as a result the Veteran's Administration set up a temporary service center to take care of the overload. I was assigned to the one in Manchester and, unbeknownst to me, this would lead me to a career that would take me through the rest of my life.

I was happy with my work at the American Screw Company, and I told Judy that I liked my job and planned to stay there. Only one day after we had had that conversation, Judy told me that Mr. Ford from the V.A. had called me with a job offer. I asked her what the job was and she told me it was as a Deputy Jailer for the Tolland Jail.

I responded adamantly: "What? But I just got out of being a prisoner of the Japs for three and a half years!"

Judy replied only, "He told me you would say that." She let me know that I had been driving by the jail almost every day at its location on the Tolland Green, then she added, "Mr. Ford wants you to call him back, no matter what." She told me that she wished that I would take the job because they had built a brand new house for the Deputy Jailer, which would be a nice perk for us. I called Mr. Ford back and he was able to convince me to at least talk to someone about the job, and once I agreed to that he informed me that Chief Deputy Sheriff Paul Sweeney would be calling me.

Not long after that I received a phone call from Sheriff Sweeney. He set up an appointment for me and I went to the jail for the interview. I was a little nervous, but when I arrived at the office and met with Chief Deputy Sweeney and the jailor, Ernest Peterson, I became more relaxed. I learned that the Deputy Jailor job also included Farm Superintendant. They asked me if I knew anything about farming and I answered, "No, but I can milk a cow." They replied, "That's okay; you'll learn."

After about half an hour Sheriff Sweeney told me that he would talk to High Sheriff Rob Hyde and get back to me. I went back home and worked and waited for three days, and on the third day Sheriff Sweeney drove to my house where we talked for awhile. He told me that I had the job, and the next day I went to work at the Screw Company and gave my two weeks notice.

I was told that we could start moving in anytime we wanted and that we could use the jail farm tractor and trailer, and could also use the inmates to help us move. We moved the next day after I got off work. It didn't take long because we didn't have much, but everything turned out great. While I was working out my notice at the Screw Company I was also learning about the operations of the jail and my job as Farm Superintendent.

The farm consisted of 114 acres about a mile from the jail as well as an additional acre that was right next to the jail. The area next to the jail was used for a pig sty and coops, one for chickens and one for turkeys, as well as a kitchen garden and a barn for storing hay and for milking cows during the winter. In the summer the cows were moved to the larger main farm for pasture and were milked there.

Again, luck came my way. We had an inmate come in just after I was hired with a one-year sentence. He had a degree in agriculture and it was planting time, so I put him to work as soon as I could and he came to be my farming teacher. He taught me how to improve the land, how to plant and fertilize, when to use insecticides, when and how to hay and how to get information from the Farm Borough for Tolland County. When I was there the jail farm was about seventy-five percent self-supporting. We produced most of our food, and as the farm began to improve we were able to raise more cows and were able to sell some every year. Judy was my main support, but I also found that the farm work, as well as working with people who were deprived of their freedom, also helped me to adjust and cope with some of the problems that came as a result of my war experiences.

My beginning salary was $125 per month plus everything that we needed to care for our family, minus furniture. When we moved to the jail we had two children, Darrell Wayne and our first daughter, Darlene, who had been born on April 2, 1949. Our youngest daughter, Judy-Gail, was born while we were living at the jail, on April 11, 1951.

I had been working at the jail for about a year when Mr. Peterson resigned. In 1951 Mr. George Schofield was hired to replace him. He and I worked together for about five years, and I learned a lot from him about farming and preserving food. Our families got to be very close and we had a wonderful relationship with them that remains strong after all these years. He and his wife, whom we called Ma, were like a mother and father to us. During the time I worked with Mr. Schofield our son, whom we called Butch, and our daughter, Darlene, started school in Tolland.

In 1955 Pop Schofield resigned and took a job as a jailer at the Hadden Jail. When he left, High Sheriff Sweeney asked me if I would take the job as jailer. I told him I would let him know; with only an eighth-grade education, I wasn't sure if I felt qualified for the job. I told Judy about my reservations, but she told me, "You take the job. I know you can do it." The next day when Sheriff Sweeney came in to the jail I told him I would take the job. After I accepted, we moved for the second time.

We moved from the Deputy Jailer's house to the Jailers' Quarters, a huge house that was attached to the jail and included the offices. While Pop Schofield was there the Tolland County Jail had taken on a new responsibility as Control Dispatcher for the Tolland County Mutual Aid. During that time we controlled the dispatching for two of the biggest fires ever in Tolland County, the Meniburn Mill in Rockville and the Stafford Hotel. We also did the dispatching during the flood of 1955.

After I was hired as a jailer the Sheriff hired George Cook, who had previously been the Jailer, as my assistant. He only worked with me for a few months before he resigned, and afterwards the Sheriff asked me if I knew anyone else that would be a good Deputy Jailer. I told him no, but I would try and find someone. The next day I went to see Mr. Roy Dimmock to see if one of his sons would be interested in the job. He said no, but his daughter Shirley had just married a young man who had just been discharged from the service and if he was interested he would be a good man for the job. Sheriff Sweeney and I discussed it, and he told me to have a talk with him. If he was interested and I thought he was a good man for the job, I was to set up a time for him to talk with us and we would hire him.

I interviewed him and then he met with me and the Sheriff together, and Richard Hills was hired as my assistant. His wife, Shirley, became a matron with Judy. Richard worked with me until Sheriff Sweeney, who was a Republican, lost the election to Democrat Nickolas Pawluk. After the election there were several months before the change took place and neither Richard nor I were asked to stay. Once again, it was time to look for a new job. The job I pursued was as a Guard for the State Prison. I filled in the application, took the exam, and was interviewed and ready to take the job. However, the evening before the change of administration, Sheriff Pawluk came over to the jail and asked me to stay. I agreed, but he said he was replacing Richard.

I wanted to keep Richard; he was very capable and he and I worked well together, but he was replaced and had found a job with the state. His replacement came, but I was sure that he wasn't the man for the job. I told Sheriff Pawluk why I thought he wasn't suited for the job, and suggested the possibility of having Richard come back and having his replacement take his job with the state. After some maneuvering we were able to have him back, and he and I worked together for about six years, until 1960, when the County Government was abolished and the County Jails became State Jails.

After the law was passed we had about two years before it took effect. During that time, Richard and I received a huge expression of appreciation for the work we had done for Tolland County. Under the county there were no benefits for retirement, so the County Commissioners decided to take some of the money that they had been saving to build a new jail and establish a retirement plan for Richard and me. The plan was in compliance with the state plan for State Police and Prison Guards, which meant that we could retire after twenty years, at the age of forty-seven, at fifty percent of our highest three years salary. When the County Commissioner and the County Attorney General finished the plan it was retroactive to the date of employment. So when I became a state employee I started with eleven years of retirement.

When the state took over, my salary with the county was six hundred dollars a month with full maintenance. It was more under the state, although not much more—I don't recall exactly how much. Under the state my title of Jailer changed to Lieutenant, and Richard went from Deputy Jailer to Sergeant. It was to remain that way until 1964 when they changed the title again from Lieutenant to Captain. During that time I was made aware that I needed at least a High School diploma, so I enrolled in night school at Rockville High and earned my GED.

Prior to the change of title, the small jails had an open examination for the position of Captain, so I decided to take it and try and see if I could pass. About thirty people took the written exam, and I passed with the highest mark of the group. I was overjoyed at the result and proud of myself for my achievement. I was offered the prime position at Montville, but refused it because I didn't want to move. In 1964 they changed the title for small jails to Captain, and I had to take the exam again and pass it in order to stay at the position I had already been in for so many years. Well, forgive me, but it's time to brag again—I not only passed, but came out first for the second time and remained in the Tolland Department.

About a year later the state changed titles again, this time from Sergeant to Lieutenant and Richard had to take that exam. He also passed, and remained at Tolland for about a year before he was transferred to Brooklyn Jail. After his transfer he made Captain and was finally promoted to Warden, where he remained until his retirement. When he transferred to Brooklyn, Sergeant Donald Cartier became my assistant until another exam was open for Lieutenant. After the exam one of my staff, Henry DaDalt, passed it and became my assistant until Tolland Jail closed in 1968. During that time, Henry and his family became friends with ours and we still remain very good friends with Henry and Marge and their three girls, Hope, Robin and Beth.

In closing this part of my life, I want to take a moment to thank my staff. Most of my small staff was able to make rank, and whether they made rank or not I was honored to have worked with them. I would also like to express my thanks to the State Police and the firemen for Tolland County; I am thankful that I was able to meet all of them when the Tolland County Jail was made the headquarters for Tolland County Mutual Aid. The small house that Judy and I moved to fifty-seven years ago is now the headquarters, and the old jail later became a historical building. The State of Connecticut sold the jail and the 114 acre farm to the Town of Tolland for one dollar. The Tolland High School is now located on what was once the jail farm.

Before I close, I would first like to go back to 1958, after the law was passed to abolish the County Government. I knew I would lose all the living maintenance and that I would have to start making arrangements for a place to live once the state took over. I started looking for a piece of land that would be large enough for a house for my family and large enough to have land left over to give our children once they were ready for it. I found eighteen acres for sale in Stafford for $2,200, and we bought it. As soon as it was ours I started cutting down trees on the land for lumber to build our new house. After it had cured for awhile, my brother-in-law Bill and I started building. By the end of 1958 we had the house finished at a cost of $12,500. Judy's sister, Sue, moved in until we were ready to move in 1960, and that is the house we continue to live in today.

In 1968 the jail was closed and I was assigned to the large jail in New Haven as Deputy to the Warden. When the Warden left the job I was asked to take his position. I refused because I did not want to move from Stafford; it was a seventy mile drive, but the state gave me a car and asked me to fill in as acting Warden for thirty days until they could find a replacement. Finally, I agreed, just for thirty days.

Thirty days went by, and they asked me to stay for another thirty. This happened a few times, and every time they would ask me to just take over the position permanently. I was becoming frustrated, and finally it was time for me to do something. I called Mr. Manson and requested that he find someone to replace me because I was going on vacation for thirty days and when I returned I wanted a position closer to home. I didn't want to use my vacation because I could get paid for it when I retired, but I felt it was my only choice. When I retired I still had sixty days on the books along with 120 days of sick time.

During the thirty days, Judy and I and our three children went to California to visit my family, as we did every other year since I had begun working at the old Tolland Jail. After we returned I went to Hartford and talked with Mr. Manson, and he told me that he thought he had a position I would enjoy. He told me that the Commissioner was going to begin a Transportation Department and that he would like me to organize and supervise it. I would be working out of the Maximum Security Prison in Somers and I would draw my staff from there.

I told him that I would take the position because it sounded as though it was something that I would enjoy doing, and it was only about twelve miles from our house. It turned out to be a challenging job, and the biggest challenge came during the race riots of 1970. In 1971 I decided to retire; after my application was approved I had been with the County and the State for twenty-two years. Between that and my six years of military service, I retired at sixty-six percent of my pay. Upon my retirement I was honored at a small party given by the prison guards who had worked for me in Transportation as well as at a large party that Henry DaDalt arranged. They presented me with a new monogrammed Remington shotgun and a membership in the Italian-American club. Most of all, I was honored by all the people that came. They came from the Department of Corrections, the State and Local Police and the Fire Department, as well as many friends who came from their work in other vocations.

Retired

Shortly before I retired, Judy and I bought a motor home. Before we were to use it as a family, I had to fulfill a promise I had made to a boy who had lost his father before he entered high school. He was Dale Clarke, my little buddy who would work my bird dogs when he went along hunting with me. Before he entered high school I told him that if he got good grades in school and stayed out of trouble I would bring him to Nebraska to go pheasant hunting. When I retired, he graduated with High Honors and was voted the most outstanding citizen of his class. I told him that I was proud of him and that we were going on our trip, but I didn't tell him that I had bought a brand new motor home to take with us. We had a great time in Nebraska, and after we returned home he asked me to take him to the Navy recruiting station. I was honored that he asked me, and after his enlistment he stayed in the Navy, achieving the highest rank possible for an enlisted man.

After Dale and I returned, Judy and I made the first of several trips that we would make to California in our motor home. It gave me a chance to spend more time with Mother and Daddy and all the others in California. On one of the trips we brought my parents back with us and they stayed for several weeks. When they were ready to go home I bought a plane ticket for them. When it was time to fly Mother was extremely nervous, but they made it back okay.

After traveling for awhile, I wanted to stay home and take some shorter, closer trips, but I was getting anxious to have something else to do. Our daughter Darlene and our son-in-law Ed Dion told us that they were ready to build a house, and that gave me something to do. We gave them a piece of land and I started building. When the house was finished they moved in with our first grandson, Eddie. About two years later they had our second grandson, Christopher, their youngest.

About two years after building Darlene's house, Judy-Gail married her first husband, and we gave her a piece of land. I helped build their house as well, and that is where our grand-daughter Stephanie was born. She was Judy-Gail's only child. Judy-Gail eventually married again; his name is Ron Gilbert, and he adopted her daughter Stephanie. As a result,

Stephanie now has two older brothers and one older sister, and we were blessed with three more grandchildren—Michael, Peter and Nancy.

Our son, Darrell Wayne (Butch) was the last to build on the land we had for him, which he did in 1988 after he and his wife Janet were divorced. When the house was finished, he moved in with two of our granddaughters. Amy graduated from Windham Tech High School and Cindy graduated from Stafford High School. Our oldest granddaughter, Jennifer, stayed in East Hartford with her other grandmother in order to graduate where she had started school.

After building Darlene and Judy's houses and before I started Butch's, I was drafted into one of the most enjoyable jobs of my life. The coach on Chris and Stephanie's t-ball team quit, and the mothers of the team drafted me to be the new coach. I coached that team all the way to the majors, and when they went to the majors I stayed as their coach and became the director of the Farm League. I enjoyed doing this job for eight years. Also during this time period a friend of mine, who was a retired State Police Sergeant, worked with me to start a new business doing renovations and repair work on homes. We did this for a couple of years, and although we didn't make much money we enjoyed working together.

Stanley Nasiatka and I had formed a friendship over twenty years before we ever started the business; he was the closest friend I ever had. When we first met he was a rookie State Trooper and I was the Deputy Jailer at the old Tolland Jail. Our first meeting was very unusual; it was the result of a minor accident that I had with the jail pick-up truck. It was a cold day, and there was snow and ice on the road leading up to the jail farm. Two of the inmates and I were on our way to feed the beef cattle, and when we reached the old one-lane road we started down. The hill was steep and had high banks on each side with a sharp curve about half-way down. As I went around the curve at only five miles per hour, I saw a car trying to come up the hill with a young girl at the wheel and two kids pushing. When I spotted them I tried hard to stop, but it was impossible; the road was a sheet of sheer ice. When the two kids pushing saw that I couldn't stop, they ran as fast as they could to get out of the way, and they were a safe distance away by the time I slid into the car. The car was being driven by Shirley Dimmock, who was to marry Richard Hills, the future Deputy Jailer. However, when this happened she was only sixteen years-old.

Because of the accident, I had to notify the State Police even though no one had been injured. The Trooper that came to investigate was Trooper Stanley Nasiatka, who had recently finished his internship and was just beginning to work on his own. He arrived at the scene and got out of his cruiser, standing tall at 6'2" and a picture of spit and polish, oozing with the confidence of a good officer. He came over and introduced himself, and I told him what had happened.

We stood at the top of the hill as he surveyed the scene and took down the information. He told me that he would need to see the scene of the accident. I said, "Sure, but just be careful as you walk because it is very slippery." He replied, "I know how to walk on ice. Just lead the way."

Well, we had just walked about ten feet down the steep hill when Stanley's leather soled shoes slid; he took a hard fall and landed on his back as his hat flew off. He wasn't physically hurt, but I know that his pride was a bit wounded. To add salt to an open wound, I couldn't resist laughing. After he was up and had retrieved his hat, he looked right at me and said, "You were right. It is slippery." He finished his investigation and we shook hands, and that was the beginning of a lifelong brotherly friendship that extended to our two families.

Getting the Message Out

When I was about seventy years-old I gave up working for other people and started spending my time reading, maintaining my home, gardening and traveling about once a year. I also started to do something that I had wanted to do since I was liberated from prison camp: tell as many people as I could about what we had suffered as POW's of the Japanese. This was a long-awaited breakthrough for me and something that I was very nervous about. Not long after I had arrived home, the son of my mother's cousin had just finished Basic Training and had come visiting. He hadn't seen a second of combat, but as we were talking he commented that every one of us who had surrendered should have been killed. I wanted to punch him out, but I refrained because of Mother. I knew that he was wrong, but at the same time I was afraid that others felt the same way and would share in his response to my story. I was also afraid of public speaking, having no experience in it. In my fear, I had kept quiet about my story all those years after being liberated.

However, that was to change, in large part because of two very good friends of mine. Bob Sullivan, a middle school teacher and friend, asked me to speak to his eighth-grade class about my war experiences. I told him that it was a gruesome story at times; I was afraid that it would be too much for the kids. He told me that I could tone it down, but I was still nervous.

Bob assured me, "You will do just fine." With those reassuring words, I was convinced to make my first public speaking appearance. When I saw those thirty eighth-graders looking at me, I was convinced that I would have been less nervous going into combat again. However, after I finished talking and got through the question and answer period, I knew that I had found something that was important to me and that I wanted to continue to do. I told Bob to count on me for next year.

A few years later, another teacher named Bruce Dutton, who taught at the high school, asked me to speak to his class. I spoke to his students every year for six years, and he and I became good friends. In fact, I was originally going to have Bruce write this story; we began it, but I wasn't able to tell it verbally. He understood my difficulty, and he and I remain good friends to this day; he continues to help me improve my public speaking. As a result of his help, I have spent the last seventeen years telling people of all generations about the way we were treated at the hands of the Japanese.

I also gave speeches at the Nathan Hale School in Coventry, Connecticut. I was invited to speak there by Mr. Tom Dzicek, for an audience of three hundred people that included students, adults and the media. I thought that such a large crowd would make me more nervous, but I found myself looking forward to telling my story each time. It was a relief to get my story out and to finally talk about something that I had been keeping silent about for so long.

The largest audience of older people that I was privileged to speak in front of was a group of approximately 125 students, adults and media at a speaking engagement entitled: "Old Men Over Sixty Along the Shore in Madison, Connecticut." My most recent speaking engagement as I write this in August 2006 was back in May of this year, when I was a host tour guide for the National Prisoner of War Museum in Andersonville, Georgia. They furnished me with a beautiful apartment on the grounds of the museum and, to make the experience even better, my brother Bud and his wife Reta flew in from California to spend the week with me. During that week I was able to speak to about two-hundred people of all ages, from all over the country. The group that I most enjoyed speaking to at my week at the museum was a group of twenty soldiers from Fort Benning, Georgia.

After my week at the POW museum we went to Lawrenceville, Georgia, and visited my grandson Peter and his wife Kenda at their home. Kenda, a teacher, asked me if I would speak at her school. I told her that instead of speaking, I would send her a copy of my oral history; the Nathan Hale School children and Mr. Dzieck had made a video of the history for the Library of Congress. I suggested that she show the video to the class and that afterwards we could have a question-and-answer session. As it turned out, the entire faculty saw the tape and decided to show it to the entire school. When I arrived I spoke to about two hundred children. It was a great session; since they had seen the tape prior to our meeting, they were able to think about their questions and write them down. Every one of them asked very good questions, and it felt good to know that I was getting my story and the truth about what had happened to us out to a younger generation.

Children of my Captors, the Enola Gay, and Washington DC

Shortly after I returned home, I went on a trip that my granddaughter Amy had planned for her father Butch, her sister Jennifer, and me. We traveled to Washington D.C. by train and had a wonderful time. It was one of the most informative and explorative trips that I have ever taken, and while I was there I had the chance to do something that I had always wanted to do—talk to young, native Japanese about World War II.

While we were visiting the Smithsonian Air and Space Museum I was looking up at a Japanese Zero Fighter that was suspended from the ceiling. Next to it was a platform for visitors to see it up close and on the platform was a group of Asian young men. I understood a few words of Japanese, and approached them tentatively.

I asked them, "Are you Japanese?" struggling to be sure to keep my voice courteous. They said yes, and I asked them if they spoke English. When they nodded yes, I introduced myself and said that I would like to talk to them for a bit. I told them that I had been shot at by planes like this one, and I told them a little bit about my experiences in the war. I told them that they weren't at all responsible for what had happened in the war, but that I wished that their teachers would tell them the truth about the war. Before I left, I shook each one of their hands.

My last speaking opportunity on our trip to D.C. came at the Smithsonian Air Museum in Virginia, where the Enola Gay is displayed. Butch and I took the bus from Washington D.C. to see the large planes displayed there. When we arrived I noticed a group of twenty people standing under the Enola Gay, where the tour guide was just beginning to speak. I couldn't hear him very well, so I worked my way to the front. I wanted to hear every word he said, because there was so much controversy about how the Enola Gay was to be displayed. I was pleased at the presentation that the tour guide gave, and when he finished and asked if there were any questions, I raised my hand. I said that I didn't have any questions, but that I would like to make a comment about the B-29 bomber. I told him that I was a former POW of the Japanese and that I was in Japan when they were being used to bomb. He called me up to where he was standing, asked me my name, and introduced me as a former POW. I spoke for a few minutes before the crowd started directing questions at me. I answered as many as I could before they had to move on to the next station. The tour guide even asked me to come with them, but I had to go in order to catch our bus back to D.C.

Counseled and Counseling

I waited until this last section to recount one of the most important things that happened to give me the confidence to keep talking about my experiences and to continue to live a productive life. About two years after the Iran hostages were released, I received a questionnaire from the Veteran's Administration asking about my health and my experiences as a POW of the Japanese. I filled it out and returned it, and about a month later I received a letter requesting that I come in for a complete physical. After I had gone through the physical, I was called in for an in-depth psychological examination. The examination was more than just questions about how I felt, but was a list of questions that reached all the way back to my experiences in prison camp. The examiner was causing me to recount some experiences, and I was so effected that I broke down and cried as hard as I had when I first came back after the war and was with my family. Once I was able to control myself once again, I felt embarrassed and angry with him. I said, "You make me feel like a baby!" The examiner looked at me with compassion in his eyes and said, "Mr. Stark, you are no baby. You are one of the strongest men I have ever met." He told me that I could get some help from the V.A. that would make the load I had been carrying all these years feel a little lighter. As it turned out, he was right.

I started with counseling and eventually became one of three men who started the first group therapy sessions for X-POW's. We had our first meeting in Newington, Connecticut. Between that meeting and the next, one of our members died, but after a year had passed we were up to about fourteen. I started to heal when I began to feel that I was helping someone else; I still go to the group every other week and meet with good friends and feel free and relaxed. As a result, I can and will talk about anything. After being in the group for sixteen years, I can tell people about my war experiences and, most of the time, I can keep my emotions in check. I am sure that if I hadn't received the help from the V.A. I wouldn't have been able to write my life story.

During my time at the V.A., I talked about the blank spots that still exist in my memory surrounding the Death March. I have been told that these blank spots are not uncommon and other X-POWs have recounted experiencing the same thing. I am sure they do, but it still bothers me to have parts of my memory missing. However, as a result of the help I have received I have been able to talk to a group of more than seventy mental health personnel from V.A. facilities all over New England. I stress why it is so important for me to talk to people about Bataan and all those who died or were affected for the rest of their lives by the ill treatment and outright murder committed by the Japanese. The thing that impressed me most was when, before my talk, I asked for those who had even heard of Bataan to raise their hands—of the seventy, only one hand was raised. That experience stresses why I feel as strongly as I do about letting people know the truth about what happened there, and I will continue to do that for as long as I am able.

The Most Important Part of my Life

Now, I would like to conclude by discussing the most important part of my life—my nearly sixty year marriage to Judy and the family we have raised together. She has had tolerance with my moods all these years, and with her strength and patience we have raised three wonderful children. I have stated, in detail, each and every one of their accomplishments to convey my absolute pride in all of them. For any readers that are not a member of my family, I hope that you will bear in mind that while this book was written to inform you and to tell my story, it is most importantly a testament for my family.

My oldest child and only son, Darrell Wayne, has been very successful. Shortly after he graduated from Stafford High School he went to work for Cummins Diesel Engine Distributor, washing parts. He worked up to sales manager and forty years later he is still with the same company. He married Janet and had three daughters with her. Unfortunately my son and

Janet grew apart later in life and separated. After their divorce Darrell met Dolores Latina, a wonderful woman who has been a part of our family for the past eight years, and the two of them are very happy together and she is loved by all of the family.

Jennifer is his oldest daughter; she graduated from East Hartford High School and after graduation she received a scholarship from Wesleyan University in Middletown, Connecticut. She graduated with a Bachelor of Arts degree in Biology and Psychology and after working for a few years she received a fellowship from the University of Ohio to pursue a Ph.D. in Neuroscience. She was awarded her Ph.D. and moved to St. Louis, Missouri to work at Washington University, where she had been doing research work for a cure for multiple sclerosis. She now works for the National Multiple Sclerosis Society in New York.

Darrell's second daughter, Amy, finished grade school in Colchester, Connecticut before coming to Stafford to attend Windham Technical School. She graduated with honors and a degree in electronics. After graduation she received a scholarship to Three Rivers Community Technical College where she earned her Associates Degree in Nuclear Engineering Technology; she was also paid a stipend of $400 per month by Northeast Utilities while in school. She graduated and went on to the University of Massachusetts at Lowell where she received a Bachelor of Science degree in Radiological Science. She now works for the University of Connecticut and has completed a Masters Degree in Social Work. Amy and her husband, Shawn Courchesne, have been married for several years.

Darrell Wayne's third and youngest daughter, Cindy, graduated from Stafford High School and attended the University of Connecticut, where she received her degree in Education. After graduating, she married Marc Carrier. As a result of that union we now have six great-grandchildren: Isaiah, Jonah, Rebekah, Deborah, Hannah and Micah.

My middle daughter, Darlene, married Ed Dion after they both graduated from Stafford High School; they have been married for thirty-seven years. She has worked for the Town of Stafford for the past twenty-eight years, the past eleven were spent as the town treasurer. Darlene and Ed gave us two grandsons, Edward Allen and Christopher. Both graduated from Stafford High School. Eddie went to a technical school for electronics and received a certificate; he now works as a Maytag Service Technician and is single. Chris worked at various jobs and also served four years in the Air Force, where he attained the rank of Staff Sergeant. After his enlistment was up he went to work at Tyco as a foreman. He married

LeQuyen Tran, and they gave us another great-grandchild, Sarah. Chris is now pursuing a degree in Business Administration and Public Speaking. He and LeQuyen met each other through Chris' Vietnamese co-worker; he was introduced to her through the Internet and went to Vietnam to meet her in person. After the meeting they became husband and wife. She is loved by all of us, and admired because of her courage to come to the United States by herself.

My youngest daughter, Judy, married Ronald Gilbert. They both graduated from Stafford High School and have been married for twenty-four years. After Judy graduated she worked for twenty-one years at AARP as an office manager and bookkeeper. Ron and Judy were both previously married, and from her first marriage Judy gave us a grand-daughter, Stephanie Alice. At the age of ten, Stephanie was adopted by Ron and, as I have stated previously, the adoption gave her two brothers, Michael and Peter, and a sister, Nancy. Stephanie graduated from Eastern Connecticut State University with a degree in Psychology and continued her studies at Southern Connecticut State University where she received a Masters Degree in Special Education. After she graduated she married John Palmer, and they have blessed us with two great-grandchildren: Stephon and Trinity.

Michael has two degrees: a Bachelors Degree in Mechanical Engineering and a Masters Degree in Finance. For many years he has held a high position for the state of Connecticut. He and Lisa have been married for seventeen years and have given us two great-grandchildren: Sean and Bryan.

Peter graduated from Stafford High along with his brothers and sisters. After his graduation he enlisted in the Marine Corps; after four years he was discharged and he and Kenda were married. Peter is a certified designer in landscaping and they have no children.

Nancy has attended culinary school and is now a certified chef. She and John were just recently married.

Now that I have finished my life story, I would like to end by sharing how I feel about myself at this point in my life. The years of hardship that I endured growing up have given me an appreciation for learning, a sense of confidence and an ability to adjust to difficult and trying conditions, as well as a determination to overcome them. The love that we had for each other in our family and for others has carried me through some very difficult times. It has given me a sense of respect for my fellow prisoners and for others, which has only grown as I write this and recount my experiences.

Writing this memoir has given me a deep sense of love for humanity and a respect for those that have endured as I have.

I know that, despite the hardships, I have been fortunate. I have had opportunities come my way that have enabled me to do wonderful things, and I have encountered kind and caring people along the way whose confidence in me has given me the ability to do what they knew I could. I am also grateful for the opportunities I have had to work with others, like myself, who lived through the POW experience; despite not having had much education myself, I know that I have made a difference to many of them. My experiences as a Prisoner of War and my love for humanity have made up for what I may be lacking in education.

During the time that I was writing my life story, I became ill and had to prolong the experience for a bit; I am happy to say that I am now on my way to a complete recovery from a triple-bypass operation.

I would like to close by saying: stick around and I will give you a complete update in twenty years. But when I do finish my life, I feel good in knowing that it has been a full and rewarding one. If I have hurt anyone in my lifetime, I ask that they forgive me, and when it is my time to go it will be much easier for me because I have already made peace with those who were mean and hateful to me in my life.

Conclusion

As I write this conclusion, I have just reached my eighty-fourth birthday. Out of those eighty-four years, four of them were spent fighting on Bataan, with three and a half as a prisoner of war. The years I spent as a POW were the most difficult years of my entire lifetime—not just for me, but also for my family who had to endure pain and suffering in my absence. The Japanese absolutely refused to work with the International Red Cross to communicate with my family about my well-being. In addition, for three and a half years I was treated like an animal and deprived of my humanity. As a comparison, the POWs of the Germans in World War II had communication with their families in the short period of time, and their death rate during their imprisonment was less than two percent. Under the Japanese, our death rate was 37.5%. The Germans have admitted their guilt in regard to the Holocaust and have made some monetary restitution. The Japanese, on the other hand, have refused to take responsibility for the inhumane treatment of their POWs and have not offered any monetary compensation. I firmly believe that if Japanese people knew the entire story, they would make amends for the things that they have done to all of us who were POWs, and to our loved ones who were unaware of what was happening to us.

The
Office of the Governor of Connecticut

To all who shall see these presents greeting.

Be it known that

Darrell D. Stark

Of the United States Army

is hereby inducted into the

Connecticut Veterans Hall of Fame

In testimony Whereof and by authority
vested in me, I do confer
upon said veteran this

Certificate

Given this 20th day of November, 2007
in Hartford, Connecticut

M. Jodi Rell
Governor

CPSIA information can be obtained at www.ICGtesting.com
Printed in the USA
BVOW021426040412

286835BV00002B/24/P

9 781436 324021